THE DESCENT ON ENGLAND

Also by John Carswell

THE OLD CAUSE: *Three Biographical Studies in Whiggism* (Cresset Press)
THE SOUTH SEA BUBBLE (Cresset Press)
THE PROSPECTOR: *Being the Life and Times of Rudolf Erich Raspe* (1737–1794) (Cresset Press)
THE CIVIL SERVANT AND HIS WORLD (Gollancz)

EDITED WITH INTRODUCTIONS:
THE POLITICAL JOURNAL OF GEORGE BUBB DODINGTON (O.U.P.)
SINGULAR TRAVELS, CAMPAIGNS AND ADVENTURES OF BARON MUNCHAUSEN by R. E. Raspe and Others (Cresset Press)
AUTOBIOGRAPHY OF A WORKING MAN by Robert Somerville (Turnstile Press)

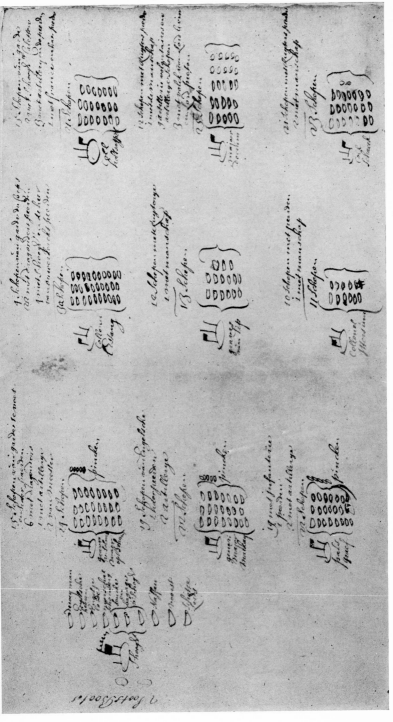

Bentinck's Logistical Diagram of the Troop-Carrying Fleet

(Portland MSS, Nottingham University Library; by courtesy of the Duke of Portland)

William, Prince of Orange

JOHN CARSWELL

THE DESCENT
ON ENGLAND

A STUDY OF THE ENGLISH
REVOLUTION OF 1688
AND ITS EUROPEAN
BACKGROUND

'Aut nunc aut nunquam'
William of Orange
in August 1688

THE JOHN DAY COMPANY
New York

First American Edition, 1969

Library of Congress Catalogue Card Number: 74–89305

PRINTED IN GREAT BRITAIN

TO
ALL AT CAMINEL
WHEN THIS WORK
WAS COMPLETED

LIST OF ILLUSTRATIONS

CONTENTS

Preface

In writing this book I have drawn for the first part on lectures on the European context of the English Revolution which I delivered in the University of Sussex in 1963. This has developed into a detailed narrative of the invasion and the Revolution itself, down to the acceptance of the throne by William and Mary.

The political and constitutional settlement achieved at the Revolution was of such importance as a point of reference that accounts of the Revolution itself, from Echard down to the classic expositions of Macaulay and G. M. Trevelyan, have had a political and constitutional flavour. They naturally dwell on the internal causation of the Revolution and produced a picture in which the intervention of William seems an inevitable incident, rather than an extraordinary adventure which could only have been undertaken and carried to success in a certain combination of European power politics.

Yet when one comes to examine the sources on which historians have relied in writing about the Revolution, one encounters a curious paradox. Although the Revolution is discussed as an event primarily of constitutional importance, at no point in history does the historian depend more on the evidence of foreign observers: primarily on the despatches of seven diplomatists in London—Barillon, Ronquillo, Hoffmann, Terriesi, d'Adda, van Citters, and Rizzini. This throws into sharp relief the relative poverty of domestic material, and its highly selective character. 5 November 1688 must have been the bonfire day for more than one collection of political papers, and the Duke of Ormonde's papers which Clarendon saw the Duchess burning on 26 November must be regarded as suffering a typical fate.

The papers of Jeffreys, Sunderland, Preston, Middleton, and Melfort for their periods of power can barely be said to exist. We have no papers for Feversham, James's commander in chief, and even Dartmouth's collection—one of the few large archives to survive—contains a significant gap. By great good luck the substance of James's great parliamentary canvass has survived, and I have attempted a tabular analysis of it; but the state papers for the reign as a whole are deplorably scanty, having in all probability been subject to two successive purges, the first by officials fearing reprisals, and the second by their successors, desirous of suppressing whatever did not tally with the approved version of events. The survival of Stewart's letters to Carstares and the fascinating Johnston correspondence is a striking exception to what may be called the general scarcity of direct evidence about the inner workings of politics.

Much work remains to be done on the diplomatic and military prelude to the invasion of 1688, and I would claim only to have shifted the emphasis still further from the purely English to the European and Atlantic aspects of this astonishing episode which opens the Augustan age of Britain and Britain's role as a world power.

References to many of the authorities I have used will be either in the footnotes or in the references at the end of the book which give the source of quotations. I have not attempted to provide a separate bibliography. Useful ones already exist, notably in Mr Ashley's recent study *The Glorious Revolution of 1688*; but a full bibliography for the reign of James and the Revolution, including the European sources, would be an extensive affair, and one much to be desired as an aid to scholarship.

I am beholden to many: to his Grace the Duke of Portland, who has deposited his manuscripts for study in Nottingham University; to the Libraries and staffs of the British Museum, Nottingham University, and the National Library of Scotland; to Mr Robert Garioch, who assisted me with the Wodrow MSS; to Professor Asa Briggs, who originally invited me to deliver the lectures on which the first part of the book is based; to Professor W. H.

Preface

Barber, for many useful hints over a long period; to Professor
L. A. Dralle, who read the manuscript and made a number of
helpful comments; to Mrs M. Ritchie, who typed the MS with
inspiring accuracy; and to my wife who read it with an enthusiasm that was always critical.

J.C.
Caminel, Lot
August 1968

Note on Dates

In the seventeenth century British reckoning was ten days behind the Continental, though the days of the week on either side of the Channel were the same. This is a considerable nuisance in a narrative which involves events on both sides of the Channel, and the usual solutions are either (1) to adopt the insular style for events in Britain and the Continental for events on the Continent; or (2) to give dates in both styles—e.g. 5/15 November 1688. The first leads to confusions, even if the letters O.S. and N.S. are used; the second is clumsy, and takes the edge off narrative. I have therefore adopted a different device. Except where I have specifically indicated otherwise, all dates in this book are given—as the point of view of the book itself requires—in the New (or Continental) Style, even when the event takes place in England. Some readers with detailed knowledge will find the results unfamiliar, but reconciliation merely involves a mental deduction of ten days.

Part One

THE POWER STRUCTURE

I

Europe

Until the railway age travel by water was on the whole safer, quicker, and cheaper than movement by land. In the seventeenth century the main thoroughfare of London was the Thames. The journey from London to Amsterdam took two days or less, but one needed a week to get from London to Exeter unless total exhaustion and great expense were to be faced. Where navigable rivers stretched far inland, or where natural waterways had been improved by canals, commerce and communication flourished. Three great waterways, the Rhine, the Danube, and the Narrow Seas of the North Sea and the Channel dominated Western and Central Europe, and carried much of its traffic.

What was true of commerce and personal travel was true also of military operations. It was, for instance, much easier for the English to hold the seaports of Ireland than for the lowland Scots to be masters of the highlanders.* Only a month after King James II wrote from Windsor to William of Orange asking for help against Monmouth's rebellion, regiments which had been at the frontier of Flanders were disembarking at Gravesend. It had taken nearly as long for the unfortunate Monmouth to march from his landing-place at Lyme Regis to the scene of his destruction at Sedgemoor. To both the business man and the military planner of the 1680's Europe appeared in terms of physical geography and trade routes, not as nations coloured on a map.

To this there was a single, huge, exception. France, unquestionably the greatest power in Europe and, with the exception

* Culloden was won by an army much of which had travelled by sea and which was provisioned from ships.

ZUIDER ZEE

Lingen

Amsterdam

The Hague
Brill
Doesburg

Mook
CLEVES
Rhine
Breda

Büren

Flushing
Antwerp

Ghent
Diest
Cologne
Brussels
Aachen
NASSAU
Herstal
Lahn

StVith
Coblence

Vianden
Mosel
Mainz
Rhine
Luxembourg
Trier
Mannheim
Philipsburg

The
NETHERLANDS
and the
RHINE
FRONTIERS
1685

Strasbourg
PALATINATE

Rhine

Basel
Miles

W. Bromage
Besançon
0   50   100

Shaded areas show the personal dominions of the
House of Orange-Nassau.

of China, in the world, had already advanced far towards the pattern of a modern nation-state. To the average man of the seventeenth century the concept was terrifying in its novelty. From the Atlantic to the Alps, from the Pyrenees to Flanders, the professed aim of the King of France was a single language and a single, coherent, centrally administered system of government for twenty million people. The few exceptions to central jurisdiction within this area, such as Avignon and Orange, were already like small islands in the national ocean, and were under constant attack. By contrast the British Isles, with a population not much more than a third that of France, consisted of a bundle of particularities. There was one predominant language (but three important subsidiary ones), and the three crowns of England, Scotland, and Ireland had one wearer. But there were three parliaments, three legal and religious systems, and an abundance of municipal, aristocratic, and corporate jurisdictions and privileges which for most people represented the substance of authority.

By 1685 France had been accustomed to efficient, centralised government for a quarter of a century. New industries had been developed with the aid of deliberate planning and subsidy behind high tariff walls. Communication between the three coast lines by the highly developed canal system was reliable; and on those three coast lines a formidable sea power had been created. When King Louis had taken control of his kingdom in 1660 Brest, Toulon, Rochefort, and le Havre had been fishing villages. Ten years later each was a major naval base. In 1661 the fire-power of the French navy was just over 1,000 guns; in 1665, 1,847, in 1674, nearly 6,500.* These ships could be built and maintained from the resources of France herself. There was no need to turn to Baltic suppliers, as the English and Dutch had to do.

The same applied to the French army—an army to which a national adjective properly belongs because, unlike most continental armies of the time, it consisted mainly of subjects of the prince it served. In 1667 it had a nominal strength of 72,000, of whom only half were fit for service in the campaign of that year. Ten years later, in the last year of the great war against the Dutch,

---

* 15 vessels in 1664, 196 in 1672, 300 in 1688. Lavisse and Rambaud, *Histoire Générale*, VI. 100.

it mustered a quarter of a million disciplined effectives. It was subject to rules of precision and subordination which are familiar to us, but were then unique in Europe. The name of Martinet, Inspector-General of Infantry, has passed into the language, and his work in devising the tactical ballet movements known as foot-drill transformed the appearance of war.

The French officer, who was paid fifty per cent more in war than he received in peace, was expected not only to obey, but to accept. In other armies officers were liable to throw up their commissions for personal or political reasons, but in France such individualism was resented. 'I think,' Louvois once wrote, 'that Montil is too wise to ask me to let him resign, because that is the way to get into the Bastille. The King does not like belly-achers (les gens chagrins).'[1]

There were still enclaves in France after twenty-five years of rationalisation. Orange was one such, though in technical terms only, and there were other properties belonging to the House of Orange dotted about Burgundy. There was the papal fief of Avignon. But on the whole, and with one important exception, corporate and aristocratic power had lost the independence it still enjoyed elsewhere in Europe. The exception was huguenotism, and the future of that exception was one of the great issues of European politics.

The great issue of the previous century had been whether France would become a Calvinist country. Calvin had been a Frenchman, born near Compiègne, in the heart of France, and his followers had been fighting the Wars of Religion not for toleration but to gain France for the reformed faith. Nor had that struggle ended in toleration. The generous words, and perhaps the magnanimous spirit, of King Henry IV in issuing the Edict of Nantes, are misleading to a modern mind about what that document actually meant. The effect of the Edict of Nantes was not to tolerate but to restrict protestantism in France to certain areas. Its two most important provisions were permission to carry on the reformed worship in areas (of which Paris was not one) where it had been firmly established in 1598; and in the houses of noblemen who at that date were committed to the Religion Prétendue Réformée—or R.P.R., which must be among the first instances of a political force being known by initials.

Being a huguenot was not a bar to public office, and to this extent non-catholics in France had an advantage over non-anglicans in England and non-calvinists in the Netherlands. The great Turenne had been a huguenot. But the cement of the French state was catholic, just as that of the English was anglican, and to a conformist Frenchman the Edict of Nantes was as much a national partition as if lines had been drawn on the map. The huguenots, once they had resigned themselves to being a minority, naturally dwelt on the guarantees of equal citizenship which the Edict contained. But Louis regarded it as the equivalent of a treaty derogating from his sovereignty, which like other obstacles in his path should first be undermined and then demolished.

The survival of huguenotism was irksome to King Louis for a number of other reasons. It had aristocratic and particularist associations, and it had loyalties, or at any rate solidarities, outside the borders of France. Orange provides an example of both. In the Wars of Religion the 'Pépinière orangeoise' had been the nursery and refuge of protestantism in the south. Twice in ten years it had been sacked by catholic armies. It had provided the fragment of sovereignty that entitled William the Silent to hoist the Orange flag on the privateering fleet which decided the struggle for Dutch independence; and the idea of such a flag of convenience had been provided by the huguenot Admiral de Coligny: 'Vous êtes Prince Souverain d'Orange,' wrote William's future father-in-law, 'cette qualité vous permet, sans faire acte de piraterie, de donner des lettres de marque pour faire la course en mer.'[2]

Another example of an international, aristocratic huguenot is Henri, Marquis de Ruvigny, who for many years filled the difficult buffer post of General Deputy for the Protestants: the official channel of communication between the Government and the huguenot community. Ruvigny's sister Rachel was married to the staunchly anglican Earl of Southampton, Charles II's first Lord High Treasurer. Her daughter, another Rachel, became the wife of Russell, the whig martyr of 1683. In the end the Ruvignys abandoned Louis altogether, and the next generation provided one of William III's commanders, the Earl of Galway and a naturalised Englishman.

The huguenot counted not only in international politics but in international trade. In February 1665 the Lieutenant General of Caen wrote to Colbert: 'Most of the business men of this town are Protestants; and since they have more access to, and contact in, England and Holland because of their agreement in religion, they handle all the business in cloth and other goods that come from those countries.'[3] His letter went on to suggest that the official cloth subsidy should be reserved for catholic traders, who were more likely to develop the domestic industry with the help, if need be, of imported skill.

But on the whole skill flowed away from France, It was no part of Louis' policy to expel the huguenots—indeed he made great efforts to prevent them from leaving—but it was his policy to gall them into conformity, The increase of pressure was gradual but deliberate, spreading over the whole twenty-five years from 1660 to the final revocation of the Edict. Profession after profession was officially closed to them, discrimination was piled on discrimination, premiums were offered for apostasy, and punishments for relapse. The effect was to add the word refugee to the English language, and over the years to establish many thousands of the most enterprising French protestants in more sympathetic lands—Britain, the Netherlands, Brandenburg, the Rhineland, and Switzerland.

Yet even in 1685 there were still a million huguenots in France; and Louis was not alone in thinking that by abolishing their remaining privileges he would add immensely to his already formidable power. For it was his power, not the power of the international catholic church, that stood to gain, and this was not lost on the European powers who feared him.

The fate of huguenot privileges was one great European issue of the 1680's; another lay just beyond the north-east frontier of France, as drawn in 1679 by the Treaty of Nijmegen, in what was left of the Spanish Netherlands. That patchwork of particularities had once consisted of seventeen provinces, but was now so tattered at one end by French erosion, and torn at the other by the federal independence of the United Netherlands, that only five were left. They covered an area considerably less than modern Belgium, especially since the Bishopric of Liège was a separate entity linked to Cologne and to France. Their commerce, once so prosperous, had been ruined by international agreements under which the mouth of the Scheldt, and consequently the port of Antwerp, was closed to commerce—a state of affairs which persisted for over two hundred years with far-reaching results on modern English history. From 1609 onwards the boundaries of the Netherlands ran—as they do today—so as to include a strip to the south of the estuary, giving the channel to Antwerp and Ghent Dutch territory on both banks. The barrier on merchant shipping, originally enforced for reasons of defence, was maintained for commercial ones, and was an essential factor in the growth of Amsterdam and Rotterdam. The Treaty of Münster in 1648 formally guaranteed Dutch control of the approaches to Antwerp, which did not finally disappear from European history until 1863, when Holland surrendered it under an international treaty (and in return for a substantial sum of money). It was in general both Dutch and English policy throughout the period from Westphalia to the French Revolution that there should be no major commercial and military port on the coast between Rotterdam and le Havre—whence the importance attached to Dunkirk. But such as they were the Belgian provinces were subject to the mad and invalid King of Spain, Carlos II. When his dim consciousness ceased those five provinces and all his other dominions, including South America, were likely to fall to the French king; and this would give Louis control both over the narrow seas and the main waterway from the West into central Europe.

Only this feeble barrier separated France from the great centre of seventeenth-century economic growth, the United Netherlands—or, as they preferred to be called, the United Provinces—where, as Sir William Temple put it 'the earth is better than the air, and profit more in request than honour'.[4] The independence of the seven provinces had been won under the leadership of the House of Orange, but with French support; whence the Dutch maxim that the Frenchman was a good friend but a bad neighbour. It might have added 'a good customer' for it was to a great extent on the French market that Dutch prosperity was built and Dutch business friendliness to France was founded.

But the polity of the United Provinces was precisely opposite to the French. In France power was conceived as flowing in a shining stream downwards from the summit to act upon individuals with the least possible interposition. In the United Provinces it was thought of as generated in the smallest corporations, and flowing upwards to the largest, leaving the maximum scope for corporate autonomy. For this was the great principle of *Vrijheid*—freedom not so much for the individual as for the corporation. It was seen in the basis of the union itself. Each of the seven provinces retained its unabated sovereignty; so that the States General of the Union consisted of delegates bound by the instructions of their provincial assemblies, each of which had to approve all major decisions before they could be acted upon. So separate were the provinces that they could hold colonies independently, as Zeeland for many years held Surinam.

The same principle ran back through the whole political system. Unfortunately—but significantly—we cannot help calling the United Provinces Holland, which was the most important of them. The others were Zeeland, Overijssel, Utrecht, Guelderland, Friesland, and Groningen. But the country also included North Brabant, which was not self-governing, and was governed by the United Provinces as a whole, whence its name 'The Generality'. Each province had a different constitution with a history preceding the union itself, and component organisms of town and rural district; and these in turn were often made up of still smaller constitutional organisms. Friesland, the most northerly, and one of the poorest provinces, was a kind of rural democracy divided into four quarters and no less than thirty-two divisions, returning deputies to the provincial assembly. Elsewhere the municipalities had the greater share of the power, and the hereditary landowners a lesser share; in some there was a nobility—represented by a curious legal fiction in Zeeland by a single nobleman, the Prince of Orange himself; in each there was a traditional office of Stadhouder, or governor, though it was not always filled. Everywhere was variety, particularity, separation of powers, and endless possibility of legal manipulation.

But from another point of view the Netherlands can be regarded as a city-state formed round Amsterdam. That great town dominated the most important province, Holland, and was by itself more significant than any of the other six provinces. It was the financial capital of Europe, the seat of the Bank whose notes circulated far abroad, the headquarters of the Dutch East India Company's commercial empire which stretched from the Cape to Formosa and possessed a virtual monopoly of all European trade east of the Straits of Macassar. For sixty years capital had been pouring into Amsterdam, and a common rate of interest was two per cent. In the words of Byland, an Amsterdammer who was accused of trading with the enemy in wartime: 'Burgesses of Amsterdam are free to trade everywhere. Commerce must suffer no interruption. If it were necessary to pass through Hell in pursuit of gain, I would risk to burn my sails.'[5] He was acquitted. In 1650 three-quarters of the sea-going merchant ships of Europe sailed under the Dutch flag. In the course of thirty years, while England had been engaged in the struggle between King and Parliament, Dutch enterprise, drawn on by the prospect of the trade in pepper, cinnamon, and tea, had destroyed the Portuguese empire in the East; established a system of indirect rule through native princes on a scale fully comparable to the British in India in the next century; embarked thousands of Europeans from every nation—provided they were protestants—in its trading fleets; and planted cabbages in a nursery garden at the Cape of Good Hope to reprovision vessels on the long voyage out.

With trade went other forms of communication. The speed, range, and output of the Dutch printing presses were unequalled in Europe, and they concentrated on foreign languages—English French, Czech, Hebrew, Armenian. The Dutch were even more than the chief printers of Europe: they were its type-founders as well, and were rapidly becoming its paper-makers. They could handle large printings, of 10,000 copies or more. The level of skill, literacy, and social welfare was high, and so were incomes. Gregory King estimated that they were more than forty per cent higher per head than in France, and five per cent higher than in England. Taxation too was high, but so were savings.[6] Civilised standards were deeply rooted and richly financed.

It would be a mistake to describe the municipal councillors of Holland—its ruling class—as business men. After three generations of astonishing commercial success the typical Dutchman holding a municipal or official position was a graduate with a private income. He had taken his degree, probably in law, at the comparatively new university of Leyden, and his income came from investments inherited from a business-man father or grandfather. The Regenten, or councillors, were thus also Rentieren, or rentiers. Their fortunes depended directly on the continued solvency of the Republic and its great commercial and trading corporations. The outlook of such a man was cultivated but legal-istic; peace-loving but lacking in imagination; benevolent but class-conscious; tolerant but timid.

Calvinist he had to be, for although all religions were tolerated in the Republic, office was limited to those of the established religion. But the Regents were on the whole broad-minded. It was quite otherwise with the ordinary people, 'unqualified and mean persons' as Jan de Witt described them, who 'have no place in the government'. Among them the hold of the calvinist clergy, who were also excluded from political power, was strong and deep. Both clergy and people were inclined to look for leaders more inspiring than the timid, conventional, and rather highbrow Regenten. Since the great war with France and the destruction of Jan de Witt and his brother by the Amsterdam mob, *Vrijheid* survived in a modified form, and the craving for leadership was satisfied by the Prince of Orange.

Between the two great waterways of the Rhine and the Danube lay the uneasy, many-membered body of German states known as the Empire. Diverse though it was, a jumble of principalities, bishoprics, municipal governments, and tiny fiefs, it had a kind of unity. The unity did not reside any longer in the Emperor. There was a clear distinction drawn between the Empire and the Emperor, who was a German prince, pre-eminent no doubt by his rank, but in no sense the ruler of the member states. They, in the words of a contemporary jurist, were *divinata confusio con-servata*, a muddle preserved by divine providence, a kind of German Commonwealth. It had its Diet, which pursued its somewhat ineffectual deliberations at Regensburg, and it had its constitutional law, as well as a common language. It did not pretend to a common policy. Among its hundreds of members some, such as Saxony, Brandenburg, and Bavaria, had European status on the strength of their German dominions. But the Em-pire also included in its membership Princes whose main do-minions lay outside its boundaries. Of these the most notable was the Emperor himself, with his interests in Italy and Hungary, as well as in Austria and on the Rhine; but the Kings of Poland, Sweden, and Denmark also held territories within the Empire.

The most efficient state in Germany was already Brandenburg, soon to be Prussia. Its ruler, the Elector Frederick William, had been educated in the Netherlands, and was William of

Orange's uncle by marriage. In 1685 he was the senior monarch in Europe, having been on the throne for forty-five years. During his reign he had created, in his poor and scattered dominions, an efficient administrative machine and a powerful army. With Dutch capital he had embarked on colonial enterprise in Africa. The bulk of his lands lay in the east and north, marching with Poland and Denmark. But the beginning of Rhenish Prussia, the Duchies of Cleves and Mark, were just over the border from the United Provinces, a few hours' journey from the Hague.*

A feature of the German side of the Rhine was the great belt of ecclesiastical states. The only lay prince of any importance between Heidelberg and Hamburg was the Count Palatine: all the rest were archbishops or bishops, of whom the most significant was the aged amateur chemist, Maximilian Henry, Archbishop Elector of Cologne. His territories included not only Cologne but the bishoprics of Hildesheim, Münster, and Liège, through which Louis had delivered his thrust to the heart of the United Provinces in 1672; for Maximilian Henry was a friend of France.†

The Emperor Leopold, an uninspiring, but underestimated man, was deeply interested in the Rhine frontier, but he had little time or strength to spare for it. Away to the east, on the Danube, he was confronted by the third great European problem developing, like the future of the huguenots and the disposal of the Spanish Empire, towards a crisis. This was the future of Hungary and the last great effort of the Ottoman Sultans to dominate all eastern Europe south of the Danube. Emperor and Pope alike were deeply involved in this conflict.

Innocent XI, Odescalchi, was one of the most formidable,

* The French preferred to invade the United Provinces from the east, rather than the south, since the damage to the Provinces themselves was more direct. Invasion from the Spanish Netherlands affected only Dutch Brabant, which had no political representation in the Federation. 'Tout le mal,' wrote Louvois to the Elector of Cologne on 28 April 1684, 'Que l'on fera dans le Brabant Hollandais ne regardant que la Généralité, leur sera fort peu sensible, tandis qu'un village pillé dans l'Overyssel ou dans la province de Groningue fera crier des hauts cris à la Haye.'—Rousset, *Histoire de Louvois*, i. 245.

† It may help a reader with the subsequent history of Prussia in mind if it is added that the Duchy of Mark, which Frederick acquired in 1666, included the (then small) town of Essen. The situation of the two Duchies was curious. The Elector, as Duke, was sovereign. But each Duchy retained its own assembly of estates; and under the Treaty of Münster Dutch troops were stationed in them.

perhaps one of the greatest, popes of modern times. He had intended as a young man to be a soldier, not a priest, and he was tall and bony. His austerity and parsimony were celebrated: on becoming pope he had refused to allow the expense of a fresh set of pontifical robes, and continued to wear those of his predecessor, though they were far too small for him. It was said that as his working costume he made the same cassock last ten years. The finances of the Church, and therefore her rights, were his special care. He strongly disapproved of worldliness in prelates, and so of the German ecclesiastical princes who danced to King Louis' diplomatic tune on the upper and lower Rhine—Münster, Liège, Cologne, Mainz, and Trier.

Innocent considered that Christendom should unite against the Turks, and this wish was not confined to catholic Christendom. He looked favourably on the labours of Spinola, Bishop of Tina, in search of a formula for some measure of reconciliation with Rome, to which the German protestant princes might subscribe. Spinola had begun his quest in 1675, just before Innocent's election, at the instigation of the Emperor Leopold, and the results were laid before the Pope in 1684. So far as the Emperor was concerned they had great political as well as spiritual importance in consolidating the Empire in his rear during the struggle against the Turks. They were therefore opposed by King Louis through the French cardinals in Rome, just as French diplomacy in Constantinople encouraged the Turks.

These were not the only issues that divided the Pope and the King of France. The struggle for authority over the Church in France itself had been refined into two great points, 'The Quarter' and 'The Régale', the first being a matter of diplomatic privilege in Rome and the other, close to the Pope's heart, the right to allocate the revenues of vacant benefices. This was the source from which King Louis found the bounties offered for the conversion of huguenots, and his indignation was great when he learned that the Pope had different views. The French Cardinal d'Estreés reported to Innocent the numerous conversions that the scheme was achieving for the true faith, and received a crushing reply:

> What is the use of demolishing all these conventicles if all the bishops are schismatics? They are going the way of England.[7]

In his reference to England there can be little doubt that the Pope was thinking not of Charles II but of Henry VIII and considered the Most Christian King with his Gallican Church was going the same way as the Defender of the Faith with anglicanism.

England, Scotland, and Ireland lay on the periphery of all these tensions—the thrust of French power eastwards and Turkish armies westwards, the involvement of papal interest and Imperial prestige, the secret ambitions of Prussia on the Rhine, and the social, commercial, and intellectual abundance of the Netherlands. Charles II, after slithering through his reign, died in February 1685. He had made war on the Netherlands in the interests of France, and he had allied himself with the Netherlands in the interests of the balance of power; and had married his niece to William of Orange partly to clear off family debts incurred while the Stuarts were in exile. His successor, James, was fifty-three, and the next male heir was William. Here was posed the fourth great European issue of the 1680's, which brought Britain and British politics into the main stream of the diplomatic conflict.

Britain had grown in weight under the tortuous reign of Charles. The restored monarchy had been a period of rapid economic growth. Between 1660 and 1685 a share in the British East India Company appreciated in capital value by a thousand per cent and still yielded ten per cent at the market price. The same sign of prosperity is found in the hearth tax, which was assessed on houses containing two or more hearths. In 1664, it had yielded £60,000; in 1685, £100,000. The increase is 66 per cent in twenty years, or 3 per cent per annum. Such figures do not allow for inefficiency and evasion, but the improvement in standards that they indicate is inescapable.[8] New industries were coming into existence, such as the manufacture of white paper, hitherto imported from France. It was looked on with typical jealousy by the French Government. 'If,' wrote Louvois to the French Ambassador in London, 'you can put forward a memorandum which will explain what needs to be done to increase more and more the decline of the British paper industry, you will do something most acceptable to his Majesty.'[9]

But even in 1685 Britain was, in European terms, a weak power. Her army was small and inexperienced in serious land warfare; her fleet was inferior, technically and numerically, to those of both France and the Netherlands; her administration was primitive, and depended too much on local notables; the revenue came in slowly and reluctantly. Above all there were great flaws in British public life which made for instability: the unresolved conflict between Parliament and the executive, which was reproduced nowhere else in Europe; a church settlement that was disputed in England and defied in Scotland; and what can only be described as an uneasiness in the possessing classes about whether the existing system was the best guarantee of their possessions. Britain, more perhaps than any other power, was penetrated by the agents and intelligence services of other European governments. She might be necessary to the balance of power in Europe, but she was not the mistress of it. 'Your Majesty knows,' wrote the French Ambassador in London to his master in February 1681, 'what use it may be to you hereafter, and how much the cabals in opposition to the Court are necessary to keep the affairs of England in a state convenient to your Majesty.'[10]

Yet there was one development of Restoration Britain that marked her out from the other European countries. The powers of the western seaboard of Europe had by the 1670's begun to take seriously the settlement and exploitation of the huge spaces of North America. William of Orange had spoken, at the worst moments of the war against France, of carrying on the struggle from the other side of the Atlantic. Even Frederick of Brandenburg had colonial interests. Colbert had not neglected colonial policy. In 1672 the French Jesuit Marquette had been the first European to see the Mississippi, and had navigated it as far south as Arkansas; and ten years later, by establishing its estuary, French explorers had claimed the whole of the Middle West as the new province of Louisiana. But the French settlers were few, despite the heroic expeditions that have left a trail of French place-names across the centre of the United States—Champlain, Detroit, Des Moines, St Louis. The British settlers were many. In the year of the Restoration the population of British America was estimated at about 160,000, of whom more than half were in the West Indian islands. In the year of the Revolution the corresponding figure was over 360,000. The population on the mainland made up nearly two-thirds of it. Never before had so large a number of Europeans constituted an organised society outside Europe. In one respect at least James, Duke of York, and his great antagonist, Shaftesbury, shared an interest, for James was the proprietor of New York, and Shaftesbury of Carolina. The intensity of the British settlement of North America shaped the future course of world history; and even had its weight in the events of 1688.

The Sinews of Power

The three elements of modern civilisation identified by Carlyle—gunpowder, printing, and the Protestant Religion—were the sinews of the conflict in which the English Revolution was the decisive episode.

Land warfare in the later seventeenth century was a matter for professionals, and by 1685 it had long been established that comparatively small bodies of hardened troops could master far larger numbers of amateur soldiers, however courageous. In the conquest of the East, which was already in progress, the foundations had been laid by the great military organisers and drill-masters: Frederick Henry Prince of Orange, William III's grandfather and the son of William the Silent and Louise de Coligny; Gustavus Adolphus; the Great Elector, Frederick William of Brandenburg; and Louis XIV's tactitians. These men devoted themselves to the problem of manoeuvring masses in close order, not for show but as an instrument which would answer accurately at the moment of conflict and extract the most out of the limited breath and muscle of man and beast. In so doing they transformed the face of warfare, from a scramble-at-arms to a linear, almost geometrical art.

The acquisition and maintenance of professional soldiers was difficult and expensive for governments. Barracks, except for strictly limited bodies of household troops, were not provided, and unless troops were quartered in fortifications they had to be billeted on householders, thus creating a political as well as a financial problem. Military policy therefore was that so far as possible troops should be assembled only when they were needed for operations; and that they should be kept, while they were in pay, outside the territory of the government who employed them. There was a European market for professional soldiers. Some of the men who landed with William at Torbay had the year before stormed Belgrade under Charles of Lorraine. The British Isles and Germany made especially large contributions to this European pool of military men.

The market for professional officers was even more cosmopolitan than the market for other ranks. Experienced senior commanders were particularly scarce. In the whole of Europe there were perhaps only a score who could effectively manoeuvre a mass of closely marshalled regiments in action. The qualifications were formidable. In the presence of considerable personal danger, and without any communications system except gallopers and his own eyes, a seventeenth-century general had to manipulate with precision the movements of twenty or thirty thousand men. His immediate subordinates might well speak a language other than his own. The maps would be primitive and inaccurate. Everything depended on the man, and it is not surprising that he commanded a high price and a great place in the world.

One such was Armand von Schomberg, who was to command the land forces in William's descent on England, find a dukedom there, and a grave on the Boyne, where he fought the last battle of his long career. Schomberg was half German, half English. His mother had been Anne Dudley, daughter of the ninth Lord Dudley, and his father a German diplomatist in the service successively of Frederick, Count Palatine and of the Elector of Brandenburg. Under the first of these masters the elder Schomberg had been concerned in negotiating one of the greatest protestant alliances of the century, the marriage of the Count Palatine to Elizabeth, Charles I of England's sister, and William III's great-aunt.

In 1685 Schomberg was seventy. His military experience of fifty years since leaving Leyden University had been immense, and now that Condé and Turenne were dead he was regarded as the leading soldier of Europe. He had served under William II of Orange in the Thirty Years War, in the Fronde under Mazarin, and as deputy to Turenne in the invasion of Holland in 1672, for which he was made a Marshal of France. He was especially skilled in the command of forces of mixed national origin, being trilingual. In 1685, fresh from the triumph of capturing Luxembourg for King Louis, he was still in the French service. But he was, like his mentor Turenne, a protestant.

The Netherlands did not lack an officer class: that class was personified by the head of the House of Orange, and the same republican measures that had been taken to exclude the Prince from power in the state were taken—and taken with greater success—to exclude the squires and gentlemen who were his relatives or dependants. Under the constitution as operated by de Witt the Dutch gentry could not hope for municipal office except in rustic Friesland and in the strongly Orangist Zeeland. William, in fact, was not alone in having to make his political fortune in the United Provinces, and in being helped to make it by the great national war against the French. His entourage was an important source of pressure for power and adventure.

Willem van Bentinck, later Earl of Portland, was typical of his class. He was the nephew of a military officer from the eastern province of Overijssel, and had been William's page during the Prince's deprived boyhood as a ward of state. He became William's closest friend, accompanied him on his first visit to England in 1670, and helped to negotiate the marriage to Mary in 1677. Where William was febrile and asthmatic, Bentinck was solid and practical, a large, pleasant-looking man with reddish hair and a country outlook. His military gifts were conspicuously those of a staff officer, not a commander in the field, and it was as William's chief of staff that he was to play a leading part in the expedition of 1688.

There were many others of the same class in William's immediate retinue, and several were related to him: for example Willem Friederich van Nassau-Zuylestein, whose father had been William's tutor as a boy and was also his (bastard) uncle; and Henrijk van Nassau, Count of Ouwerkerk, who traced his illegitimate descent from William's great-uncle, Maurice of Nassau. Zuylestein, who was a handsome professional cavalry officer, was bilingual, being half English through his mother, Anne Killegrew. He too had been a friend of William's since boyhood. Ouwerkerk was rather older—in 1688 he was over forty—but he had been attached to the prince since at least 1670. He was not, like Zuylestein, solely a careerist, but had substantial estates and influence in the Orangist province of Zeeland, where another of

Everaard van Weede
Heer van Dijkvelt

Raadpensionarius
Gaspar Fagel

William Carstares,
as Principal of
Edinburgh University

Sir James Stewart
of Goodtrees,
as Lord Advocate

William's relatives, the devious Nassau Odijk, had been the leading figure since 1668. Completing this group of Orangist military
men was the captain of William's personal guard and his maternal
uncle, Henrijk Trajectinus, Count von Solms-Braunfels, who was
to be the first officer ashore at Torbay. Nothing could be further
from the mark than to picture William's expedition as sober,
middle-class, and respectable. Its heart was an adventure of
military aristocrats.

The native Dutch troops were raised and paid by the Provinces, and much care was expended on deciding precisely
which provincial government bore the cost of which units. But
there were two special ingredients in the Dutch forces: William's
personal troops, the Blue Guards, and the Anglo-Dutch Brigade.
The Blue Guards, both horse and foot, under Solms, were in
themselves a formidable force, and they were maintained entirely
from the Prince's personal revenues. The Anglo-Dutch Brigade
was even more important militarily and politically.

There had been English and Scottish soldiers in the service
of the Dutch Republic from its earliest beginnings,* and by 1685
as many as three generations of the same family had served in
these regiments. The first Balfour, for instance, had been commissioned by William the Silent in 1561. All his five sons served—
four of them as lieutenant colonels. His grandson, Bartholemew
Balfour, commissioned in 1676, commanded a regiment in 1688,
and was killed commanding a brigade at Killiecrankie. Such
families were, after so long, partly Dutch, but they remained,
English-speaking; the regiments prided themselves on carrying
British colours and marching to British music; and their ranks
were constantly filled by recruits from Britain who were either
driven by persecution, seeking their fortunes, or anxious to gain
military experience.

The regiments had been many times reorganised and

---

* These forces are fully documented in the Dutch archives, the information
being summarised, as regards the Scottish regiments, in James Ferguson.
The Scots Brigade in the Service of the United Netherlands 1572–1782 (Scottish
History Society 1899) The extent to which they served as a school of arms for
English soldiers in the seventeenth century is most notable. Among others
Philip Skipkon, Thomas Fairfax, George Monk, had served in the Brigade.
The roll includes a Lambert, two Fleetwoods, and two Cromwells. See also
An Historical Account of the British Regiments . . . in the . . . Dutch Republic
(1794) and Mackay, J., *The Old Scots Brigade.*

rearranged; but by 1685 there were six—three English and three Scottish. They mustered nearly 4,000 of the most seasoned infantry in Europe, well found, adequately paid, and carefully trained. Their status was peculiar. Although they were paid by the Republic, their prime loyalty was to the House of Orange, and when that House was excluded from power following the settlement between Cromwell and the Dutch republicans, the Scottish regiments had refused to drink the wine issued to them for the celebrations. But this was not the only peculiarity. When, more than twenty years later, princes of Stuart blood were re-established in both the Netherlands and Britain, and the two branches were united by the marriage of William to his cousin Mary, the ambiguous convention grew up that the regiments technically formed part of the British army (though on loan to the States) and should be available to the English king if he required them. This convention was—or was thought to be—enshrined in an agreement signed by William and Thomas Butler, Earl of Ossory, who between 1677 and 1680 combined the posts of British ambassador to the States and commander of the Anglo-Dutch Brigade.*

The ambiguity of the Brigade's status made it a source of contention between the two branches of the House of Stuart. The first signs of this had emerged as early as 1680, when on the death of Ossory King Charles wanted to use the vacancy to provide for the Earl of Dumbarton, while William was resolved to appoint Henry Sidney, who was to play so strategic a part in the events of 1688. But the Brigade was not merely a source of political friction. It was a factor in military calculation. The English Stuarts regarded it as an important reserve for their own forces; William attached special importance to it for its intrinsic value, and because it was British. James Stewart, writing to Carstares on 29 January 1687, recommended purging the six regiments of their catholic officers 'for in case of a brush with England, here they would have six regiments the most proper in the world, to make division by invasion, and consequently most formidable

---

* Ferguson (p. 559) gives the text. The commander was to be British, but was to be responsible to the Prince of Orange. The troops were not to be reduced in number, and were to be available to the King of England if required. Their pay was to be increased by 2d a day, and the pay and allowances of the Commander were fixed at the level payable to the elder Zuylestein as a general in the Dutch service.

to the present Court'. A week later he writes 'if a breach should happen there are in this country, who on the appearance of the six regiments well modelled, might direct and manage a diversion'.[1]

The British army was hardly stronger on paper than the Dutch, and a good deal less experienced. King Charles had run it down for reasons of economy, and in 1685 it numbered less than 20,000 men, of whom about a quarter were mounted. Much of this force was employed on what would today be called internal security, and such overseas experience as the units possessed came from garrison duties on tropical stations such as Tangier. It was unthinkable to find from it a field force on the continental scale. The officers, in particular, left much to be desired. Many, like Sir John Reresby, were military amateurs whose main interest in a commission was the pay and influence it provided. The Englishman who wanted to rise in the military profession had to go abroad and serve in a foreign army. Many of those who distinguished themselves in the war that followed the Revolution had served in the Anglo-Dutch Brigade: Cutts and Talmash, and the two adversaries at Killiecrankie, Claverhouse and Mackay. Marlborough had served with the French army; the Duke of Berwick, at sixteen, was to learn warfare in Hungary against the Turks.

At sea the British and Dutch were rather more evenly matched. Both navies were founded on the existence of a large merchant marine, with its consequent pool of seafarers; and were at a fairly high pitch of efficiency. In Holland the navy was the concern of the Republic acting as a central authority, and in England steps towards naval efficiency were regarded with less jealousy than any corresponding moves for the land forces. Even so there was in England a strong amateur element in the ships, the men, and commanders. Since mobilising the fleets meant adapting large numbers of merchantmen, it was computed that in any encounter between the Dutch and British navies only some twenty-five per cent of the vessels in either had been purpose-built for war. The Dutch admirals were professionals. But the British had developed a tradition of putting land commanders in charge of fleets, sometimes with success. Blake had gone to sea at the age of fifty-four after a successful career as a soldier on land; Montagu, first Earl of Sandwich, had first

distinguished himself at Naseby; Monk, who was probably th
most distinguished British soldier between Cromwell an
Marlborough, twice commanded fleets; Prince Rupert forsoo
the cavalry for sea service in 1666; such 'generals at sea' tended t
depend on professional sailing masters for strategical and tac
tical movements.

In 1685, therefore, when James became King of England, th
military balance between him and his nephew William wa
comparatively even. For both powers the use of open force
whether on land or sea, was a matter for specially assembled effor
prolonged mustering of men and material, slow movemen
of cumbersome columns moving twenty miles or less a day ove
badly maintained roads, or less painfully, if no more quickly, b
water transport. Only France, among European powers, had th
large professional force, the administrative machine, and th
internal communications, that would allow the secrecy and spee
that achieve surprise.

In such conditions intelligence and propaganda were essentia
weapons. Of the intelligence networks by far the most effectiv
was, of course, the French. The professional diplomatists c
King Louis, Barillon in London, Villars in Turin, D'Avaux a
Amsterdam, the Duc d'Estrées at Rome, the Abbé d'Estrades a
Venice, Verjus to the Germanic Diet at Regensburg, were node
of a diplomatic service such as no other state possessed. The
maintained regular contact not only with the centre at Versailles
but with one another through the copying of despatches to othe
posts, so that the tactics of each could be concerted with those o
his neighbours. All operated according to a common strateg
of seeking deliberately to maintain the internal political tension
of the states to which they were accredited: between King an
Parliament in England; between the Regenten of Amsterdan
and the House of Orange in the Netherlands; between anti
protestant and anti-Turkish outlooks in Vienna. Each had fund
at his disposal, and employed a squad of agents.

But if the French diplomatic service had the brilliance an
prestige of superior organisation, William's intelligence networl
had two countervailing advantages: it was integrated with hi
personal military and political following, and it was linked witl
—almost indeed it was identical with—a propagandist organisa
tion. The agents of Louis worked according to a commor

strategy, those of William within a common philosophy—that of protestantism—supported by the unrivalled Dutch printing industry. The ability to churn out pamphlets from what Madame de Sévigné called the 'lardonnerie hollandaise', or Dutch sausage-shop, was among William's most effective weapons throughout his progress to power.

William was himself the centre of his intelligence and propaganda service. His deep sense of personal mission, his capacity for paper-work, and his gift of inspiring confidence in others without ever fully imparting his own to anyone, suited him well to the task. But he depended especially on two men—Bentinck, with whom he was more at ease than with any other person, and Gaspar Fagel, Grand Pensionary of the States of Holland.

It was through Fagel, in 1672, that the renegade English diplomatist and passionate huguenot, Peter du Moulin, was introduced to William's service, and until his death six years later this disagreeable but intelligent man did much to mould William's views on English affairs. In a series of memoranda* du Moulin analysed English affairs on lines that emphasised the baleful influence of James, Duke of York, as an inveterate enemy of the Netherlands; the pro-French policy of Charles; and the need to counter it both by propaganda and intrigue among parliamentarians. There can be no doubt that William read these memoranda with approval, and authorised the tactics they recommended.

When du Moulin died in 1679 an agent who was to be even more influential in William's intelligence service had already been enlisted and been trained under him. This was William Carstares,† a bulky, blond, mild-looking Scot with a covenanting background and degrees from the universities of Edinburgh and Utrecht. His father was a refugee minister in Holland, and Carstares himself claimed to be in holy orders, though when he came, by William's patronage, to occupy a succession of important ecclesiastical posts, first in Holland, then in Scotland there was

---

* These memoranda, and all du Moulin's other papers, were seized on the day after his death by Fagel's agents, and placed in Fagel's private archives. They provide the basis for Mr W. H. Haley's excellent study, *William of Orange and the English Opposition* (1953).
† For Carstares see McCormick, J., *State Papers and Letters Addressed to William Carstares* (1774), R. H. Story, *William Carstares* (1874) and Ian Dunlop, *William Carstares* (1967).

some difficulty in finding out exactly when and where he had been ordained.* He seems first to have come to William's notice as early as 1669, through Fagel, who in turn had the introduction from Dr Rumpff, a German, who was a secret agent as well as William's personal physician.

Carstares was the most apt pupil du Moulin bred. Within three years of recruitment he was concerned, with another Scottish refugee, James Stewart, in the pamphlet *The Accompt of Scotland's Grievances*, for distributing which he was arrested in London in 1674. It was aimed against the Cabal (in this case especially against Lauderdale) and like its predecessor on the same theme *England's Appeal*, which du Moulin himself had written, it had been printed in Amsterdam, and smuggled into England. As a result of this affair Carstares spent six years a prisoner in Edinburgh Castle, before a turn of the political wheel in 1679 brought about his release and immediate return to intelligence activity. In 1680 he appeared successively in Ireland and at Cheshunt; and then, after a series of journeys between Scotland, London, and Utrecht (where his contact was the Rev. James MacWard, minister of the Scots congregation there), he returned to England to become involved in the widespread, inchoate set of conspiracies known collectively as the Rye House Plot. He was not concerned primarily as a conspirator. He shrewdly analysed the weaknesses and differences of aim that motivated the variegated group of republican enthusiasts, whig intellectuals, and dissatisfied Scottish noblemen, and transmitted his findings to his masters, Fagel and Bentinck.† When, soon afterwards, he was arrested and put to the torture, his chief anxiety was that he might betray his true role and his true employers. To protect that secret he was prepared to give information to the Scottish Privy Council which led to the execution of one of the conspirators, Baillie of Jerviswood.

The chief weapon of such men as Carstares and du Moulin

* It seems probable he was ordained in Holland, but the only documentary evidence is a certificate of 1681 given by a number of Scottish ministers that Carstares was 'to our knowledge a lawful ordained Minister'. (Dunlop, p. 36)
† 'It is certain, in particular, that, from the time he left Holland until he was apprehended in England, he maintained a correspondence with Pensionary Fagel and Mr Bentinck.' This is ascribed to the admission of Carstares himself after the Revolution. (McCormick, J., *State Papers and Letters Addressed to William Carstares* (1774) p. 24.)

was not conspiracy or espionage, but the written word. Propaganda had played a part in the critical summer of 1673, when William was swept to power over the constitutional dykes the republicans had built to contain the House of Orange. He had confidently refused the offer of his English uncles to provide him with a principality of his own out of a Netherlands truncated after French conquest; but he printed his uncle Charles's letter making the offer and blaming the war on the folly of the Dutch republicans. By that time the storm of pamphlets was already rising against the de Witt régime, and on 15 August, only five days before the de Witts were butchered by the mob, came the publication of the King of England's letter. When, in the winter of 1672–3, William's new leadership of the war against the French was passing through its first critical test, the ravage of the defenceless villages of Bodegraven and Zwammerdamm by French troops became universally known in a matter of weeks in the account by the journalist Abraham de Wicquefort and the brilliantly horrific illustrations of the engraver Rousseyne de Hoogh. The effect on Dutch morale was noticeable. At almost the same time the stirring letter from William to Admiral de Ruyter was ready printed for circulation through the fleet as soon as the admiral had read it from his own quarterdeck. Many other examples could be given. William had a strong sense of public relations, the means to make it good, and a supreme gift of timing.

King Louis relied on display rather than subversion. His achievements, the mass of his force, the efficiency of his organisation, the invincibility of his policy, composed a huge canvas that he painted to impress Europe. The panoply of his court, and the often derided ceremony of his personal military interventions, were all part of this purpose. With William it was otherwise. He used propaganda like a stiletto, waiting for the opponent's error, and then exploiting it by striking swiftly at a vulnerable point.

The propaganda weapon of which William and his servants were masters was not, however, soulless. It was deeply rooted in a sincere international protestantism—'the protestant interest', or simply 'the interest'. Those convictions were summed up in the words of the unsophisticated John Erskine of Carnock when he decided, at the age of twenty-three, to throw up his

studies at Leyden and join Argyll's disastrous expedition against
James II in 1685:

> Neither could I see how I or any man . . . could refuse to
> venture all he had in the world for the interest of Christ
> against so mighty enemies—the liberties of the nation, the
> property of the subject, and the lives of all our honest
> countrymen and friends, being inseparably joined with that
> great interest; yes I may say the standing or falling of the
> Protestant interest in Europe depended in great measure
> upon the event of this undertaking in Britain.[2]

Such a man as Carstares was older and harder, but he was no less
devout. He possessed a substantial library of theology despite
his constant comings and goings on intelligence work, and in
1686, writing in his private notebook, he vowed he would 'read
a particular portion every day of my compends of Philosophie
and Theologie. I would spend 2 houres a day upon what I
design for a just vindication of myselfe, principles, and friends,
from the aspersions cast upon them in the narrative of the plot
printed in England.'[3]

Disaffected English gentry, ambitious Dutch soldiers, anxious
Amsterdam business men, elderly republican plotters such as
Rumbold and Wildman, surviving from the days of the Commonwealth, the secret society of exiled Covenanters,* all played their
part in the Williamite Revolution and its preliminaries. But the
world of the Scottish exile in Holland had a peculiar significance
as the Revolution's nursery. Ever since the early years of the
century Scottish churches had been established in the Netherlands, and since the 1660's a steady stream of refugees had filled
their congregations and made them foci of emigré opposition to
the Stuarts. They were men with direct experience of the Scottish
régimes of Lauderdale and James, Duke of York; and so of
repressions far more savage than any inflicted in England. The
emigrant churches, which were financed as part of the Dutch
established church, were collecting points for information, and
bases for the exiles in their perpetual travels. Among the exiles

* The more extreme of the Covenanters, including a group associated with
the Argyll undertaking, were organised in a secret brotherhood, with signs,
code-names, and the like (See Erskine 211–12). Among these was James
Wishart, a contact of Carstares, who had commanded Argyll's ship, the *Anne*,
and later—under Queen Anne—became an Admiral of strong tory outlook.

themselves there was strong competition for these curious in-
cumbencies.* The Scottish churches in the Netherlands are the
propagandist counterpart of the Scottish regiments in Netherlands service.

For William Carstares, though outstanding in this society,
was not untypical. We shall meet many other Scots of his kind:
James Stewart, the slippery son of a Lord Provost of Edinburgh;
John Hutton, the herd-boy of Caerlavercock, who rose to be
William's personal physician and Bentinck's chief adviser on
German affairs; James Johnston, son of Archibald Johnston of
Warristoun, and a cousin of Burnet, who provided the energy and
drive for the handsome, idle Henry Sidney; and Gilbert Burnet
himself, an episcopalian by adoption, (and on that account still
more useful to William), but a Scot in upbringing and political
connections. All these were able Scots in their forties and fifties
who were drawn into William's service. In most cases they had
spent many years on the Continent.

Many of them had been educated there—Carstares had studied
at Leyden, Johnston at Utrecht. Hutton's degree was from
Padua. But above all—and this they had in common with the
military part of William's retinue—they were professional in
their approach to politics. There were idealogues among the
exiles—Ferguson, for instance, and Fletcher of Saltoun. But the
aim of those whom William attached to himself was professional
success, and when the Revolution made their political fortunes
they showed themselves well fitted for it. Carstares became successively Moderator of the General Assembly and Principal of
Edinburgh University, besides remaining William's confidant
for the rest of the King's life. Stewart, after many tergiversations,
finished as Lord Advocate and died in the odour of sanctity.
Hutton amassed a large fortune, was Fellow of the College of
Physicians and of the Royal Society, a Member of Parliament, and
Physician General to Marlborough's army. Johnston, after the
Revolution, was successively ambassador to Brandenburg and
Secretary of State for Scotland, in which post his letters show him
to have been a brisk man of business. Such men despised the

---

* In 1675, for instance, there were three candidates for the post of second
minister of the Church in Rotterdam—William Carstares, John Brown, and
Robert MacWard. All were refugees. The last was appointed. W. Steven,
History of the Scottish Church in Rotterdam (1833).

grandees who occupied the front of the stage. 'My advice is,' Johnston wrote to Carstares not long after the Revolution, in a letter about appointments in the army, 'since these regiments are in the country, to make the nobility colonels, and to give them men of experience to be lieutenant-colonels and majors out of the troops in Flanders.'[4]

King James, with his plans for a more modern state, would have been glad of such servants. It is among the paradoxes of the Revolution that the professional support for what King Louis regarded as a backward-looking particularism should have been far more effective than the service at the disposal of that worshipper of efficiency, King James. But it is not the only paradox. The King who wanted to broaden the religious basis on which his authority rested was to be chased from his throne as a bigot and a persecutor. The Revolution from which so much of liberal tradition of Europe flows was to be accomplished by the skilful use of a formula limiting toleration.

The Princes

Henry IV, author of the Edict of Nantes, which reconciled the huguenots in a catholic state, was a common ancestor of all the three princes most closely concerned in the English Revolution. Louis XIV was James II's first cousin and William of Orange's first cousin once removed. The relationship between William and James was even closer. William was James's nephew, and the closest in succession to the English crown after James's daughters Mary and Anne. And since William had married Mary he was also James's son-in-law.

On this dynastic point it is important to bear in mind that William's right of succession could be made more remote if James had any more children; while Mary's (and Anne's) would be damaged only if James had a son. Next after William came Maria Louisa, Queen of Spain, grand-daughter of Charles I and Louis XIV's niece.

The three princes had more in common than descent. Each had lost his father when quite young (William before he was born) and had spent childhood in deprivation, youth in the struggle to gain power. Louis, titularly king at the age of four, had grown up as the ward of Mazarin in the confusion of the Fronde. James had been twelve years old at his parting from the doomed Charles I, and had passed the next thirteen years in penurious exile. William had been born into a political climate that was deeply hostile to his family and all that it stood for—the climate of de Witt's republicanism. Fatherless, and from the age of ten motherless also, he had from early childhood been driven into self-dependence. His opportunity had come at the age of twenty-three. All three princes believed profoundly in divine right, but not, one may suspect, entirely on grounds of inheritance. To each the design of providence appeared from the success of his own early struggles. All three were self-made men.

In 1685 King Louis XIV was just entering the sixth decade of his stately life. Versailles was complete, not only as his home but as his capital, replacing a Paris that reminded him too much of his youth and of the Fronde. He had married Madame de Maintenon, and was firmly settled in his routine of gorgeousness and hard work. His passion for regularity and order had achieved an expression, both in his immediate surroundings, and in France itself, that drained away initiative and obliterated diversity. He had made France great, but that was incidental to his main purpose in life. 'La nation,' he once said, 'ne fait pas corps en France. Elle réside toute entière dans la personne du roi.'[1] It is difficult to call Louis a patriot. He did not identify himself with his country, but his country with himself. Observers were struck by his lack of emotion, his disregard for the feelings of others, his dryness of soul. As others have a passion for the accumulation of money, Louis was a miser in the accumulation of power.

One of his earliest acts on attaining his majority had symbolised what was to follow. In 1660 the young Louis paid a ceremonial visit to the Principality of Orange on the Rhône, the patrimony of his even younger cousin William. He climbed to the highest bastion of the formidable fortifications, then considered among the strongest in Europe, 'comprimant son indignation à la vue de cette orgueilleuse citadelle placée comme un défi au milieu de ses états'.[2] He looked out over the houses of the tiny enclave that had been a seed-bed of protestantism, a city of refuge for huguenots, the seat of the only university on the Continent west of the Rhine where a non-catholic could take a degree; and beyond he saw the continuous realm of France. Taking a small stone he cast it down into the moat as a symbol that demolition should begin, and solemnly descended. The fortifications, apart from the Prince's own palace, were pulled down, and it was announced that during the minority of the reigning Prince of Orange the protectorate of the Principality was undertaken by the King of France, to whom all revenues would be paid.

As Louis accumulated power and felt the strength of the machine which he controlled, its manipulation became his deepest interest. But because his ultimate objectives—apart from gathering more power—were obscure, there was a kind of incoherence about his skill. To Louis the conception of alliance on any footing of genuine equality simply did not occur Supporters he tolerated, but other powers, even when their interests might coincide with his own and therefore support some aspect of his policy, were fundamentally opponents to be undermined. Hence, as Mazure pointed out, he pursued simultaneously not only a French policy but, at times, a policy that would have been suitable for one or other of his rivals.* There was no bottom to his policy. In his eagerness to succeed the Emperor he pursued, before that objective had been achieved, a policy towards the protestant German states that would have been appropriate for the Emperor Leopold. And until it was too late he worked against his obvious ally, King James.

King James had mounted the thrones of England, Scotland, and Ireland at the comparatively late age of fifty-three. But he was still robust, a soldierly, or perhaps rather a sailorly figure, for there was always something of the quarterdeck about him. He took regular exercise, and kept regular hours. He had a reputation as a good manager, who meant what he said and got things done, unlike his brother Charles. James had glimpses of great achievements, which he felt he was not too old to attempt. He was aware of the latent strength that was developing in his kingdoms as a result of economic growth over the past twenty years. The prospects of imperial development in America and the Far East interested him deeply. He considered that Britain, if she was united at home and possessed an efficient central government, could play a much more independent part in the world than the jackal's, to which his brother's policy had consigned her. For these reasons he cast admiring eyes at the France of Louis XIV.

But James's glimpses of great possibilities were accompanied by a gross miscalculation of his own capacities and the nature of the difficulties he had to deal with. He placed too high a value on will-power: too little on patience. The tendency of his mind was to find several reasons for the policy he wished to pursue,

* Louis XIV voulait tout à la fois continuer, contre la cause protestante le système de Charles Quint, et contre l'Autriche le système de Richelieu. Mazure, F. A., J. *Histoire de la Révolution de 1688 en Angleterre* (1825).

rather than to adopt a policy for one good reason, so he became entrapped in inconsistency and accusations of hypocrisy. He justified his plans for religious toleration on the ground of humanity, on the ground of national unity, on the ground of economic advantage, on any ground, indeed, except the true one, which was his own deeply felt wish to enfranchise his catholic co-religionists. He never measured the weight of political feeling objectively, preferring to give parties a subjective importance derived from the stereotypes of his own mind. He seems to have thought, for instance, that the hold of the Church of England was far weaker than in fact it proved to be, and the sympathisers with Rome or dissent more powerful than they were. He considered, until it was too late, that he and William of Orange had a community of interest in maintaining 'the monarky' as it was: his gruffly avuncular letters to William recur endlessly to the family theme. Worst, almost of all, he supposed that policy could be reversed at will without weakening confidence. Tortuousness need not be evidence of cunning. In James's case it was the outcome of stupidity.

This is the context in which James's catholicism must be considered. His personal devotion had the narrow passion of a convert. Although he insisted on one of the most precisely traditional coronation ceremonies ever carried out, he was also crowned and anointed in private by his confessor before it began. While he could not ignore the political disadvantages of his religious position, he made a virtue of parading it, and almost seems to have persuaded himself that the political obstacles it presented were not material. In fact his plans for toleration and enfranchisement were irreconcilable with his other main objectives of strong government both at home and abroad. Toleration could only be achieved in the teeth of an established order, with all its vested interests, lay and ecclesiastical. That battle could not be fought at the same time as other battles, and yet James seems to have supposed that completion of his favourite plan, by demonstrating his authority, would strengthen and support his other aims.

James was confirmed in his over-estimate of his powers by the favourable political situation at the outset of his reign. Faction seemed to have spent itself in the struggle to exclude him from the succession three years earlier; and the possessing classes as a whole had swung round to the idea that the due succession they considered so important for their own estates was best guaranteed by a similar transmission of the crown. He was able to treat his first encounter with Parliament, in which his known opponents had been reduced to a handful, in the stereotyped manner of a new colonel taking over a regiment. 'The best way to make me meet you often,' he told them, 'is always to use me well.' His nephew William might be younger by eighteen years, but he was a bad life. James might well survive him; and in fact the two men died within a year of each other, the elder in spite of exile and failure, the other kept alive by success.

By contrast with James, who was a tallish, fair, conventional man, William was a very odd creature indeed. He was somewhat stunted in appearance, his legs being disproportionately short, so that he appeared at his best on horseback. A severe illness in 1675 had left him with a chronic cough, his teeth were unusually bad, even for the period, and he suffered acutely from piles. His one recreation, to which he gave as much of his time as he could, was hunting. He had indomitable energy, and no regard whatever for his personal safety.

He was certainly not Dutch. By ancestry he was as much an Englishman as James, who was half French, a quarter Danish, and a quarter Scots. The nearest analogy to William's chequered genealogy is the ancestry of the Emperor Charles V who, like William, had been born in the Low Countries and always felt at home there. William spoke and wrote fluently but incorrectly in four languages—Dutch, German, English, and French, the last being probably the one in which his thoughts worked most readily, for he spoke it to Bentinck on his deathbed.

His many quarterings had made William a great territorial magnate in his own right, with a standing wholly independent of his political position in the United Netherlands. Altogether he was master of more than thirty territories and jurisdictions in many parts of Western Europe. They were managed as a single estate under a 'Domains Council', over whose weekly meetings, held on Tuesdays, the Prince himself usually presided. The income from one hundred and two sources of revenue was paid into one account, and with patient financial management, redeeming debts, and recovering loans, the Prince became one of the wealthiest men in Europe.

Orange was not much of a financial asset—for most of William's lifetime its revenues were diverted to Louis—but it conferred the great treasure of sovereignty. William never visited Orange, but the status it gave him was never far from his thoughts and calculations. Many protestant Orangeois found their way into his household or on to his pension list. Louis' pressure on it, ending with formal abolition of its status in 1681, was never forgotten or forgiven, any more than its counterpart, Louis' sneering reference to his cousin as 'le petit sieur de Breda'. The restoration of Orange was carefully included among the peace terms of Ryswick in 1697 by the man who by that time had for nine years been King of England, Scotland, and Ireland.

The House of Orange had other properties in France—six manors in Franche-Comté which had been seized without compensation when Louis took over that province in 1668; and the hereditary burgraveship of Besançon, which came under the hostile scrutiny of Louis' lawyers in the 1680's, and was suppressed as repugnant to royal jurisdiction.* But most of William's property was either in Germany, in the United Provinces, or in the Spanish Netherlands and their adjoining principalities.† The first group made him a substantial figure in the Empire. As a result of the second he wielded personal influence in local politics, especially in Zeeland, where there was a situation not unlike English borough patronage in the following century. The third group, which was much the most important financially, gave him a personal stake in the future of the border lands that can be measured by the fact that during the war of 1673–9 his domain income was reduced by something like two-thirds. The only moment when William was seen to waver in his attachment to

* 12 September, 1684, 'Sa Majesté ne s'estant pas expliquée sur la Jurisdiction.' *Correspondance Administrative sous la Règne de Louis XIV*, II. 104.
† In Germany: Nassau, a substantial principality between Mainz and Siegen, and its dependencies Katzenellenbogen and Dietz (shared with his cousin); Vianden in eastern Luxembourg; Meurs, in Westphalia; Lingen, an enclave in the Bishopric of Munster, where William launched a university. In the United Provinces: Lingdam, Ter Veere, Flushing (all in Zeeland); Doesberg and Beuren (Guelderland); Naaldwijk (Holland); Isselstein (Utrecht); and at least a dozen places in 'The Generality' or North Brabant, which was governed by the Federation as a whole—including Breda, Gertruydenberg, Graves, Diest, and the fortress of Willemstadt. In the remainder of the Netherlands and Liège William's possessions included St. Vith and Herstal. The possessions in the United Provinces were administered separately from the Provinces in which they lay. See map, p. 4.

the Dutch Republic was when, in 1672, the panic-stricken Regenten were on the point of sanctioning a peace offer to Louis including cession of these hereditary possessions of the House of Orange.

In a good year of peace the income from the estates and jurisdictions alone exceeded a million guilders, of which one-third was ploughed back, one-third put to reserve, and one-third assigned to education and religion. The reserve found William his household expenditure, but it was also available for public works and special improvements in the estates such as the Oranjepolder land reclamation scheme and the fortifications of Willemstadt. This huge estate was, of course, kept quite separate from William's substantial salary and expenses as Commander in Chief and such additional sources of income as the three and a third per cent holding in the proprietory of the Dutch East India Company, which had been voted to him in recognition of his leadership during the struggle against the French.

King James once remarked wryly that the Prince of Orange was a rich man—richer than the King of England, and it was true.[3] But the nature of William's wealth was even more important than its amount. The fact that it was private gave William an independence and a freedom to pursue his own ends that James lacked. He recruited and paid his own household troops, selected his own advisers, entered into personal agreements, without reference to anyone. The French diplomatist Pomponne inferred there was something ungenteel and almost mean about the interest William took in his private fortune. This was a gross misreading of a man who was generous both naturally and as a matter of policy. William's care for money was based on his knowledge of the independence it gave him.

But this was not the only historical importance of the Nassau estates. They lay in the path of Louis' pulverising system, and their very existence, in the shape of jurisdictions, enclaves, royalties, hereditary feudal rights, made them typical victims of Louis' machine. From Louis' point of view the 'petit Sieur de Breda' was a French nobleman who had failed to come to Versailles, 'a man I never see', a Frondeur. But for the very same reasons William appealed to the Dutch and to the English landed gentry as that long-lost ideal, a prince who could really live of his own, who would not constantly be asking for money to pay for his palaces and his pleasures; above all a prince who understood what it was to be a landed gentleman because he was one himself, who understood pluralism because his own power and wealth depended on it.

These financial, geographical, and hereditary facts made William's career possible, and to some extent determined it. But it would be wrong to say that William's predominant motive was self-interest. He once significantly distinguished between what he called his interest and his obligation. His obligation might require him to sacrifice, or at any rate to risk his fortune, his short-term objectives, or even his life, all of which he included under the heading of 'interest'. Such had been the case when in 1672 he had declared it would be better to die in the last ditch (a phrase he has added to language) or even carry on the struggle from America, rather than concede what would amount to a French protectorate over the protestant United Netherlands.

William's obligation, for which he was willing to risk everything else, was the defence of protestantism as an established religion, and the system of particular rights—corporate, princely, traditional, that made this possible. In this sense he is the last representative of a sixteenth-century outlook, rather than a pioneer of the age of reason. Like other great men he marks both an end and a beginning, the transition from particularism to the world of interest. It has often been said that William was interested in England only as its possession counted in his personal duel with Louis, and he probably felt little of what he called 'obligation' towards the British episcopalians as such. But England, like his private fortune, was peculiarly important in furthering his great obligation, since without it the struggle to which he considered he was destined could not be carried on.

William rarely, if ever, discussed his decisions before they were made. They emerged from him after what one must assume was a careful calculation of the alternatives, and utterance was the moment of commitment. It was his habit to have subordinates make their submissions in the form of questions, to which he would enter the answers in the margin. It is consequently very difficult to say with certainty when the possibility of a particular operation first occurred to William. He kept possibilities in mind long before they became practical; and when he committed himself it was only to one stage of the new course at a time, again keeping open a choice between its various possible developments. His other leading characteristic, which contrasts oddly with his calculating, reserved methods of business, was loyal and generous friendship. Personal devotion to him commanded a warm and reliable response. Throughout his life he was surrounded by the friends and companions of his childhood, whom in the days of his success he rewarded handsomely with titles and money. But his dependability went far further than this. No service was ever forgotten, though the period might be long before protection, promotion, or patronage discharged the Prince's obligation. He understood the nature of patronage and manipulated it expertly. The possession of one of his frigid letters ending 'be assured of my friendship' was as good as a promise to pay. Failure, on the other hand, or disloyalty, were ruthlessly punished, regardless of earlier service. He was, in fact, a highly expert party politician, with experience of party intrigue, discipline, and the manipulation of corporations far exceeding any English politician's. The fact that he was a soldier as well, by necessity, has concealed his gifts as a party leader, which were greater than his gifts as a general.

This shy, ugly, reserved man, whose days were so fully occupied, had a gift for friendship: he not only felt warmly, but commanded devotion. His wife, Mary, identified her fortunes completely with his, and although he was not an undeviatingly faithful husband, all the evidence shows him to have been a loyal one. Bentinck remained his chief of staff throughout his career. But the most remarkable case is undoubtedly that of Gaspar Fagel, Grand Pensionary of Holland. Because he was William's most unlikely and most decisive friend, Fagel completes an account of William's character. He was older than William, and a typical member of the second generation of Vrijheid. Born at Haarlem in 1629, he was bred to the law for a public career, which he took up at the age of thirty-four as Pensionary of his native city, that is to say its permanent delegate to the States of the Province of Holland. In this capacity, and no doubt under the political influence of de Witt, he had been an extreme republican and one of the two proposers of the Perpetual Edict of 1667, whereby the Stadthoudership of Holland was permanently abolished (in fact the Edict endured for five years), and to all appearances the future of the House of Orange was finally

blocked. Three years later Fagel became Clerk of the State
General of the United Provinces, still as a safe adherent of the
republican régime. His moment came in 1672 when William
stood on one side for resistance to the French invasion and the
majority of the States General on the other for peace at any price
He had refused to authenticate the decision to ask for terms
which he considered to have been irregular, and told the emissary
to Louis, in language which had all the more force because o
its middle-class metaphor, that 'he might have sold the house, but
he would find it difficult to give possession'.

On 20 August 1672 Fagel succeeded the murdered de Witt a
Grand Pensionary of the Province of Holland. This was the
strategic post from which de Witt had directed the affairs of the
Republic. In form it was that of permanent delegate from the
Province of Holland to the States General. In Fagel's hands i
became the vital link between William's executive and military
authority and the representative machinery of the Republic
His lawyer's mind kept them distinct, yet ensured they acted in
concert: on matters of importance in the States General it became
the form for the Prince's advice to be sought before a resolution
was passed, and for a copy of the resolution to be sent to him fo.
his information. Within the framework of what remained a
diarchy, Fagel came very near to being William's chief minister
It was Fagel who negotiated the Peace of Nijmegen in 1679
Fagel who was reelected for successive five-year terms in 1677
1682, and 1687; Fagel who stood at the centre of William's in
telligence network; and Fagel whose skill was called upon again
and again to adjust differences between William and Holland
William and Amsterdam. The part he played in the English
Revolution was indispensable.

By 1685 William, though not the sovereign of Holland, and
still capable of distinguishing between his official position and
his personal interest, was established as the leading figure in the
politics of the United Provinces. He had held his own once
against Louis. His belief in his destiny and the charmed life he
bore had been confirmed. He had encountered the deepest
discouragement without flinching, in the conviction that persistence was bound to succeed in the end. During one of the
worst moments of the French war, in 1676, when even Fagel
had begun to speak of peace, William had told Temple that—

he had seen that morning a poor old man, tugging alone in a little boat with his oars, against the eddy of a sluice, upon a canal; that, when with the last endeavours he was just got up to the place intended, the force of the eddy carried him quite back again; but he turned his boat as soon as he could, and fell to his oars again; and thus three or four times while the Prince saw him; and concluded, this old man's business and his were too like one another, and that he ought, however, to do just as the old man did, without knowing what would succeed, any more than what did in the poor man's case.[4]

* * *

The action of the English Revolution turns on these three princes, each with his own web of interests and ambitions yet each interlocking in interest and ambition with the others. But serious historians are in a curious way the last of the mysogynists, the last believers in the subjection of women. Unless a woman occupies a political position in her own right it is enough for them to mention her as little more than a twig in a family tree. This may be partly because historians take their protective colouring unconsciously from their periods, during most of which the formal position of women was subordinate; and partly because documentary evidence about women tends to be confined to the domestic and the peripheral. As a result women in history are usually treated separately from the history of events, and by authors who are more interested in personal relationships, passion and intrigue than in the historical process as a whole. Yet Mary Clorine, wife of William and elder daughter of James by his first wife; Maria Beatrice, James's second wife; and Françoise d'Aubigné, Madame de Maintenon, Louis' second wife, were an integral part of the history leading up to 1688.

In 1685 all three were childless—though Maria Beatrice had borne several children none of them were then living. All three, also, were deeply influenced by religion, though it worked on them in different ways. In Mary Clorine it took the form of submission to her husband; in Maria Beatrice devotion to her church; in Madame de Maintenon admiration for morality and discipline.

Mary Clorine was twenty-three years old—eleven years younger than the husband to whom she had now been married for seven years. Her education had been rudimentary, her dynastic marriage, at first, loveless. But her mild, dependent nature, which

readily lent itself to harmless fantasies and single-minded attach-
ments, very soon fell under the domination of her strange husband. He liked her—even, in the end, came to be devoted to
her—but politically he treated her like a piece on a chessboard:
with care, but without discussion. 'He comes to my chamber,'
she wrote, 'about supper time, upon this condition, that I should
not tire him more with multiplicity of questions, but rather
strive to recreate him, over-toil'd and almost spent, with pleasing
jests, that might revive him with innocent mirth.'[5] And even in
this role she fell short. In Bentinck's sister-in-law, the ugly but
clever and graceful Betty Villiers, William found a companion
who was more his intellectual match. Sixteen-eighty-five saw the
dénouement of this infidelity, and William did not give up either
woman. Mary's struggle of indignation was brief, and she became as devoted to her husband as before. An incidental political
result was to enable William to get rid of several spies whom his
father-in-law James had planted in Mary's entourage.

The marriage of Maria Beatrice d'Este to James had also
been dynastic. As a girl of fourteen in Modena she had decided
to be a nun, and only the personal intervention of the Pope had
persuaded her to accept the duty of marrying a foreigner some
thirty years her senior whom she had never met. 'We therefore,'
Clement X had written, 'earnestly exhort you by these presents to
place before your eyes the great profit which may accrue to the
Catholic faith in the above-named Kingdom, and that inflamed
with zeal for the good which may result, you may open to yourself a vaster field of merit than that of the virginal cloister.'[6]
That had been in 1673, and in twelve years of married life she
had tried to do her duty, conscious that she had been sent to one
of the outposts of the true faith. She had weathered the fury of
the Popish Plot agitation, during which she had been accused of
treason and attempted murder, all with a wan Italian dignity;
and she had lost five children. But Isabel, her second, had lived
to be five years old, and Charles, Duke of Cambridge, a perfectly
healthy boy, had perished in infancy only because of the folly of
his half-sister Anne, who kissed him before she was out of
quarantine for smallpox. The record, though sad, was far from
unusual, and Maria Beatrice was still only in her twenties. The
idea that she could not have a child that would survive was as
absurd as it was to be politically important.

Françoise d'Aubigné was as different as possible from these two young dynastic wives. She had achieved the greatest triumph of her remarkable life by getting the Sun King to marry her when she was fifty. It is true that he did not make her his queen, or ever explicitly acknowledge their morganatic marriage, which probably took place in 1685. But her influence over Louis was far greater than that of the acknowledged wives of William and James over their husbands.

She had been born into a huguenot family, and had at one time been a practising calvinist: she was therefore, like James, a convert. Her rise from comparative obscurity had been managed by determination and force of character, and by cultivation of the clergy. Her central desire had never been concealed: 'Je voulais être estimée: l'envie de me faire un nom était ma passion'; and again 'je voulais de l'honneur'.[7] Over a period of seven years 'l'amie de l'amie' had edged her friend, Madame de Montespan—through whom she had been brought to court—out of Louis' favour, and when Louis' Queen died in 1683 the way was open to her great achievement.

Measurement of her influence on decisions is difficult. She was certainly consulted on everything. 'Qu'en pense votre Solidité?' the King used to ask her at meetings with ministers, or 'consultons la Raison'. But whether her advice was solid or reasonable is open to doubt. So far as her influence can be measured it was in the direction of propelling Louis along paths he was already inclined to tread, though sometimes against his better judgment. She approved of the policy that led up to the revocation of the Edict of Nantes. She believed in centralisation and in war. So Louis, as he approached old age and settled down to an unexciting domestic life, did not mellow. As his political plans grew vaster and more complex he became more angular and austere, buttressed by this clever and forceful woman who believed in him. Almost as much as Louis himself, Françoise de Maintenon symbolised the middle age of the system that it was William of Orange's mission to destroy. Yet the words St. Simon wrote of her might almost as readily have been applied to William:

Polie, affable, parlant comme une personne qui ne prétend rien, qui ne montre rien, mais qui imposait fort.[8]

France

In 1685 Europe was on fire at one end, and smouldering at the other. In the east the Emperor Leopold was at grips on the Danube with resurgent Turkey, while in the west an uncertain truce had since 1684 damped down the renewed flickers of war which had broken out in the Low Countries and on the Rhine since the great European settlement of 1679. Although the Truce of Regensburg had a formal duration of twenty years, nobody believed it could endure for as many as five.

That summer of 1658 all European eyes were fixed on the Danube and the Christian army operating under Charles of Lorraine against the Turks. Two years earlier the Turkish armies directed by the Grand Vizier Kara Mustapha had been at the gates of Vienna, and the fortunes of the House of Hapsburg had been at their lowest ebb. The Emperor had been forced to leave his capital city. On 12 September 1683 that celebrated siege had been raised by an international force under the command of John Sobieski, King of Poland, with Prince Waldeck, who was William of Orange's chief collaborator in German politics, as his chief of staff, and Charles of Lorraine, whose main object in life was to recover his duchy, now incorporated in France, as field commander. Large sums of Dutch money had helped to finance the Imperial forces, and the campaign can in truth be said to have owed its success to Christian Europe as a whole. A captured Turkish standard, erroneously believed to be the original holy flag of the Prophet, was sent in triumph to Pope Innocent, and reverently laid up in the Vatican.

The Turks, shaken but by no means defeated, still clung to the

fortresses on the Danube that covered the approaches to the
Balkans and the kingdom of their Hungarian calvinist ally,
Tököli. But at Linz in March 1685 Pope Innocent and the
Emperor, with Poland and Venice, formed the alliance which
was permanently to cripple Turkey as a major European power,
and has been called the Fourteenth Crusade. It was the last great
Christian coalition against Islam, the crowning achievement of
the militant Pope. Charles of Lorraine took the field on the
Danube with further success that summer, and the Venetians invaded Albania and Greece, where their operations led in due
course to the destruction of the Parthenon. In August 1685,
when Jeffreys was on circuit in the West of England dealing out
retribution to the broken adherents of Monmouth's rebellion,
King Louis was preparing the revocation of the Edict of Nantes,
protestant and catholic alike throughout central and western
Europe were unaffectedly celebrating the news of the fall of the
great Turkish fortress of Neuhäusel.

These Turkish setbacks were not satisfactory to King Louis,
for a number of reasons. The pressure of the Turks on the
Emperor had been invaluable to Louis' erosive tactics on the
Rhine, and had helped to put Leopold in a suitable frame of mind
to accept the Truce of Regensburg, under cover of which these
tactics could conveniently develop. Moreover Turkish preoccupation with the Danube diverted the attention of Constantinople from other parts of its huge empire. Louis' eyes were already turning towards Algeria, and for this purpose he was concentrating his fleet in the Western Mediterranean, with consequences that could not have been foreseen. And yet Louis valued
his role as a Christian champion, and he found the results of his
benevolence to Turkey embarrassing, especially now that Turkey
was faced by a Christian coalition. Europe smiled when the
Christian King's ambassador to Constantinople was received
with special marks of favour, including the coveted honour of
the sofa, while his ambassador to the Pope was perpetually involved (on instructions from Versailles) in undignified wrangles
about diplomatic privilege. It is difficult to believe that the
desirability of making a specifically catholic gesture in response
to these critics did not enter into Louis' calculations that autumn.

For six years now, to the mounting indignation and alarm
of his neighbours, he had been improving piecemeal on the

advantages he had gained from the Treaty of Nijmegen. That comprehensive settlement, arrived at with so much effort and ceremony, formed the minds of a generation of European statesmen, and served as a perpetual datum line for later negotiations. The hall at Nijmegen where it had been signed was a showpiece, with portraits of those who had achieved the peace preserved on its walls. France had reaped great gains there from the Empire and old-fashioned particularism. The acquisition of Franche-Comté had been ratified and with it what is still today, with only minor modifications, the French frontier with Switzerland; while further to the north only some remaining rags of Alsace now separated France from the Rhine. Further north still Louis had acquired the whole of Lorraine, evicting its Duke, and the substance of what is now the French part of Flanders. In producing a France very much the shape it is today, the negotiators of Nijmegen have been justified by history.

The techniques employed by Louis to exploit these gains were then unfamiliar, and deeply disturbing. In the first place he proceeded to introduce into his newly acquired territories the same forms of centralised administration that applied in the rest of France. The old order could accommodate itself easily to changes in the sovereignty of counties, duchies, and even villages (by marriage, inheritance, or agreement) because it was tacitly accepted that under a new sovereign local government continued very much as under the old one. For instance the King of Sweden had come to be Duke of Zweibrücken on the Rhine but that did not mean Zweibrücken was ruled as part of Sweden. The King of Spain ruled Brabant, but he did so under a local constitution, the Joyeuse Entrée. There were Dutch troops stationed in the strategic counties of Cleves and Jülich, beyond the frontier of Overijssel, but the constitutions of those counties were unaffected. But Franche-Comté, Flanders, and the Rhine Provinces were simply absorbed, as rapidly as possible, into France. The medal struck by Louis in 1681 to mark his progress in Alsace bore the uncomfortable inscription *Alsatia in Provinciam Redacta*.

Worse still, at the same time as he trampled on particularism, Louis turned its own weapons of law and custom against it. As soon as a territory was acquired his lawyers began a systematic scrutiny of its legal history with the purpose of determining which places, in the interminable convolutions of feudal law, had ever depended on it, and then claiming those as part of the acquisition. The same method was employed, on a more modest scale, and at the same time, by Louis' English pensioner Charles II, when legal teams were set to work scrutinising municipal charters for flaws which would enable them to be forfeited. It was a world in which those who thought they had unquestionable rights suddenly realised they might not be safe.

One such 'reunion' concerned Orange, which Nijmegen had formally returned to William, who promptly directed that its fortifications should be rebuilt. But the Treaty had scarcely been sealed before Louis' lawyers were engaged on research into the medieval history of Orange with the aim of demonstrating that its sovereign status had no legal foundation. On 15 August 1682 a regiment of French dragoons under the Lieutenant General of Languedoc occupied the place and had the new fortifications removed. So angry was William that when, in October, he received a visit from Lord Cornbury, his uncle James's nephew by marriage, he refused him a room, made him stay at an inn, and would not speak a word to him at the meal which protocol required to be taken with the young man sitting next to him: all to demonstrate his indignation at his uncles of England, who had acquiesced in this breach of the terms of Nijmegen.

For Nijmegen had, on balance, weakened William. The war had, it is true, established him as perpetual and hereditary Stadhouder in most, though not all, of the Seven Provinces (his cousin, the Prince of Nassau-Dietz, with whom he was on bad terms, was Stadhouder of Friesland); but the stadhoudership, and William's military offices, meant far less in peace than in war. And republican sentiment, which was still strong, suggested that William, who had profited so much politically from the state of war, would have prolonged its expense and sufferings if he could. The Dutch wanted to settle down to a period of calm and peaceful prosperity. They considered that so far as they were concerned the terms of Nijmegen were not unsatisfactory. They retained possession of the vital frontier fortress of Maastricht; Dutch troops were stationed in the chain of towns beyond their frontiers to the south, known as 'the Barrier'; and above all Louis had conceded them free trade: an immense concession from an economic nationalist who in other circumstances had gone so far as to

order his own son's dress waistcoat to be burned when he found
out that it had been made from foreign cloth. The concession
was, of course, a calculated one, for the purpose of developing
two self-balancing foci of power in the United Provinces, and to
provide the French ambassador, d'Avaux, with a basis of operations.

Orange bothered nobody but William. The cases of Luxembourg and Strasbourg illustrate better the kind of action that
troubled Europe almost more than direct old-fashioned aggression. Strasbourg, with its bridge over the Rhine, had retained its
ancient status as an independent municipal republic, even though
surrounding Alsace had been acquired by France. Two years after
Nijmegen more modest 'reunions' in the neighbourhood of Strasbourg left it an enclave. There were other grounds, apart from its
strategic significance, for eliminating its independence. It was
protestant, and had become, like Orange, a haven for huguenots
retreating before the constantly increasing pressure exerted by
Louis against their livelihoods, their family life, and the exercise
of their religion. The plans for the final blow were prepared by
Louvois. Fifty thousand men, dispersed in comparatively small
bodies over a wide area, were destined for the operation, which
was thrown into motion by the issue of a single secret order on
10 September 1681. A fortnight later Strasbourg was besieged.
The French resident there, who had not, of course, been told
what was to happen, could give no satisfactory explanation to the
city authorities; but the commander of the French forces, who
was better informed, announced to the magistrates that Strasbourg
was part of Alsace, and refusal to recognise this fact would result
in immediate bombardment. Next day Louvois, who had been
officially on a hunting holiday in the neighbourhood, arrived,
and on 30 September Strasbourg accepted the inevitable. The
town was incorporated in France. The cathedral was restored to
catholicism—a measure which Louvois reported to the French
ambassador in Regensburg with a direction to make a point of con-
trasting it with the Emperor's apparent willingness to compromise with the Hungarian protestants. A new incumbent for the
reclaimed cathedral was also in readiness in the person of Franz
von Furstenberg, brother to the coadjutor of the Archbishop of
Cologne, Cardinal Wilhelm von Furstenberg. Both members
of this Rhenish princely family had attached themselves to Louis'

fortunes, and were spearheads for the penetration of Western Germany.

The coup de main at Strasbourg and the installation of Bishop Franz von Furstenberg was duly noted by William in a letter to his collaborator and kinsman Prince Waldeck on 23 October. He lamented the feebleness with which the German princes were reacting, and enclosed a copy of an agreement he had just signed with Sweden for preserving the status quo: 'c'est un pied pour faire une ligue'. Waldeck's efforts in this direction were unceasing, but they achieved little.*

The campaign against Luxembourg was opened while the secret moves for the annexation of Strasbourg were already in train. In this case Spain was the victim, since the Duchy of Luxembourg was part of the Spanish Netherlands. In July 1681 French official lawyers mounted a claim to the County of Chimy, which formed a sizeable part of the Duchy, and when this claim was resisted four French cavalry brigades entered Chimy and lived there at the expense of the inhabitants. After a few weeks of this the Spanish governor conceded the French claim, whereupon he was presented with fresh claims, based on profound feudal research, that virtually the whole Duchy, with the exception of the town of Luxembourg itself, had formally depended upon, or been subject to, medieval Counts of Chimy, in whose shoes King Louis was now acknowledged to stand.† Troops were moved accordingly. The capital was not entered, but traffic to and from it was so impeded by military patrols that life became very difficult for its inhabitants. Protests were met with the bland response that the policing of roads on French territory could not be discussed with a foreign government.

Matters had remained in this uneasy state until October 1683, when Spain was goaded into declaring war. It was a month after

---

* See William to Waldeck, 23 October 1681 in Müller, P. L., *Wilhelm III von Oranien und Georg Friederich von Waldeck* (1880) p. 115. Sweden's interest in the Rhine arose in an acute form when Charles XI, in April 1681, inherited the Duchy of Zweibrücken, in the Bavarian Palatinate, and found himself promptly faced with a legal claim that it had originally depended on the bishoprics of Metz, Toul, and Verdun (since 1679 incorporated in France). The claim was dropped in the interests of Louis' Baltic policy, but not before Charles had entered into an agreement with the United Provinces to preserve the settlement of Nijmegen.

† Including the Lordship of Vianden, which was a personal fief of William of Orange.

Sobieski's great victory at the gates of Vienna had given the eastern Hapsburgs a breathing space. The Spanish Netherlands were at once invaded, and from 22 December to Boxing Day Luxembourg was subjected to bombardment. During those four days more than three thousand mortar shells were fired into the town as a demonstration of French striking power, and in the spring the place was besieged and captured in form. In August 1684 the Hapsburg monarchs accepted Louis' offer of a truce of twenty years, coupled with recognition, de facto if not de jure, of all French acquisitions since Nijmegen, including Strasbourg and Luxembourg.

King Charles of England had not played a creditable part in all these transactions, as was well known to his nephew William. Charles had been a guarantor of the Nijmegen settlement, but in the spring of 1681 he had entered into an informal arrangement with Louis under which Charles would gradually disentangle himself from these guarantees, and would receive from Louis a quarter of a million sterling over the next three years—an amount equal to rather more than ten per cent of the annual public revenue of England at that time. Since it was obvious that such an agreement implied Louis' intention to proceed with annexations as and when it suited him, Charles had specifically stipulated that the agreement did not extend to French aggression against Strasbourg or Luxembourg.

Within a few months Charles had to digest both—the latter with a very wry face and the solace of an additional £40,000. But he did nothing to help Spain, indeed he agreed to play the hypocritical part of an arbitrator whose good offices are unacceptable, for which Louis had cast him. The matter had been handled with great virtuosity by the French ambassador in London, Paul de Barillon, whose penetration of English politics was so deep that during his embassy he can almost be regarded as an English politician in his own right. Within a week of opening the Luxembourg affair to Charles he had an English opposition politician, Montagu, on his doorstep offering, in return for financial support, to get up parliamentary pressure against any move by King Charles to adhere to his treaty obligations towards Spain. Barillon recommended Louis to invest in this piece of hedging, but Louis decided to give up the plan of pensioning both sides in England, or even one of them. He was now satisfied that Charles would stand anything, and could be brought to heel if need be, either by going slow on the existing subsidy, or by blackmail. Indeed after the Truce of Regensburg had been concluded there was very little that Louis wanted the King of England either to do or to abstain from doing, except keep quiet. Nor was the French financial position in the early sixteen-eighties of a kind to encourage unnecessary expense.

King Charles's death in February, 1685, and the accession of James, were therefore unwelcome to Louis. James, in accordance with his picture of himself as a strong man, hankered after a positive policy. Although a catholic, he was more nearly related to Louis' irreconcilable opponent William than Charles had been, being his father-in-law as well as his uncle: and because an open catholic, he was less susceptible to blackmail than Charles had been. Louis' stipulation in the secret Treaty of Dover that Charles should in due course declare himself a catholic had been designed to cause Charles domestic trouble at a time to be selected by Louis. No such obligation could be laid on James. A compliant House of Commons, the ignominious failure of the rebellions of Monmouth and Argyll, the possibility that after all some kind of compromise fitting the catholic king into a protestant establishment might be worked out—all these gave Louis ground for concern. Additional funds were therefore once more put at Barillon's disposal, and he was instructed to give James £40,000 as a preliminary gift; but no more was to be offered unless, to use the ambassador's words, 'I see the Parliament dissolved, and the King of England reduced to make his subjects submit by force.'[1] In the meantime he was to do his best to produce that state of affairs. 'Vous vous servirez,' wrote King Louis a few months later, 'de toutes les occasions qui se présenteront pour insinuer au roi d'Angleterre l'intérêt qu'il a d'employer son autorité au rétablissement de la religion catholique.'[2] At the same time opposition leaders were to be assured that the King of France would never support James in forcing England to become catholic, and that they could freely oppose King James's policy without fear.

By contrast nothing could have been more respectful or correct than William's behaviour during the first months of the new reign. He did not actually make the voyage of congratulation himself, but he sent his close collaborator and kinsman Ouwerkerk

with a friendly message protesting future goodwill and regretting
past differences. He even agreed to remove a number of officers
from the British Brigade in Holland, on the ground that James
considered them politically unsympathetic. They were quietly
found commissions in other mercenary regiments, either in the
Dutch service, or in the forces of some German prince friendly
to the House of Orange. He politely declined, however, to replace Henry Sidney as the Brigade's commander, although
James considered the post should go to his new ambassador to
the United Provinces, Sir Bevil Skelton.

It is impossible that William was not aware, through his own
intelligence sources, of the attempt to be made by Monmouth
and Argyll. But he certainly gave it no official encouragement.
He had every reason for wishing it the complete failure that in
fact overtook it. Its sponsors were precisely the kind of men
whose success would produce the unstable England William
wished to avoid. An eye was kept on them through Carstares,
whose contact Stewart drafted Argyll's manifesto,* but when, a
month after the expeditions sailed, William received requests
from James for the loan of the six regiments to help in suppressing the rebellion, he hastened to comply. The requests
were promptly referred to the States General who (Friesland
dissenting) approved the transport of the force under William's
direction and, of course, at James's expense. James was also to
pay for the regiments while employed in England, and in due
course an exact repartition of the sums owing to the treasuries
of each province was worked out by the Council of State.

The operation was carried out with great speed and efficiency.
Bentinck was in charge, and within a month the first three regiments had disembarked at Gravesend. James reviewed them at
Blackheath only three days later, and was heard to say more than
once that he had never seen finer soldiers. But Sedgemoor was
won, and the rebellion crushed, before they could join the main
army, and by the end of July the Brigade was ready to re-embark.
The farewell review was made the occasion for executing two

---

* See the entries in Carstares' notebook quoted (I have not traced the
original) in McCormick, p. 35, which show that Carstares made disburse-
ments on behalf of William to Wishart, who commanded one of Argyll's
ships. Wishart is spoken of as a man 'of whose honesty and willingness to
serve his Highness I am fully assured'. It is probable that this was an intelligence payment, rather than help for the rebels.

Willem van Bentinck,
as Earl of Portland

Marshal Armand von
Schomberg, in 1689

Henry Compton,
Bishop of London (Knelle

Lieutenant-General-
Admiral Herbert

soldiers, who had been condemned for drinking the Duke of Monmouth's health, but this was the only unhappy note in an exercise which ended in mutual professions of gratitude and esteem on both sides, and no doubt afforded Bentinck valuable experience in the logistical problems of transporting large numbers of troops across the North Sea at short notice.[3]

William's co-operation had been quite wholehearted. His instructions to Bentinck were to emphasise the identity of interest between the two branches of the House of Stuart, reserving only the point that William was entitled to the patronage of the Brigade. So dutiful had William been that he had offered himself to attend the expedition, but James had rather condescendingly declined the idea. 'I do not think it at all proper,' he wrote, 'at this time for our common interest, it being as necessary for you to stay in Holland at this conjuncture, to keep things well there, as it is for me to stay here in London.'[4]

This was true. For some time past William had been working quietly to reconstruct and strengthen the exposed position in which Louis' Truce of Regensburg had left him. Through his authority as Stadhouder to confirm elections to town councils he had carried out a ruthless purge of Orange supporters who had shown weakness over acceptance of the Truce: years of faithful attachment did not excuse disloyalty in this respect. And he disposed of the family feud with Henry Casimir of Nassau-Dietz, Stadhouder of Friesland. As recently as 1684 there had been suggestions that Henry Casimir should be installed as Stadhouder of Holland. But on 30 March 1685 William was able to write that 'All obstacles have now been removed which have till now prevented so close a relationship between us as was due to our proximity of blood and interest.'[5]

In May William was occupied with far more important business than the Monmouth expedition, then just dropping out from the Texel to its inevitable fate. This was the visit of Paul von Fuchs, a Minister of the Elector of Brandenburg, to Holland. Von Fuchs, Leyden-educated like his master, a lawyer and talented pamphleteer, was not untypical of the modern-minded men whom the Great Elector Frederick had enlisted to improve his dominions.

On the whole, though with important periods of exception, Frederick had been content to accept French subsidies and the role in the French scheme of things that King Louis assigned him. For most of his career he had been pre-occupied with building up the economic strength of his dominions, and adding territory quietly to territory, and he had no wish to incur the permanent enmity of the most powerful king in Europe, whose methods he was, in certain respects, imitating. But by 1684, with immigration and annexations, he had raised his state from a mere 200,000 inhabitants, barely populating a territory of 600 square miles, to nearly a million, covering 2,000 square miles. Moreover he was troubled by Louis's eruptions on the Rhine.

A central feature of the Great Elector's policy had been toleration. It went hand in hand with the encouragement of immigration. His gain was King Louis' loss. As the restrictions on the huguenots tightened, and despite the laws against movement out of France, greater and greater numbers were attracted into the Elector's dominions: and just as huguenots were not the only objects of French persecution, they were not the only recipients of Frederick's hospitality. Jews, banished from Paris, settled in Berlin. Dutch settlers also were encouraged. On 29 October 1684 this liberal policy was crowned by the Edict of Potsdam, which offered to every settler from abroad his travelling expenses, land, building materials, loans, and ten years' tax exemption. The response was considerable. A hundred years later, in 1770, it was calculated that one-sixth of the Prussian population at that time were the descendants of huguenot refugees.

Fuchs's visit to the Hague established the second link in the power structure that made the English Revolution possible. If the link between the House of Orange and the Republican régime in the United Provinces was the first of these, the second was undoubtedly the entente between Brandenburg and the United Provinces that stemmed from Fuchs's work in 1685. This took the form of a pact eliminating all outstanding financial claims in return for a large payment to the Elector; and a defensive agreement which was to last for fifteen years. At the same time— and no less important—Fuchs offered his services as mediator between William and the town of Amsterdam, and succeeded in settling a number of differences which had been carefully exploited by the French Ambassador d'Avaux.

One other event in the first half of 1685 contributed to the explosion three years later. In March Charles, Elector Palatine of the Rhine, the last of his line and unmarried, died. His dominions straddled the middle Rhine, just north of Strasbourg, and Charles is remembered in history, like so many of his contemporary German princes, for a pro-French policy throughout the five years of his reign. King Louis' interest in the future of the Palatinate was reinforced by the fact that his brother's second wife was the sister of the Elector Charles's predecessor. But much to Louis' fury the Emperor Leopold managed to instal the lawful heir; and this heir, the Duke of Neuberg, happened to be the Emperor Leopold's father-in-law. This friction on the Middle Rhine, which was sharpened by a dispute about the family furniture, was later to produce one of the most wanton acts of destruction in European history. But for the moment no forward move on the Rhine was possible for Louis. The Emperor's renewed interest in the Rhine frontier unquestionably strengthened William's position.

That autumn King Louis' main preoccupation was at home. He had decided, in response to the pressure of the established church, that the time had come for a final solution of the huguenot question. On 17 October he revoked the Edict of Nantes. On the thirty-first of the same month young Erskine, just back in Utrecht after his adventures with Argyll's rebellion, saw refugees arriving there: 'several hundred were in a few weeks come to this town, and many more to Amsterdam'.[6]

The Revocation, as has been often emphasised, was not a sudden measure, but the culmination of a policy pursued over a considerable number of years. But the moral effect, both in France and in Europe, was immense. The pace of emigration quickened. Vauban, the great engineer, computed the total loss of population as 100,000, taking with them not only their skills but capital funds estimated at 60 million livres. Among them was Armand von Schomberg, who surrendered his marshal's baton and entered the service of the Elector of Brandenburg. It is easy to see what Louis lost. On what gains did he reckon?

One factor, certainly, was a strengthening of his Christian position, at home and abroad. Revocation was the darling demand of the most loyal element of his own clergy. The words of Cosnac, Bishop of Valence, at the General Assembly of the French clergy in the summer of 1685, ingeniously mingled flattery with blackmail: 'We ask nothing except in the name of the Lord, and for

His Glory, and we ask it from a Prince who can do anything he wishes, and who wishes above all things the re-establishment of the reign of Jesus.'⁷ When the Revocation had been signed the King received clerical homage in the most elaborate and grovelling terms. He was Theodosius, he was Constantine, he was Charlemagne. There can be no doubt that as a step in gaining full control of the organs of public opinion and education within his own kingdom Revocation was valuable; and abroad it helped to recover some of the ground lost through his abstention from crusading alongside the Emperor and the Pope against the Turks. He even had a polite letter from Innocent XI.

Louis did not regard his act as a measure of persecution. To him, and to the clergy who recommended it, the Revocation was a reunion, similar in nature and in the techniques by which it was accomplished, to the 'reunions' on the frontier. It is only by making this conceptual shift that an apparently insensate and disastrous decision can be understood as entirely consistent with the rest of Louis' policy. To him the Edict of Nantes was not a charter of toleration or a fundamental law, or (to use the contemporary English phrase) an indulgence to tender consciences. It was a treaty which his predecessors had agreed to, conferring certain privileges and exemptions on a section of their subjects. Such a treaty could be denounced. The period of 'legal persecution' leading up to the Revocation—premiums for conversions, dragonnades, restrictive decrees professing to interpret the original Edict, all have their parallels in such episodes in external policy as the seizure of Strasbourg and Luxembourg. From this point of view the Revocation itself was only the last step in a familiar orderly process. Louis was almost certainly himself misled by the rosy statistics about the success of the earlier measures. The storm of indignation, and the outpouring of emigrants, were quite unexpected. He had accepted the Archbishop of Paris's argument that there was so little protection for the huguenots left in the Edict that its disappearance was no more than a piece of administrative tidiness which would have a beneficial effect on majority opinion.

To Louis, therefore, Revocation seemed administratively sound, politically wise, relevant to his foreign policy, and in accordance with his own personal piety. There has rarely been a better example of a calamitous error being made for a combination of apparently good reasons; nor of an act of apparently internal policy having more widespread international repercussions. Wherever the refugee huguenot travelled he was the symbol of persecution and of abrogated rights. Protestantism and particularism now had a common wrong, and their common champion, William, a refurbished case.

In England the Revocation dangerously weakened the position of the complacent James, fresh from his triumphs over Monmouth and Argyll, confronting his first and fervently loyal Parliament. He did not, of course, approve Louis' action in public. He even extended official sponsorship to the raising of funds for the refugees. But confidence was shaken. People began to look to their rights. The climate in which equal rights for Roman Catholics in England might have been achieved without the use of force suddenly clouded over.

Suddenly, too, it became possible to believe in the existence of a vast, international catholic plot under the direction of the Pope and the King of France to reclaim North-Western Europe for the true faith. The infection of plots was endemic: now every action of James or Louis could be interpreted in this conspiratorial sense. The interpretation was ludicrously wide of the mark: the aims of Louis and James were in many respects opposed, and the Pope, who was in any case far more interested in Eastern Europe at that moment, was hostile to Louis and distrustful of James. Nevertheless the vague general picture had the charm of simplicity, tradition, and excitement. The foundations of Revolution had been laid, though the decisions had not yet been taken. In November, however, General von Spaen, the Brandenburger Governor of Cleves and Mark, visited the Hague for conversations about strengthening the fortifications on the Dutch Eastern frontier.

Part Two

THE POWER STRUGGLE

Britain

Just one month after the revocation of the Edict of Nantes, with King James doing his best to maintain an impression of broad-minded generosity to the streams of refugees arriving in England, his parliament assembled for its autumn session. It contained many new faces in senior positions. A new Lord Chancellor, Jeffreys, presided over the House of Lords. However much his loyal service in dealing with the Western rebels was approved—and there were many members of parliament who thought the rebels had got no less than they deserved—he was a disagreeable contrast to his cultivated and reliable predecessor, North. He was only thirty-seven, he drank too much, his self-confidence overran decency, he did not command respect. Neither did the Speaker of the House of Commons, Sir John Trevor.* And it was even less acceptable that the management of parliamentary business had been entrusted to two Scottish peers sitting in the Commons for English constituencies, Lord Middleton, the Secretary of State, and Lord Preston.† Both had served their political apprenticeship under James in Scotland, where methods of parliamentary organisation were very different, and a great deal cruder. But among those surrounding the throne in the new state of

* Bramston, the experienced Essex country gentleman, who sat in this parliament for Maldon, repeatedly comments on Trevor's inadequacy in the Chair.
† Charles, Earl of Middleton, was forty-five, and a man of charm and wit, though his political experience was limited. Richard Graham, Viscount Preston, was only thirty-seven, and was English by origin, though a Scottish peer. He had only just been recalled from the Paris Embassy, where he had been throughout the Luxembourg crisis.

affairs the most conspicuous was the other Secretary of State, Robert Spencer, Earl of Sunderland. His savage dynamism, lack of scruple, and shortage of ready money, his ruthless desire for power and his knowledge of foreign affairs, were already making him the indispensable minister of the new reign.

The middle eighties, in fact, saw one of those rifts in the succession of political life, such as Namier notes during the early years of George III. Most of the men who had been through the Cromwellian age and dominated the politics of the restored monarchy had gone: Lauderdale in 1682, Shaftesbury and Essex in 1683, Arlington and Leoline Jenkins in 1685. Henry Coventry was to die in 1686, and Buckingham, already in retirement, a year later. Of that generation Danby still lived and hoped, but he had nothing to hope for from James. Apart from him and Sunderland only three major politicians with experience of high office were available—the King's two brothers-in-law, the Earls of Rochester and Clarendon; and the Marquis of Halifax. It is not surprising that James found himself employing new, unfamiliar men, but the fact emphasised the change of monarch and demanded the establishment of fresh confidence.

Halifax had been removed from office shortly before Parliament met. He is one of the most remarkable, puzzling, and attractive politicians of his century. If Clarendon and Rochester represented the fixed centre of a political spectrum, Halifax was the shifting one. As political opinion extended towards one extreme or another, so he sidled gently to resume his position precisely between the two new extremes. He lived for politics almost as an artist lives for art.

His father had been a loyal Yorkshire cavalier, and by careful management Halifax had become immensely rich and well connected. His estates in six counties covered nearly eight thousand acres. His maternal uncle was Sir William Coventry, one of his sisters was married to Sunderland, and he had himself married a sister of Shaftesbury. His sources of information were numerous and good, and his own family was widely spread, one daughter being married to a huguenot nobleman now a refugee in England, and one son fighting with the Emperor's army against the Turks on the Danube. In the seventies, when the monarchy had been under attack, Halifax had stood against the Shaftesbury faction, opposing the Test Act and the exclusion of James from the succession. Now that monarchy was at its strongest, Halifax was evolving away from it and casting cautious, oblique glances across the North Sea. He was an agnostic in politics, a reader and admirer of Montaigne. But if Halifax had any conviction it was hostility to France; and this hostility was fully reciprocated by King Louis.*

Sunderland, by contrast, tended to extremes, and there can be little doubt of the model he was now setting himself: it was Louvois, the implacably efficient instrument of King Louis' ambition. But although Sunderland did not lack political gifts, he was more implacable than efficient. His strength lay in his freedom from personal prejudices and a willingness to go to the limit. His weakness was indifference not merely to administrative detail (though that was to prove important) but to probable political consequences. In December 1685 this fatally well-cast minister added the Presidency of the Council from which Halifax had been dismissed to the Secretaryship of State he already had; and a year later he was to displace all other competitors in the confidence of his master.

The English parliament was still a remarkably compact and homogeneous body—far more so than the parliaments Namier has analysed. The House of Lords was a small enough assembly— about 150 lay and 26 spiritual peers—for the views and move-ments of every active member to be known and followed without much difficulty.† The lower house, with 513 members, was nearly as large as the Commons of today, though of course it covered only England and Wales. At this number it was able to muster something like a five per cent sample of the landed proprietors that made up the overwhelming bulk of its member-ship. Its outlook was therefore difficult to vary by a fresh choice, as the King was to find.

* Barillon to King Louis, 5 November 1685 (Fox, cxxx–cxxxi) reporting Halifax's dismissal and suggesting that Halifax's sympathy for the United Provinces and Spain had been responsible for the 'honeymoon' relationship between James and William; and King Louis to Barillon (Fox, cxxxiii) in which the King agrees that Halifax's dismissal has been 'fort avantageux à mes intérêts.' Reresby was also quite clear about Halifax's opposition to French policy (*Memoirs* 308, 309).
† The list prepared for Dijkvelt showing the political complexion of the peerage in 1687 (see K. H. D. Haley in E.H.R. for April 1954) lists 137 lay adult peers and 24 bishops (two sees were vacant), a total of 161. This list has 8 omissions. Catholic peers, of course could not sit.

James hectored his parliament, but he considered it important to carry it with him. In this, as in other things, he displayed the naïve strain in his character. He was a man who believed that opposition to an objectionable request would fade away if only the point was put frankly and firmly enough. But there was also a strong element of international calculation in James's desire to enlist parliamentary support for his policy. He had learned from experience that the English government lost weight abroad if it was at loggerheads with parliament, and lost still more if—because of such differences—there was no parliament at all. He had no doubt that he could, if he wished, legislate on his own authority for his own realm, but the subjects on which he wished to legislate most were the expansion of the armed forces and the repeal of the Penal Laws and the Test Act; and these were matters of international significance. On religious policy, in particular, parliamentary endorsement would relieve him both of blackmail from Louis and criticism from William. There was thus a paradox. In his race against time to achieve his programme, the absolutist King James bent every effort to assemble a parliament that would approve it; while to William every day that passed without a parliament was a day gained.

Despite its initial friendliness to the King, the parliament of 1685 jibbed at his proposal to repeal the Penal Laws and the Test Act. The historian—most unusually—can write with confidence that the state of public opinion among people who counted was deeply opposed to any relief of this kind; and this was the issue, nationally and internationally, that was to precipitate the Revolution. It is not at first sight obvious why the preservation of rules imposing religious disabilities should have been the pretext for a Revolution which is very generally supposed to have ushered in a period of greater tolerance and reasonableness—as in fact it did. Such, nevertheless, was the case.

The English were not a bigoted or even particularly zealous people in 1685, though they were subject to certain illusions. Two years later almost every man of substance in the country answered affirmatively to the third of King James's celebrated questions—'Whether he will support the King's Declaration for liberty of conscience by living friendly with those of all persuasions?' No doubt many of the answers were made for the sake of peace and quiet, but they show at least that expression of intolerance was no longer an acceptable political attitude in public. The reply of the Hon. John Darcy, one of the magistrates for the North Riding, was typical of hundreds: 'It has been my desire, and ever shall be, to live peaceably with all men, as becomes a good Christian, and will ever do so.'

But Darcy, again like many of his fellow magistrates replying to the same questionnaire, expressed it as his 'present opinion not to repeale the penall Lawes and the Test'.[1] These two were wholly different in nature and impact. The original Penal Laws stretched back to the Tudor Settlement, though some—mainly directed against non-conformity—were as recent as the restored monarchy. Together they made up a vast code imposing fines and other punishments on all who did not conform to the national religion. They punished non-conformists and Roman Catholics as such, since in principle nobody could deviate openly from the Church of England without incurring their penalties. Given the structure of society and administration such laws could be enforced in patches only. All enforcement depended on the outlook of the local magistracy, so that in some districts the penal laws (or some of them) were enforced, in others they were selectively applied, and in others again they were not applied at all. Public opinion was already moving away from them.

But the Test Act was much more recent, and it was easily enforced because it was almost self-enforcing. Certainly it did not depend on the outlook of local magistrates for its effect, which was to disqualify catholics and non-conformists from any significant office: from commissions in the armed forces, from the magistracy, from the universities, and from parliament.* To most Englishmen—indeed to most Europeans—it was in the nature of things that the exercise of authority in society should

* The Act (25 Car. 2, cap. 2) required people covered by it (broadly all office-holders, but not 'inferior officers' such as the rank and file of the army, constables, and churchwardens) publicly to take three oaths: of allegiance to the crown, of acknowledgment of the crown's ecclesiastical supremacy, and against transubstantiation. The last excluded catholics. They were also required, before taking the oaths, to produce a certificate of having taken anglican communion—which excluded catholics and many non-conformists. Failure to take the oaths automatically disqualified for the office. Exercise of the office while disqualified involved a fine of £500 for the benefit of the informant, and loss of certain civil rights. The disqualification did not extend to the right to vote, for which the oaths were not required. A subsequent resolution excluded catholics from both Houses of Parliament.

be reserved for those who accepted the state's religion. Even to such an advanced thinker as Locke, the Test Act was no affront to liberty of conscience. Religious observance was not merely a matter of individual belief. It was the bond and the guarantee of society itself. Those who gave little thought to religion—and they must have been many—could not conceive how society could exist without it. To millions the Sunday sermon was the only broadcast they heard, the only news they took in; and the clergyman was the only welfare officer they could turn to, the only schoolmaster they could hope for. It could not be right that a man who did not accept the very basis of the society in which he lived should have any official power over his fellow-citizens.

To this deep-seated general conviction about power as inseparable from membership of an established church, the Englishman added two other beliefs which influenced him in favour of the Test Act. Both rested on memory: one recent, the other more distant but not yet remote, and both were concerned with property. Thirty years before, within the personal memories of a large part of the population, protestant extremism had carried the day. Office-holders had been ejected, property had been forfeited. Every year, on the 30 January, congregations were reminded of those dreadful days when 'cruel and unreasonable men' had gained the upper hand, and listened to the prescribed Epistle and Gospel: St Peter's 'Submit yourselves to every ordinance of man for the Lord's sake'; and the parable of the husbandmen: 'This is the heir, come, let us kill him, and let us seize his inheritance.'

The other memory went back to the far-reaching changes in ownership that had accompanied the Reformation. By a curious illusion we suppose that a period which is far removed from us in time seemed just as remote to people who lived in an intermediate period between it and our own. It is all 'history'. But the relationship between periods alters with the passage of time. To the squire and clergyman of 1686 the reign of Elizabeth I stood roughly in the same relationship as Queen Victoria's to us. In 1688 Elizabethan coinage was still in circulation.* The plays of Shakespeare and Ben Jonson had the same kind of period flavour as (to us) those of Ibsen or Chekhov. The great Acts of

* W. Lowndes: *A Report containing an Essay for the Amendment of the Silver Coins* (1695), p. 105.

Uniformity and Supremacy, the dissolution of the monasteries, the settlement of the prayer-book, all stood in the same sort of relation as the Reform Bill, Catholic Emancipation, and the Tolpuddle Martyrs today.

Hence the slogan 'religion and property', which seems cynical to us, but was entirely natural to the possessing classes of the late seventeenth century. The anglican settlement underpinned count-less property rights, as Shakespeare no doubt had in mind when he wrote the speech of a scheming pre-reformation Archbishop:

> If it pass against us,
> We lose the better half of our possession:
> For all the temporal lands which men devout
> By testament have given to the Church
> Would they strip from us; being valued thus:
> As much as would maintain, to the King's honour,
> Full fifteen earls and fifteen hundred knights,
> Six thousand and two hundred good esquires . . .*

The clergy were no less conscious than the earls and squires that religion backed property. When Dr Hough, the President of Magdalen, was deposed by King James's commissioners his pro-test was not in the name of academic freedom. He said 'My Lords, you have this day deprived me of my freehold.' It was with anxiety that Narcissus Lutrell, in the spring of 1686, noted a rumour that 'there has been some enquiry into what lands belonged anciently to the church'.[2] At almost the same time Carstares, travelling on the Rhine, and eager as ever for informa-tion, carefully noted the opinion of a catholic priest that it seemed likely James 'would in the ensuing parliament take some course for taking away all fears of the restitution of Abbey lands to the Church of Rome'.[3]

Two opinions, one correct, and the other mistaken, about contemporary movements in Europe, shored up these feelings about religion, property, and order. One was the dread of central-ism on the French pattern. England was a country of corporations and country gentlemen, deeply hostile to intervention of any kind in their affairs. They looked with suspicion on the men of

---

* *Henry V*, Act I Sc. 1. Gregory King estimated (1696) a population of 1,400 baronets and knights, 3,000 esquires, and 12,000 gentlemen; and 10,000 clergymen.

humble origin and administrative ability whom the Stuart brothers had been gradually bringing forward: men such as Godolphin, Pepys, Blathwayte, and Lowndes.* People readily believed, and it was indeed true, that James was trying on the French model to create a machine at the centre that would drain power away from the squirearchy and impose uniformity on administration.

The other commonly held opinion was one which coloured, or perhaps one should say darkened, all the last three decades of the century in England; but events made belief in it especially attractive in the middle sixteen-eighties. This was the belief in the existence of a vast international catholic conspiracy. The alliance of Pope and Emperor in the Holy League on the Danube reinforced it, even though the alliance was directed against the Turks—and indirectly against France. The revocation of the Edict of Nantes, which was of course accompanied by great professions of catholic enthusiasm by Louis, seemed to confirm it.† Finally the personal catholicism of James made the supposed plot seem menacing. The discord between France and the rest of catholic Christendom, which in fact made the Revolution possible, was ignored in favour of the exciting notion of the two great forces of popery and French tyranny being united to reverse the Reformation and reconquer England. This was the strain that du Moulin's propaganda had exploited and done so much to perpetuate fifteen years earlier. And it was to produce one of the oddest ironies of the Revolution itself, during which virtually the only serious damage done by a revolutionary mob was to the Spanish embassy, at a time when the unfortunate Spanish ambassador was actively engaged in promoting the cause of William.

The orderly, propertied, state of affairs that country gentlemen

* In 1686 Godolphin was a Treasury Commissioner, Pepys Secretary of the Navy. Blathwayte's field was the army and colonial affairs (Secretary at War, Clerk to the Privy Council, Auditor General of Plantation Revenues). Lowndes had just joined the Treasury (1684) and was to serve there for the next forty years. James overlooked the fact that officials can be as permanent as landowners, and that they owe their permanence in large measure to their readiness to change their allegiance.

† One of them, certainly, being the last outbreak of anti-catholic feeling in England in 1679, which made a great impression on French opinion. The execution of Plunket, Archbishop of Armagh, was regarded by the French as particularly dreadful.

so valued was still symbolised in 1685 by the presence at the centre of affairs of the King's two brothers-in-law, the Earls of Clarendon and of Rochester. Clarendon, until December, when he was superseded and sent as Lord Lieutenant to Ireland, was Lord Privy Seal; and Rochester was Lord High Treasurer. They were not exciting figures: the importance of the Hyde brothers was what they stood for, rather than what they were. They represented the centre of gravity of the régime established in 1660, and, with their celebrated father, a whole tradition of English politics stretching back to the early years of the century. The old Earl of Clarendon had already embodied that tradition in his *History of the Rebellion* which his sons—both of them born before the Civil War—were to publish in the reign of their niece Anne, the last Stuart. Their special relationship to the sovereign gave them a position in society which is difficult for us to grasp. Ever since the early eighteenth century almost all our sovereigns have taken their consorts from abroad, so that their relations by marriage tend to be outside the main stream of English life. James II was unique among modern English kings in having two entirely English brothers-in-law, who at the beginning of his reign were also his leading ministers.

It was the objective of Sunderland to undermine and destroy the political power of the Hydes, and his success in doing so was an important contributory cause of the revolutionary situation three years later. Neither Sunderland nor James himself appreciated how, by destroying the position of the Hydes, they were weakening the basis of obedience on which their whole policy was founded. James far overestimated the depth of commitment by the Church of England to obedience. Was it not the central doctrine of Anglicanism? How many sermons had been preached to the favourite text, Romans XIII v. 1:

> Let every soul be subject unto the higher powers. For there is no power but of God: the powers that be are ordained of God. Whosoever therefore resisteth the power, resisteth the ordinance of God: and they that resist shall receive to themselves damnation.

Among much else, the English Revolution is one of the most remarkable instances in history of the triumph of political pressure over ideological commitment.

The two deviations from Anglicanism—Catholicism and
Dissent—were spread unevenly over the kingdom and over the
social structure. Perhaps five per cent of the population were
protestant dissenters, and an even lower percentage were catholics.* But whereas the catholics were, on the whole, gentry, the
dissenters were to be found either at the very top of the social
scale, or near its bottom, and possessed in their ministers a quite
highly integrated organisation. Both forms of dissent shaded into
anglican conformity to some extent, and it was a matter of specu-
lation how much divergence of either kind was latent because of
social and legal pressure. The bishops who conducted the religious census of 1676 chose to minimise Dissent: King James
preferred to exaggerate it. But nobody really knew how much
the established church would be weakened by relaxing the in-
centives to conform with it. That question was to be much discussed; but like most questions that have no answer, it was not
the central issue of religious policy. In the conditions of the
seventeenth century the Church of England, as an established
church, was either part of the fabric of government, or it was
lost. To the Roman Catholic it was heretical, separated from the
traditions and glories of the historic faith. To the non-conformist
it was 'Blanch'd Romanism'. The roots of the Church of England
lay in politics. Its achievements in liturgy and theology, great
though they were, were the flowers and fruit. King James was
never willing to admit that there was a dilemma in trying
to treat a church whose doctrines were secondary to its
political existence as if it were one of a number of religious
opinions.

This, the central domestic problem of James's reign, was governed as much by the situation outside England as by the relative
religious strengths within the kingdom. The situation of the
other two realms of Scotland and Ireland was crucial. In both of
these the attempt to impose the anglican compromise had manifestly failed. Scotland remained solidly presbyterian, with tinc-
tures of catholicism: Ireland obstinately catholic, with an indi-
gestible focus of presbyterians. Scotland and Ireland, with their
opposite religious magnetism, exercised a disturbing influence
on what might otherwise have been a fairly stable situation in

* The Religious Census of 1676 appears in G. Lyon Turner, *Original Records of
Early Nonconformity.*

England, and this thought was never far from the minds of the leaders of Anglicanism.

Scotland, though a poor and undeveloped country in comparison with England, possessed its own political system, but it was a system which lent itself far more readily to direct management than the English. Rougher methods were traditional, and it would not be unfair to say that the later Stuarts treated Scotland as a proving ground for courses that might later be tried in the more sophisticated political climate south of the Border. No need was felt—or at any rate none was displayed—to achieve a broad basis for the government of Scotland, and the permanent hostility of a large part of the population was a fact of life. Argyll's expedition had been no more than a jet of flame from embers that never ceased to smoulder. 'Mr Steinson,' wrote young Erskine of Carnock in February 1686, 'reckoned the best gunsmith in Utrecht . . . had this week sent 400 musquets to Scotland, and was now preparing 300 dragoons' pieces' for the same destination.[4] The imperfect hold of the government in Scotland, grappling as best it could on to the internal feuds and jealousies of the great families, was an important weakness in the Stuart system that William and his advisers knew well how to exploit, and had serviceable instruments for exploiting.

Ireland was a colonial country. It possessed a parliament, but only in a technical sense, for there had been no session for twenty years, and virtually the last act of the Irish parliament had been the Settlement, by which the greater part of Ireland had been parcelled out to settlers from England and Scotland. The authorities in Dublin were to all intents and purposes a branch of the government in London, whose main object was to preserve the land settlement. To the English and Scottish settler the link between religion and property seemed even more intimate and fragile than it did to his counterpart in England, and he followed events in England with this anxiety uppermost in his mind. The Celtic Irish he regarded as savages, and the horrors of the rising of 1641 had not been forgotten.

But James's realms were not confined to the three kingdoms, and he himself was deeply interested in his transatlantic possessions. With the capture of New Amsterdam in 1667 the whole coastal strip from New England southwards to Virginia was settled by communities under the British crown. New

Amsterdam had been acquired by an expedition managed by James when Duke of York, and had been renamed New York in his honour and as his personal possession. For the next twenty years it was developed under his supervision and gave him an opportunity in miniature for applying the ideas he was later to develop in England when he became king.

Central to these ideas were religious toleration under what was known as the Duke's Law, and authoritarian government. As soon as James became king he set to work extending the benefits of this policy from New York to other colonies. Time did not allow him to touch the southern group (dearly as he would have loved to check whiggery in Carolina or the West Indian islands) but by 1687 he had abolished the charters of five of the northern colonies*—Massachusetts, Connecticut, Rhode Island, New Hampshire, and Maine—and had consolidated them into a single 'Dominion of New England' with no local assemblies, an omnipotent governor, and, of course, religious toleration. In 1688 New York and New Jersey were merged in this aggregate, which was restored to its original seven components after 1688.

In the last months of 1685, with parliament on the shunting line of prorogation and Sunderland Lord President as well as Secretary of State, James committed himself to a series of decisions to press on with toleration at home and an independent foreign policy. The nature of these decisions can be inferred from a series of acts early in 1686, which had consequences both at home and abroad.

In February, acting on instructions, Sunderland informed the Spanish ambassador, Ronquillo, that Anglo-Spanish understandings of the last reign (these of course related especially to the Netherlands) would not be renewed. In the same month he wrote to William that James had now exhausted his good offices in negotiation with Louis over the question of Orange—a piece of news which William took very badly. There was also an exchange of envoys with the Pope. Roger Palmer, Earl of Castlemaine, a Stuart hanger-on now advancing in years (he had married Charles II's cast-off mistress Barbara Villiers, who had insisted he

---

* In May 1686 proceedings were opened also against the charters of Carolina and Pennsylvania. But those against Pennsylvania were stayed in the following month.

should be made an Earl) had been sent to Rome; and the in-offensive Ferdinand Count d'Adda had arrived in London, though he had not yet been given any official status. In his despatches to the Vatican he expressed the opinion that James would be sensible to limit relief of the catholics to abolishing the Penal Laws, and to leave the Test Act alone.

In March James granted an amnesty to all those imprisoned under the Penal Laws—mainly Quakers—and more than a thousand of them were released. The act was entirely legal, being an exercise of the prerogative of mercy. But what was doubtfully legal was the accompanying grant of numerous commissions in the army to Roman Catholics, together with dispensation from the Test Act's penalties.* But James sought to get legal cover. As a test case Gooden, the coachman of one of those granted commissions in this way, Sir Edward Hales, was put up by the government as informer against his master. The decision of the Court of King's Bench in *Gooden* v. *Hales* in April was that the royal dispensation was valid. The way was in fact clear for James to appoint whom he chose in defiance of the Test Act, and Sunderland told d'Adda that repeal of the Test Act itself could now only be a question of time. D'Adda expressed pleasure, but felt anxiety. Only with French help, he wrote to Rome, would James be able to enforce the kind of toleration he desired. Halifax, with characteristic subtlety, observed that it was no longer necessary for James to press him to support repeal of the Test Act, since the courts had allowed that it could be dispensed with.

James had not in the meantime overlooked the other arm of his programme, the improvement of his armed forces. That May and June, while *Gooden* v. *Hales* was being decided in Westminster Hall, regiments from all over England concentrated in a tented camp on Hounslow Heath. Hounslow had been selected partly because it provided a good training ground, and partly, perhaps, because it was midway between London and the King's favourite residence of Windsor. The enterprise was a large one. Two square miles were covered with tentage accommodating 15,000 men—by far the greater part of James's regular army. One

---

* As early as January 1686 James had granted dispensation to nearly 100 catholic officers. S.P. Dom. 1686–87 item 101 gives 96 names, many of them Irish, as recipients of dispensation. They include five peers.

of the objects was undoubtedly to improve standards and carry out the kind of battle training in formation that was impossible for regiments and squadrons on detachment. But one may also guess at operational reasons. Macaulay's suggestion that the purpose was to overawe London is unconvincing. There was little sign so far of resistance in the capital to James's policy, and his relations with the City government were reasonably cordial. But if, even at this comparatively early stage, James considered it would be useful to have a field force at his disposal against foreign invasion from the east or south, Hounslow was well chosen. It lies on the hinge of the three great internal highways, the Great West Road, the Great North Road, and the Portsmouth Road.

It was about this time that a significant character in this narrative decided to settle in the United Provinces and attach his fortunes to the Prince of Orange. Gilbert Burnet was a Scot brought up to Calvinism, who had made his career in the episcopal church. He was at this point forty-three and the author of a best-seller, the *History of the Reformation in England*, which had brought him the friendship of many prominent anglicans. No man of the times was more articulate than Burnet, whether in speech or writing. As preacher at the Rolls Chapel, the fashionable church in London of which he had charge for ten years, he drew crowded congregations who cheered when he turned the hour-glass over with a flourish at the end of sixty minutes and preached the next hour out as well. Utterly self-confident, he even talked down Louis XIV when he was introduced to him—perhaps the only man ever to do so. There had been an idea that Burnet should write the French King's biography in English, which came to nothing. But it was not ill-conceived. Burnet admired gallicanism, and strongly disapproved of the huguenots.

He had always dabbled in politics, first as an admirer of Lauderdale, who had helped him to the Chair of Divinity at Glasgow, then for a short time as a protégé of James when Duke of York. During the Exclusion controversy he had contributed the idea of 'Limitations' which had attracted King Charles and the compromiser Halifax; and with Halifax, Burnet remained in touch when he set off on his travels in 1685. The importance of his arrival in Holland in May 1686 may have been exaggerated. William had his own and trustworthy sources of information about the development of affairs in England. But Burnet was a recruit of a new style, neither a presbyterian refugee nor a republican plotter. If not exactly a native member of the English governing class, he knew their ways.

William and the Germans

When Burnet arrived at the Hague early in the May of 1686 and found 'the Prince was resolved to make use of me', the elements of a new resistance to French expansion had already begun to take shape. The first foci appeared not in the Netherlands, but in Northern Germany. That January a convention had been signed between Brandenburg and the Emperor Leopold by which a contingent of 8,000 Brandenburgers was provided for the coming year's campaign on the Danube; and, almost simultaneously, a Dutch officer, Colonel van Heyden, paid a visit to Berlin. Almost at the same time, too, David, Earl of Leven, whose father, the Earl of Melville, had been living quietly in Holland since the time of the Rye House Plot, appeared in Hamburg, and a little later in Berlin. He was armed with an introduction to the Elector Frederick William from the Electress of Hanover, Sophia, and proposed to enter the Brandenburg army, but he remained in touch both with William of Orange and with disgruntled members of the Scottish nobility. In March the convention between the Elector and the Emperor Leopold was carried a stage further by the conclusion of a secret agreement for mutual defence, including a promise by the Elector to vote for Leopold's son at the next imperial election. Frederick William's previous promise had been to vote for Louis XIV.

The picture, therefore, had changed greatly since Burnet had set out hurriedly for the continent in May 1685 in the apprehension that the impending invasion of Argyll might involve him in trouble. He had avoided the United Provinces, where the official attitude was still one of almost effusive friendliness to James, and had made instead for France, where the Edict of Nantes was still unrepealed. He had then descended through Switzerland to Rome, and even as far as Naples, seeing the sights, visiting libraries, and meeting everybody. In Rome, he had met Queen Christina who had smilingly described herself as 'one of the antiquities of this city'; and, more important, had conferred with the leading English catholic, Cardinal Howard, who received him with 'a goodness that went far beyond common civility' and confided in him the Curia's anxiety about the excessive zeal of some English catholics, which, they feared, would weaken England and strengthen the hand of Louis. Burnet also noted the heavy taxation in the Papal States, and attributed it to ecclesiastical avarice. He made no allowance for the demands of the papal war-chest which was being used to finance the Emperor's operations against the Turks.

His return through southern France and Switzerland had almost coincided with the revocation of the Edict of Nantes, 'and what I saw and knew there from first hand, hath so confirmed all the Ideas that I had taken from Books, of the Cruelty of that Religion, that I hope the Impression that this hath made upon me will never end but with my life'.[1] All his former sympathy for gallicanism evaporated in a deep and genuine revulsion. As he made for Holland up the Rhine in the spring his mind dwelt grimly on the details of the fortifications he passed, to an extent unusual in a clergyman:

> The fortification [he noted at Breisach] is of huge compass. . . . The bastions are quite filled with earth; they are faced with brick, and have a huge broad ditch full of water round them: the counterscarp, the covered way, which hath a palisade within the parapet, and the glacis, are all well executed: there is a half-moon before every cortin; the bastions have no orillons, except one or two, and the cortins are so disposed, that a good part of them defend the bastions. The garrison of this place in time of war must needs be eight or ten thousand men.[2]

The probable cause for a renewed war was already implanted in what Burnet described as 'one of the sweetest countries of all Germany' as he passed through the Palatinate. The Rhenish principality had now a tradition of tolerance—the three forms of

Western Christianity all flourished there, and so did Judaism. The change of Prince that had taken place in 1685 made no difference to this policy. The new, anti-French Elector, although a catholic, strictly maintained it, as Burnet approvingly and pointedly noted. In the light of what was soon to happen, Burnet's lyricism has a bitter irony— 'The way from Heidelberg to Frankfort is . . . the beautifullest piece of ground that can be imagined; for we went under a ridge of little hills that are all covered with vines; and from them, as far as the eye can go, there is a beautiful plain of cornfields and meadows, all sweetly divided and enclosed with rows of trees.'[3]

Throughout his journey he had maintained contact with Halifax, and on arrival at the Hague, towards the end of May, he found that through Halifax's intermediacy invitations had been issued to him to attend as an adviser of William of Orange. He was warned, on presenting himself, that he was to be a respectable adviser, and was to keep clear of the revolutionary English and Scottish refugees of whom the country was now full.

Burnet arrived just in time to witness an event which Colonel van Heyden and Leven had been concerned in preparing earlier in the year: a formal meeting between William and the Elector of Brandenburg. But others had a hand in the arrangements as well. Twice, on 20 February and on 11 March, the Scottish refugee Erskine of Carnock noted that his friend William Carstares (it was to him that William of Orange left less respectable contacts with the underworld of exiles) visited Cleves, the Brandenburg possession just across the Dutch frontier. That trusted agent was also in evidence, though naturally in the background, at the meeting itself, which took place towards the end of June. The Elector arrived first, on June 29. He was now a very old man, 'sore bowed and decrepid, but had a lively countenance'. Included in his suite were the Emperor Leopold's ambassador, Count Holstein, and the Earl of Leven. The Bishop of Strasbourg, as courtesy required, paid a ceremonial visit, departing on the same day: 'not very well taken with, being a follower of the French interest'.[4]

For almost a fortnight the Elector remained the sole centre of attention at Cleves. During that time he received news of heavy casualties to his forces on the Danube, where the siege of Buda had been opened by Charles of Lorraine's international army of 40,000 men. The attention of Europe was concentrated on that great operation throughout the summer, and can never have been far from the minds of those meeting at Cleves. But other news also reached the Elector at Cleves, and William at the Hague, from which he was now on the point of setting out. At Augsburg on 9 July a number of the leading German states, the Emperor, Spain, and Sweden, subscribed to a league for the defence of the status quo. This league, it was provided, should have an army.

On 14 July the Prince of Orange arrived, accompanied by Bentinck, Henry Sidney, and his new adviser, Burnet. The earnest Scottish exiles, peering up from the crowd, were deeply suspicious of the professional politicians surrounding the man who was already their hero. The Elector, Erskine thought, did not pay much attention to Burnet, assiduously though the little Scot applied himself to everyone present; and some of the exiles thought Sidney was 'here on no good design, but sent here by the King of England', though he was much with the Prince, and sat at the Elector's table.[5] Only one great personage who might have been with William was missing—Mary had been left behind at the Hague. The reason given was that William had desired to avoid awkward questions of precedence between his wife, who was heiress presumptive to a throne, and the Electress. It was, however, his policy then, as later, never to allow Mary's possession of a higher formal status than his own to obtrude where he himself formally and publicly engaged in politics.*

The conference at Cleves lasted for nine days and was then adjourned across the Dutch frontier to the Mookerheide, where the greater part of William's army—some 22,000 men—was assembled for review in a tented camp covering more than a mile and a half of frontage. Thirty regiments of infantry, twenty-four of cavalry, and ten of dragoons were inspected by the veteran Elector the next day, and performed an elaborate mock battle in which cannon were fired, infantry engaged one another in platoon firing, and the cavalry exhibited a sham flight and counterattack. Soon afterwards the Prince and the Elector returned to

---

* It is not clear from Burnet's narrative when the famous interview took place at which Mary made it clear that she would never exert her better title to the English throne except in subordination to her husband. The short interval between Burnet's arrival in Holland and his presence at Cleves, however, suggests that it was after Cleves.

their respective capitals. But the army remained concentrated at Mook. It was, among much else, the answer to Hounslow.⁶

The conference and its military sequel impressed, and was meant to impress, the rest of Europe, especially King Louis, whose ambassador had been present, and King James. The gesture showed that the means of intervention in England were not wanting; and it was made against a rapidly developing military and diplomatic situation. The cannon fired in practice at Mook echoed those being fired in earnest against Budapest under the superintendance of Antonio Gonzalez, a Spanish gunner lent to the Christian forces by the Governor of the Spanish Netherlands, and a Franciscan monk who was also an expert artillerist. On 16 July Gonzalez's guns scored a lucky and decisive hit on the Turkish arsenal, destroying a great part of the garrison's ammunition. In the accompanying infantry assault Halifax's son, young Henry Savile, was shot in the stomach. The Turks hung on, but the end could not be far off.

The Prince and the Elector were not rigid or hasty planners. Both believed in keeping alternatives open for as long as possible, and intervention in England was no new idea. The meeting at Cleves produced no formal document. It made a possibility probable. But it also produced the certainty that if such intervention took place, it would have the support of Brandenburg. This was crucial. The major problem in the invasion of England was protection of the home base from a French attack. The army of the United Provinces was not strong enough to provide both an expedition of the required strength and a covering force at the same time, nor would the republican assemblies, on whom William had to rely, ever permit their country to be exposed yet again to invasion. It must have been clear to the Prince and the Elector that any move against James must wait for victories on the Danube that would release Imperial and Brandenburg strength for the Rhine; for further evidence of the internal weakness of James's position; and, as a possible bonus, for some indication of a false move by King Louis. Until then the alternative of an understanding with James if he consolidated his position was still open.*

---

* Reliance has been placed by some authors on Burnet's record (*History of my Own Time*, p. 440) that soon after his arrival he advised William 'to put the fleet of Holland in a good condition'; and this has been taken as implying

Great news came from the east in the autumn. Buda, having refused to surrender, was stormed on 2 September. It was one of
the greatest military operations of the seventeenth century. In the
burning city, which now returned to Christian rule after nearly
a century and a half, the scholar-soldier Marsiglio of Bologna
rescued armfuls of priceless manuscripts and books from the
palace of the Turkish governor. George Lewis of Hanover, at this
time a dashing officer of twenty-five, took prisoner and granted
quarter to the two Turks whom he was to bring in his train to
England when he ascended the throne as George I thirty years
later. The Emperor Leopold was almost master of Hungary and
the Dual Monarchy—that great European stabilising force for
the next two and a half centuries—was about to be born.

And all the time James persisted in his idea that he could keep
both Louis and William in play, when his only hope lay in
closing with one or the other. In August he had been tackled
by the Dutch ambassador in London, van Citters, about an
alleged memorandum advising James to espouse a pro-French
policy, exclude William and Mary, and embark with Louis on an
attack against the United Provinces before German forces could
be released from the Danube: 'Better,' this alleged memorandum
had said, 'a vassal of France, than a slave of the Demon.'* 'Vassal
of France!' James shouted at the ambassador. 'If Parliament had
wished it, if it is yet prepared to wish it, I would bring the monarchy to a degree of consideration never before achieved under
the Kings, my predecessors, and your country would perhaps
find thereby its own greatest security.'⁷ The fact that van Citters'
despatches were regularly intercepted by French agents and copied
to Versailles did not improve the effect of this demonstration.
Yet James could not resist a gesture in the opposite direction a
month or two later, when he boasted that his navy, on which he
was now spending £400,000 a year or a fifth of his revenue,

a virtual decision on the invasion plan in the summer of 1686. Yet it is im-
probable that even Burnet envisaged such a move at this stage. 'I am further
than ever,' he wrote to James Fell on 26 September 1686, 'from all things that
lead to drawing the sword against those in whose hands God has put it.'
(Quoted by Cranston, *Locke*, p. 285.)
* Van Citters was complaining of a document supposed to emanate from
James's private group of catholic advisers. Professor Kenyon is inclined to
regard the paper as genuine. Whether genuine or not, William, into whose
hands it soon came, saw to it that it had a wide circulation.

'would keep my neighbours from insolencies in all parts of the world, though never so remote'.[8] This remark, so obviously aimed against the Dutch, was promptly reported to Bentinck. A further step in the same direction in the field of colonial policy was taken in November, 1686, when James concluded a general treaty of co-operation with France in America, involving a mutual recognition of the possessions of each power in the New World, and a significant provision that hostilities which England and France might undertake on opposite sides in Europe should not extend to America.[9]

William had hardly returned from Mook when he was confronted with a letter from James suggesting that an Irish catholic nobleman, Lord Carlingford, should take command of the flower of the troops that had just been shown off to the Elector, namely the British Brigade. William did nothing in haste. The letter, obvious as its reply was, lay unanswered for three weeks—three weeks, incidentally, during which the news of the capture of Buda broke. In the meanwhile a new emissary from England had arrived in Holland to open the winter campaign which was to be decisive for James: the campaign over his religious policy.

This emissary was William Penn, the Quaker. Many as are the characters in the English Revolution, he is probably the most singular. He had long been known to James, and his father had been one of James's favourite naval officers. As an undergraduate he had been converted to Quakerism, and ever since he had devoted himself to furthering its cause. Penn was not only for total toleration: the whole principle of established religion seemed to him wrong. He was a large, shrewd, persuasive man, yet he was in some ways surprisingly naïve and loose in his thinking.* As an idealist he found it hard to grasp the motives of others. This interesting man had gained a considerable ascendancy over James, had taken a house near Windsor, and, though occupying no official position, had become one of James's leading advisers on religious policy. To Penn's advice James owed the notion which increasingly possessed his mind that winter. This was to throw the protestant dissenters into the balance along with the catholics to outweigh the Anglican Church and achieve the

---

* See, for instance, Locke's comments on Penn's draft constitution of Pennsylvania quoted in Cranston, op. cit., pp. 261–2. Each note of Locke's shows up Penn's shallowness of thought.

toleration on which his heart was set. The plan—as was needful in an issue that was not only domestic but international—was calculated to appeal to William as a devout calvinist. To Penn also James probably owed the theme that was always associated with this policy—that toleration was good for trade.

Penn stayed some time in Holland, and saw a good many people. He saw Burnet, whom he unsuccessfully tried to coax back to England as a supporter of the new toleration policy; he saw Locke; he moved among the revolutionary exiles, who greeted him with suspicion;* and he saw William.[10] To each he explained that James was resolved, if possible with parliamentary approval, to sweep away all religious disabilities and restrictions in England and Scotland. The Penal Laws were to go, and so was the Test Act. From William he sought an assurance that he and Mary, as heirs to the throne, would support this policy; and he may have accompanied this with hints that in return for such an assurance William could expect James's support against Louis. William's reply, as recorded by Burnet, was a carefully worded approval of repeal of the Penal Laws and disapproval of the repeal of the Test Act, which 'he looked on . . . as such a real security, and indeed the only one, where the King was of another religion, that he would join in no counsels with them that intended to repeal those laws'.[11] At almost the same time William sent off a letter firmly refusing to consider Carlingford as commander of the British Brigade; but Penn was also asked to carry back a message of goodwill to James.

Before Penn returned to England he had mustered one recruit in Holland. This was Carstares' friend James Stewart, the covenanting refugee who had been an adviser to Argyll. 'Jamie Wylie' is one of the least attractive, but not among the least important personages in the prelude to the Revolution. He and his elder brother, Stewart of Cultness, had both forfeited their estates in Scotland and had been living hopefully in the Low Countries for some years. James, indeed, who was a lawyer by trade, had spent most of his life abroad, first as correspondent at Rouen for the wine business run by two of his other brothers, then as a collaborator with Carstares in the pamphlet warfare of the seventies. The Prince of Orange, in accordance with his settled policy

---

* Erskine of Carnock, p. 203 (22 August). The reference is undoubtedly to Penn, though mistranscribed 'Raw'.

on refugees, refused to have any direct contact with him, but he was one of Carstares' sources, and what was written to Carstares was shown also, if it was of any importance, to Fagel and to the Prince. During most of the winter Stewart continued to write intelligence letters to Carstares, though with an increasingly plaintive note about the arm's length at which he was kept. His brother, for whom Penn had coined the nickname 'Gospel' Cultness, had already returned to England with the prospect of a pardon. There can be little doubt that Stewart hung on in Rotterdam only in the hope that he might extract better terms through Carstares from the Prince of Orange. On 8 March 1687 he wrote announcing that he too had decided to accept favour at home. He was to be the unwitting instrument for destroying any possibility that the policy Penn had expounded to William would succeed.

Henry Hyde, Second
Earl of Clarendon

Sir John Powell,
Justice of the
King's Bench

The Seven Bishops. The large portrait in the centre is
Sancroft. The smaller portraits are—top row: Lloyd of
St Asaph (left) and White of Peterborough (right); middle
row: Lake of Chichester (left) and Ken of Bath and Wells
(right); bottom row: Turner of Ely (left) and Trelawny of
Bristol (right).

Dijkvelt, Magdalen, and the Stewart Correspondence

The fast-sailing little yachts or 'scoots' could cross the North Sea in a night, and ensure that any significant event in London was known at the Hague within forty-eight hours. But at the turn of the year 1686 still closer contact was needed for William to maintain his strange dual role as leader of the anti-French interest in Europe and embryo head of a party in England. A special observer was required, and the choice fell on Everard van Weede van Dijkvelt.

The portrait shows a genial yet subtle face, ductile, double-chinned, with a flicker about the lips. He exuded sympathy and amiability, and got more out of any conversation than he gave. Burnet called him 'the smoothest man that ever was bred in the Commonwealth'. He had been long in politics, both international and domestic, and, like Fagel, had originally been a supporter of de Witt's republican régime, though he belonged to the land-owning class. During the French war he had been the spokesman of his native town, Utrecht, to the invaders, and those seven years had led him to transfer his support to the party of unity and war. Already, before he was sent to London early in 1687, he had carried out important diplomatic missions there and in Paris. Ten years later he was to be William's principal negotiator at the Peace of Ryswick.

One reason for sending Dijkvelt to supplement the efforts of the regular Dutch ambassador van Citters (who did not correspond officially with William, but with the States General) was the menacing international situation. William told the Dutch politicians—and there were good grounds for saying so—that war in the west that spring was probable, and might well take the form of a concerted attack on the United Provinces by France and England. There was Hounslow Camp; there were James's massive naval preparations, and the friction between the two maritime powers in the Far East; there was the Anglo-French colonial agreement; and there was the obvious possibility that King Louis would strike before his opponents had concerted their arrangements and disengaged themselves on the Danube. But there was also the dramatic change in the English political scene to be considered. The events that made William decide in the first half of January to send Dijkvelt had occurred in London in the second half of December, and had left Sunderland virtually sole minister to King James.

The Hyde brothers had failed. Rochester had been relieved of the Treasury on 30 December, and Clarendon of the Viceroyalty of Ireland on 11 January. Clarendon's place was taken by the apoplectic Irish soldier, Tyrconnel: Rochester's by a commission. These changes mark the political turning point in James's reign. More than any other political figures Clarendon and Rochester represented a continuous tradition of stability, of which the Anglican Church, the monarchy, and the doctrine of obedience were the main pillars. Until now James had been able to appeal to this tradition, and even to rely upon it. From this point onwards he was driven into appeals based on his personal position, and reliance on the religious extremes of the nation.

Dijkvelt's briefing lasted for nearly a month. The French ambassador in the Hague noted constant conferences with the Prince and Bentinck, occasionally bringing in also Halwijn and Frimans, one of William's intelligence agents on English affairs. Fagel, who announced Dijkvelt's appointment to the States of Holland, was also concerned in these consultations, and Dijkvelt had separate talks with the new English envoy, the Marquis d'Albeville, otherwise Ignatius White, a highly untrustworthy Irish catholic adventurer.* Burnet contributed too, but his statement that he drew up Dijkvelt's instructions must be judged against the scope of these other consultations. There can be no doubt that Dijkvelt was given very great discretion, and it is a

* In almost every way—including his Jesuit christian name—the least acceptable envoy that could have been sent. Nobody trusted him. The French Intendant of Marine, Bonrepaux, considered him 'un intrigant', and d'Avaux took the same view. He appears to have accepted money from both the French and Dutch secret services.

matter of considerable interest that neither his briefs nor his reports survive.

Dijkvelt arrived in London on 21 February 1687, and his visit was not the only sign of European interest in the affairs of Britain. London was now the centre of intense diplomatic activity. The regular French envoy had been reinforced by a leading expert on English and naval affairs, Bonrepaux. At the end of January, after a ludicrous adventure at Haarlem where he had been mistaken for the Prince of Transylvania through wearing a Turkish caftan, Kaunitz, the Emperor Leopold's foreign minister arrived in Whitehall. His object was to combine with the Spanish and papal representatives in persuading James to place a general defensive coalition against France higher on his list of priorities than toleration for the catholics.[1]

But this was precisely what James was not prepared to do. Dispensation with the requirements of the Test Act was now a settled policy in full operation. The greater part of the King's time in January was spent in interviewing peers and members of parliament individually to establish whether there was a chance of getting a majority for repeal. And the result of these consultations had been to decide the King to proceed on his own authority. The day after Dijkvelt arrived the first results of this decision appeared, characteristically, in Scotland, with the publication of a declaration setting aside all the laws against catholics and presbyterians. With the woodenness that was typical of him, James included in this document a paragraph promising on his royal word that the owners of land formerly belonging to abbeys and other churches of the Roman Catholic religion would retain their property in accordance with the Acts of Parliament which had conferred it. What security, it was freely said, did that give, embodied as it was in a declaration which itself unilaterally set aside Acts of Parliament? And what confidence could there be in royal words since King Louis' denunciation of the Edict of Nantes?

Dijkvelt had plenty of time to look about him before James would see him. He had to wait until 13 March for his first substantive interview.*

---

* It seems that he had one interview with James soon after arriving. (James to William, 1 March 1687 (O.S.) in Japikse II. ii. 746.) The long interval before they met again was attributed by James to Dijkvelt's having hurt his foot. The injury may have been diplomatic.

Even without the need for conferences, a number of interesting things happened in those three weeks. Two significant men who had been canvassed by the King—the Earl of Shrewsbury and Vice-Admiral Herbert—resigned their commissions. Herbert's resignation was especially noticeable, since he was a professional sailor whose whole career had developed under James's guidance. In Ireland the collapse of confidence had been spectacular. Trinity College Dublin, that symbol of the ascendancy, had arranged to ship its plate back to England, only to be prevented by the new viceroy. Nor were they mistaken in expecting that the universities were to be one of the battle-grounds with the new order. Nearer home, Cambridge University was screwing itself up to resistance over the King's request that they should admit a Benedictine monk, Alban Francis, to the degree of M.A. without imposing the required religious tests, and there were rumblings at Oxford where James had succeeded in imposing a new Dean on Christ Church who was not only a Roman Catholic but a layman.

Nevertheless, Dijkvelt's interview with James, when at last it came, was cordial: cordial despite the publication at the Hague of a fresh best-seller from Burnet's pen, in the shape of the letters describing his European tour and the fatal consequences of catholic rule on living standards: it went to several editions in a few weeks, and efforts were made to suppress it in England. But James thought well of Dijkvelt. With singular fatuity he told the papal nuncio that although William was cunning and obstinate, William's envoy was an experienced and reasonable man who would not adhere literally to his instructions. Dijkvelt courteously said what he had to say, reciting the formula about the Test Act which Penn had already elicited, and enquiring gently about the purpose of James's naval preparations and the likely outcome of affairs in Ireland. In return he got advanced sight of the proposed English Declaration of Indulgence (it was published on 14 April), and vague expressions of goodwill in return for accommodation on the religious issue. It was clear that no business was to be done; that James was set on a course that would split his kingdom; but that a war that summer involving England was unlikely.

So it was that James, on 28 March, deferred the meeting of his parliament until the following autumn, and wrote in surprisingly genial terms to William:

I see you are satisfied that the peace of Christendom would be preserved at least for this year. I am of your opinion too, and you know was all along of opinion, that France would be quiet, believing it not to be their interest to be otherwise. I have this day resolved to prorogue the Parliament till the 22 November next: and that all my subjects may be at ease and quiet, and mind their trades and private concerns, have resolved to give liberty of conscience to all dissenters whosoever, having been ever against persecuting any for conscience's sake. [2]

Publication of the Declaration of Indulgence in England followed a fortnight later: but it did not produce ease and quiet either in England or the Hague, where d'Avaux noted renewed conferences between William and his advisers on English affairs. At this momentous cross-roads even William hesitated. Surely, he suggested to Fagel on 30 March, it would do no harm if Dijkvelt, while of course repeating that William and Mary could not be associated with the Indulgence policy, should soften the blow by giving an assurance that there would be no victimisation of catholic office-holders if and when William and Mary came to the throne. Fagel clearly thought otherwise, for on 13 April William agreed that Dijkvelt should adhere strictly to his original line. It is most instructive that at this critical moment Fagel saw more clearly even than William where the delicate balance of policy lay; and that William deferred to his advice. [3]

This was the juncture at which the death of the President of Magdalen College, Oxford, set off a celebrated train of events. Old Dr Clerke, whose 'lazy and idle' policy had been to let the outstandingly wealthy foundation of which he was head 'rule itself', died on 24 March* while on a visit to his married daughter in Lancashire. Lady Shuttleworth, the President's daughter, appears to have been wise in the ways of the world, for she delayed writing the sad news to the college for a few days, but sent advance notice of it to a certain Dr John Younger, who was

---

* For convenience of comparison with the documents the dates in this account of the Magdalen affair are given in Old Style. The affair is given in some detail since it illustrates so clearly the underlying realities of the anglican opposition to the Test Act. Macaulay's account is at many points biased and inaccurate. The documents are collected in Bloxam, J. R., *Magdalen College and James II*.

indeed a fellow of Magdalen, but resided in London, where he was chaplain to Princess Anne. As a result Dr Younger knew of the vacancy on 26 March, but the college did not learn of it until the 29th.

Dr. Younger was an experienced ecclesiastical politician and pluralist and a very suitable recipient for this kind of private news. Besides his fellowship and his chaplaincy he held the living of Easton in Northamptonshire and a canon's stall at Canterbury, and was looking forward to the death of the aged incumbent of Bishopstone in Wiltshire. He decided very quickly that he did not himself wish to compete for the vacancy thus thoughtfully brought to his notice by Lady Shuttleworth: perhaps he foresaw it would be a troublesome business. He therefore mentioned it, the same day, to a friend of his, Dr. Thomas Smith, another fellow of Magdalen who happened at that time to be in London. Smith, like Younger, was a don of the world—an orientalist who had beeen chaplain to the British embassy in Constantinople and to Charles II's Secretary of State, Sir Joseph Williamson. It is hardly conceivable that Younger did not also mention it to the man who had been responsible for Princess Anne's religious education and his own appointment as her chaplain: Henry Compton, Bishop of London.

Compton was an unusual bishop, though there were one or two others like him on the episcopal bench, as we shall see. Before taking holy orders he had been in the army, and he had retained something of the outlook of an officer in managing his clergy whom he assembled at regular conferences to discuss current topics. His career in the Church, where he had successively been Bishop of Oxford and of London, had owed much to his almost exact contemporary Danby, as well to his own decisive character. He was strongly anti-catholic, and as strongly anti-French; had carried out the religious census of 1676, and a year later had been strongly tipped for Lambeth. But at the time of the Magdalen vacancy he was under a cloud, having been suspended from his functions in the previous year for defying James's religious policy. The suspension, imposed by James's new machinery for disciplining the Church of England, had stopped short of depriving him of his rank and revenues, and only a few days before President Clerke's death Compton had put in an application to have the suspension removed.

Compton was also in touch with Dijkvelt, and, through Dr William Stanley, whom he had placed as Mary's chaplain at the Hague, with William.* It must have been obvious to Dr Younger, Bishop Compton, and anyone else who heard of the Magdalen vacancy, that a candidate would be recommended to the college by the King—Dr Clerke had been elected following just such a recommendation—and that in the present state of affairs the proposed candidate was likely to be a catholic. The opportunity therefore offered itself to make a demonstration against James's religious policy while Dijkvelt was still in England. This is not to depreciate the courage of the fellows of Magdalen in the battle that followed; but without the connivance of higher authority in the Church that courage would have been in vain; and the knowledge of it may well have stiffened the resolution of those members of the college whose ingrained habit was to oblige the government.

Even if one assumes that Whitehall learned of the vacancy on the same day as Dr Younger, which is probable, the government acted with breakneck speed. The royal mandate was despatched to Magdalen on 5 April, the day following the issue of the Declaration of Indulgence announcing the King's general intention to suspend the Penal Laws and dispense with the Test in suitable cases until the position should be regularised by parliament. The mandate called on the fellows to elect a certain Anthony Farmer, incorporated the now customary words exempting him from the required oaths, and ended with the usual formula mingling compliment with menace: 'and so not doubting your ready compliance herein, we bid you farewell'.

It is not known who suggested Farmer. He was of a modest family,† and although he was now a Roman Catholic 'de covenance' he had once taught at a non-conformist school at

* The Rev. William Stanley (1647–1731), later Master of Corpus Christi College Cambridge, and Dean of St Asaph's. He had been one of Compton's clergy and a canon of St Paul's before replacing Dr Covel as Mary's chaplain in 1685. The correspondence between Compton and Stanley is in Rawlinson MS 983 (Bodleian).
† His matriculation (1672) at Trinity, Cambridge, gives his native place as Frowlesworth, Leicestershire, but his brother, also at Trinity, came from Slatemore, Bucks. Anthony Farmer seems to have been an associate of Obadiah Walker, the catholic Master of University College, and one of James's advisers on university affairs.

Chippenham. He was only twenty-nine, and had a reputation for uproariousness. He was not a fellow of Magdalen or of New College (which was a qualification required under the statutes), and it is difficult to see how anyone who reflected for a moment could have thought him suitable to be head of a college. Sunderland had given the anglicans their chance by proposing not only a catholic but a catholic who was manifestly unsuitable.

But if Sunderland acted quickly, his opponents had acted more quickly still. The news that Farmer was to be recommended reached Oxford before the official mandate, giving the fellows the chance to put in a protest against the King's intentions before they had to consider his instructions. Nor did the news go to Oxford alone. It went to Farnham Palace, the residence of Peter Mews, Bishop of Winchester and Visitor of Magdalen College, whose protest in the same strain was written even before the college had written theirs.

The intervention of Mews is the crucial evidence that an important section of the Anglican Church had decided to do battle over Magdalen. Mews, like Compton, was no bookish divine. As a young man he had fought in the royalist army at Naseby, and during the Commonwealth he had been employed, much as Carstares was now, as a secret agent in the Low Countries and in Scotland. The Restoration had brought its rewards: President of St John's College Oxford, Vice-Chancellor, Bishop of Winchester. His military experience had been drawn upon as recently as Monmouth's rebellion, when he had turned out against the rebels in person and directed a battery at Sedgemoor. His part in this new rebellion was to be indispensable.

The more senior fellows were nervous about the act of defiance that was now impending, but time was running out. A new President, according to the statutes, had to be elected before 15 April. On the 14th a college meeting was told by the emissaries who had delivered the protest to Sunderland, 'that the King expected to be obeyed, and he had no more to say'. There is evidence for suspecting that Sunderland had never troubled his master about the college's or the Visitor's reaction, but there can be little doubt that James would have given similar instructions even if his minister had been more punctilious. Quavering suggestions from some of the more senior fellows that they might send another protest rather than hold an election in defiance of the King's instructions were overborne by a large majority of younger men who said some very rude things about the King meddling in the college's business.* President Clerke's mild rule had bred independence. In the first free election held at Magdalen for many years they chose Dr John Hough, the most junior of the senior fellows, who was aged thirty-six.

Hough set off for Mews's palace of Farnham Castle that very day to receive the formally indispensable confirmation of the Visitor, which was given on 16 April, just as Sunderland was writing a letter to Mews forbidding it. Congratulating Hough and his colleagues 'on their courage' the Visitor dismissed them, and the next morning, on receiving Sunderland's letter, wrote courteously regretting that it had come too late. The anglican revolt had been launched without the Declaration of Indulgence being so much as mentioned in the official correspondence. It was launched, what was more, by an act of deliberate defiance from a quarter where the King had always had his own way; and that had affiliations with clergy scattered throughout England's twenty thousand parishes. A reasonable estimate of the number of Magdalen men at this time would be fifteen hundred—most of them beneficed clergy.

It is impossible that the significance of these events was lost on Dijkvelt, who had already turned from his fruitless talks with James to a systematic exploration of the English political scene which was to last for two months. Someone, probably Lord Willoughby d'Eresby, provided him with a complete list of the English peerage, categorised into sympathisers and opponents of the Indulgence policy.† In the course of his soundings he saw Halifax, Danby, Shrewsbury, Compton, and Herbert. We catch a glimpse of him dining with four noblemen and two important commoners, and deploring, when the cloth had been cleared away, the weakness of English foreign policy in letting King

---

* The fellows should not be thought of as a group of grey-beards; most of them were in their thirties, and had never known the bad times of the Commonwealth. A majority even of the thirteen 'seniors' were under forty, though the Bursar, the formidable Dr Pudsey, was fifty-six.
† Printed and analysed by K. H. D. Haley in E.H.R. for April 1954. It is now among Bentinck's papers, and was undoubtedly available to William and his advisers from June 1687 onwards.

Louis get away with Luxembourg in 1683.* He allowed himself
to say to the Spanish ambassador, Ronquillo, that on the strength
of advice 'from a group of notable persons in the English Church',
he had little doubt that James's religious policy would lead to a
revolution and a republic. At the end of April his reports on
conversations with 'the most accredited gentlemen, both secular
and ecclesiastical' were being scrutinised at the Hague by the
triumvirate of William, Fagel, and Bentinck.[4]

William's activity following on the news of the Declaration of
Indulgence had not been confined to the Hague. At Dieren, in
Rhenish Prussia, he had a three-day conversation with the veteran
Marshal Schomberg, who had now laid down his baton in the
French service and was offered a command in Prussia. Immediately afterwards the Marshal made his way to Berlin, whither he
was followed by Pensionary Hop of Amsterdam. The Pensionary's journey was as significant as the Marshal's. Until now the
contacts between Brandenburg and the Republic had been handled
by William and his personal machine. Now the town government of Amsterdam, the countervailing force to Orange on
which the French had so long relied, was being drawn into the
network.

Dijkvelt took his leave of James and returned to the Hague
early in June with a collection of friendly, if guarded, letters
from English notabilities, most of which referred to the ampler
oral account Dijkvelt would be able to give of their views.
Danby suggested a personal meeting. Halifax took the opportunity of putting in a thoughtful counterblast to James's assurances that the Indulgence policy was going to succeed. But the
most telling part of Halifax's analysis was the stress he put on the
evolving European situation as the determinant of English
politics:

> Our affairs here depend so much upon what may be done
> abroad, that our thoughts, though never so reasonable, may
> be changed by what we may hear by the next post. A war
> in Germany, and much more if one nearer to us, will have
> such influence here, that our councils must be fitted to it;
> and whether or no we shall have a part in it, it is pretty sure

---

* Evelyn, *Diary* 2.5.87. The other guests were Middleton, the Secretary of
State, Preston, Leader of the House of Commons, Pembroke, Lumley,
Colonel Fitzpatrick, and Sir John Chardin.

we shall have a leaning to one of the parties; and our resolutions at home are to be suited to the interests abroad, which we shall happen to espouse.[5]

The attitude of William to the Indulgence policy was thus a critical item in his whole system of diplomacy against France. On the strength of Dijkvelt's report he decided, when asked formally by d'Albeville to make his position clear, that he would continue to throw his weight behind the anglican church. He therefore wrote to James in very much the same terms as the replies he now knew were coming in from the English notabilities that James was canvassing:

> Upon this head your Majesty will give me leave to repeat, what I formerly had the honour to write to you, that there is no person in the world who has more aversion than I have for all sorts of persecution on the score of religion, and that certainly I will never in my life put my hand to it; but at the same time I can never resolve to do anything contrary to the interest of the religion which I profess; and that therefore I cannot concur in what your Majesty asks of me.[6]

The reply was private; and James was not the man to disclose his lack of success. For William to have published it would have given James a plausible ground for grievance. But d'Avaux, the astute French ambassador at the Hague, saw what was likely to happen:

> 'I am persuaded,' he wrote to Louis on 6 July, 'that the Prince of Orange does not act after this manner, from an impulse owing to his nature and constitution, but there is affectation and design in his conduct. He has a mind that the protection he grants to the Protestant church may be made public, the more to encourage that party, and to induce them the more boldly to oppose whatever the King of England shall be inclined to attempt.'*

* D'Avaux *Negotiations*, vol. iv, p. 126. The idea of a public intimation of William's position on the Indulgence policy can be traced back as far as February 1687 and Lord Polwarth's memorandum to William dated 12 February. 'In the present', writes Polwarth, 'it is wished by many judicious and honest men that the Prince of Orange would in a ful, plaine, and modest letter to his Majestie, without touching much upon the succession, expostulate with him freely upon the great encouragements given to papists and

No doubt Louis agreed with his ambassador's assessment; but he welcomed, rather than disliked, anything which tended to weaken and divide any neighbouring power. If William's policy undermined James, so much the less, on Louis' calculation, was any danger from England in the coming European struggle.

The instrument by which William could openly put himself at the head of the opposition to James was by this time already in England. It will be remembered that James Stewart, the exiled covenanter who had advised Argyll, had decided to make his peace with the new régime in England, and to help in building the bridges between it and the dissenters both north and south of the Border. But although he changed sides, he maintained his correspondence with his old friend Carstares.* It had been broken off temporarily on 8 March when he wrote from Rotterdam announcing his defection, but is resumed on 12 July, only a week after his arrival in England. He had already been to Windsor and met King James, whose chosen instrument and mouthpiece he clearly now is:

> I assure you by all I can find here the establishment of this equal liberty and ease is his Majesty's utmost design . . . and have ground to believe that his Majesty will preserve and observe the true right of succession as a thing most sacred.

The dissenters, he assures Carstares, are beginning to fear the Church of England more than the toleration of popery.

---

discouragements to protestants and represent to his Majestie, that the effects may prove dangerous to his government . . . though the Prince should goe no further in it, such a letter to be published to the world after it was sent to the King is most necessary and would much endear the Prince to the nations and incourage the people in caize of Parliaments and in one day would prevaile more than private practising can do in a yeare; whatever is given in commission to Mr Dijkvelt.' (Japikse, I. ii. p. 91.)
* The complete correspondence is preserved in copies taken by Wodrow from the Carstares Papers (Wodrow MSS 30 National Library of Scotland). This important phase of the political struggle between James and William has been misdescribed by Burnet, Macaulay, and Echard as a correspondence between Stewart and Pensionary Fagel. The implication of Carstares tells much about the organisation against which James was pitting himself in this last (and no doubt in his opinion ingenious) attempt to persuade William to support the Indulgence policy. The replies of Carstares, which were framed to squeeze as much as possible out of the correspondence, have not been preserved.

Discontented Church of England men are not the truest
informers; and mynheer Dickvelt, I fear, conversed too
much with such while he was on this side; and therefore left
his Majesty so ill satisfied . . . I hope you will consider and
make your best use of all these things.

The letter ends with a barely veiled hint that James's policy will
be carried through with parliamentary approval if possible, but
without it if need be. 'Parliaments will be called and the liberty
endeavoured to be established. But I am not yet assured of the
event; only remember that Parliaments are but Parliaments.'

James's object in opening this new channel was to undo the
damage Dijkveld's report had clearly done, and continue pressure
on William without either commitment on his own part or loss
of face after the frosty private rebuff of 12 June. On the very day
Stewart began the correspondence, James had dissolved the
parliament he now despaired of canvassing into acquiescence, and
was embarking on the supreme effort of assembling one based on
dissent, catholicism, and what was left of the anglican doctrine
of passive obedience. Stewart's next letter developed the theme
of the Indulgence policy's popularity: 'even by the court reckoning three parts of four are judg'd to favour and comply with it . . .
the papists at court say that they know how many do embrace
this liberty, how little it favours the growth of their religion,
and how likely they are to have a protestant successor'. Everyone, he urges, recognises that the Penal Laws are due for repeal,
and since the judges have decided dispensation with the Test
Act is lawful, it is no more than a quibble to stand out against
James's policy. Indeed 'upon the whole it may be found that if
the Prince continue obstinate in refusing his Majesty he may fall
under suspicions of the greatest part of England and all Scotland,
to be too great a favourer of the Church of England, consequently
a person whom they have reason to dread'. The dissenters, he
said, may have seemed few during the period of anglican re-
pression, but toleration showed how numerous they really
were. An entente between William and James could only reassure
everyone that there would be continuity of policy between
James and the 'Protestant Successor'.

The next letter, still more urgent in tone, was written on 29
July from Windsor itself, where Stewart was probably staying

with his mentor Penn. Its object is to convey James's sincerity: 'I have further found such free, positive, and emphatick declarations of his Majesty's sincerity in this matter, both from himself and others, and have also had such occasions to observe all the marks of countenances, behaviour, coolness of spirits and others whereby sincerity may be discerned, and that in men of all fashions and persuasions, that I am confident no man could resist such an evidence, but would plainly conclude with me, that certainly his Majesty apprehends and designs this affair of liberty in the right manner.' William 'thinks papists should not be admitted to publick trusts': but as a matter of realism, how can one prevent a King delegating power to whom he pleases? William will have his turn in due course, and once the few determined anglican opponents of toleration have been dealt with 'you may shortly see places and imployments more equally distribute'.

The letter ends with an invitation:

> I expect you will make all I have written so fully understood at the Hague, specially with the Prince, . . . The main thing I expect from you is to have your mind whether or not his Highness may be so disposed as that a well-chosen informer sent to himself might perfect the work . . . wherever the Prince be you know who are to be spoke to and how; but keep all close, for the air on that side hinders men to judge aright.

We do not possess Carstares' reply but we do know, with some precision, how it came to be written. 'I am passive in the whole of this affair' he wrote, in his submission to Bentinck, enclosing Stewart's letter; but he made it clear that in his opinion the correspondence ought to be kept up, and that what Stewart said about the popularity of the Indulgence policy in Scotland was true.[7] After careful consideration by William, Bentinck, and Fagel, Carstares was authorised to write refusing the offer of an emissary, and urging reasoned objections to Stewart's arguments. Stewart was not discouraged. Will Carstares not come over himself, incognito— 'if you have a secret permission from the Hague it would promise more'. He makes it clear that the offer has James's personal authority, though given with a 'well, well but you will find him inflexible'.

These suggestions are all the more interesting in that there was at that very moment a personal emissary from William in England. Count Zuylestein had arrived early in August, ostensibly to condole on the death of the Queen's mother, but in fact to maintain and enlarge William's contacts with his anglican advisers, to whom Zuylestein delivered a series of personal letters. The replies to these showed a consensus of opinion that James would not—at any rate that winter—succeed in assembling a parliament that would back his policy: a matter on which William had clearly expressed some anxiety.* But Zuylestein entered into no conversations with James. As Halifax observed in his reply to William, Zuylestein was not 'wanting to make such observations as may be useful for your service, by which he layeth a foundation of being so well informed of our matters here, that he may prove to be a very good instrument to be further employed when the oêccasion shall require it'. Far the most important sequel to Zuylestein's mission was the establishment at the Hague of an accredited representative of the anglican opposition. This was the Earl of Shrewsbury, one of the most enigmatic figures in English political history.

Shrewsbury—shy, handsome, wealthy, yet curiously lacking in definition—is encountered at each turning point in the politics of his time. He ushered in the Revolution, and it was into his hand that the dying Queen Anne was to press the staff of Treasurer and the responsibility for organising the accession of the House of Hanover. He was trusted. Now he was sent to the Hague with a letter from Halifax which reads almost like the letters of credence of an ambassador: 'I shall only say in short that he is, without any competition, the most considerable man of quality that is growing up amongst us.'

William's hardening resolution towards James reflected the evolution of affairs that summer in eastern Europe. Hungary had now been virtually cleared of the Sultan's forces. The Turkish-sponsored calvinist monarchy in Transylvania had collapsed. The Emperor Leopold in his hour of triumph had behaved moderately, restraining the victorious catholics and conceding at any rate a measure of toleration to the Hungarian protestants. In April the

---

* These letters are in Dalrymple, Appendix to Bk V, pp. 74–85. Maria Beatrice was sincerely attached to her mother (her father was already dead) and her identification with James from this point onwards is noticeably closer.

Hungarian Diet had offered the crown of St Stephen to the House of Habsburg, and Leopold's little son, who was nine, had it placed on his head by the ninety-year-old primate. The Dual Monarchy, with all it was to mean for Europe, had come into existence, and on 13 August the seal was set upon it at Mohacs in southern Hungary, where nearly two hundred years earlier the last Christian king of Hungary had been killed and his army annihilated. On this same battlefield Charles of Lorraine now destroyed the last Turkish army on Hungarian soil. But it was not only in eastern Europe that the consequences of Mohacs were considered. In the letter to William introducing Shrewsbury Halifax wrote:

> We are full of the news from Hungary, which is not equally welcome to the several princes of Christendom. We think it may have a considerable influence upon this part of the world, and if the season was not too far advanced, we are apt to believe France might this very year give some trouble to its neighbours.

In other words war in 1688 was regarded as certain; yet at Windsor King James, almost insensible of foreign affairs, was preparing for his tour of the provinces. Before he set out one more letter—the longest yet—was sent to Carstares. Dated from Windsor, its tone is sharper, less wheedling than its predecessors, and those who read it at the Hague must have noted with satisfaction the unguarded words used in a text clearly authorised by James himself. 'I cannot but regret that this should be hindered from your side, and I am sure by suggestions of Church of England men, that will never be sincere in such matters, especially since you and all the world may think that self-preservation will prompt all concerned to guard against a seen hazard.' Stewart's emphasis on the advantages Scotland would get from toleration and the ruin of episcopal privilege must also have been marked as useful combustible material. Yet although William's attitude was hardening, and he was openly offering commissions to officers displaced by the reorganisation of the English and Irish forces as well as pushing on with naval rearmament, there is no evidence that he had yet made up his mind that an understanding with James was out of the question.

Late in August, accompanied by Maria Beatrice and Sunder-

land, James set out westwards, his mind filled with his plans to
bring about what was now the one object of his existence. His
unwieldy court trundled along with him, an object of dislike to
the local authorities, who were made to provide it with board and
lodging. King and Queen parted at Reading, she continuing to
Bath, he striking southwards through Winchester for an inspec-
tion of his main channel fortresses that brought him by Portsmouth and Southampton to Bath at the end of the month. But
he stayed only a day or two, touching with great ceremony for
the King's evil and listening to a missionary sermon from the
catholic Huddleston from the pulpit of Bath Abbey. Then he
pressed on, staying at Gloucester on Monday 1 September,
at Worcester on Tuesday, Ludlow on Wednesday, and on Thursday at Shrewsbury, where the corporation offered a handsome
civic welcome and a pecuniary gift. Orders replacing the Lords
Lieutenant of two of the counties through which he passed had
preceded him.*

On Saturday the King arrived at the most northerly point of
his journey, Chester, the port for Ireland and the town from
whose walls his father had watched the last action of the Civil War.
There Tyrconnel was waiting for him. If catholicism had been
advancing painfully in England, even with the help of royal
patronage, in Ireland it had bounded forward like a spring
released. Until now James had been cautious about Tyrconnel's
plans for altering the land settlement in Ireland; but he had not
been able to prevent the Lord Deputy from carrying on a virtually independent policy of demolishing protestant power in the
parliamentary constituencies and pursuing direct negotiations
with the French Intendant General of Marine by which, in certain
circumstances, Ireland would become a French base. During
the three days James spent at Chester, Tyrconnel managed to
bully him into agreement not only to a change in the land settlement but into consideration of the idea that Ireland should be
formally separated from England if a protestant succeeded. But
the Lord Deputy did not disclose the negotiations with France,
which had been kept a secret even from Barillon. If any of this

---

* Shropshire (Viscount Newport replaced by Jeffreys) and Somerset (Duke
of Somerset replaced by Lord Waldegrave). In Leicester, in the same batch
of replacements, the Earl of Rutland was replaced by the catholic Earl of
Huntingdon.

became known to William, with all its bearing on the security of the seaways in case of war, it must have caused him serious alarm: and it probably was known. As early as February the Papal Nuncio d'Adda had noted that one of Dijkvelt's objectives was to discover how far Tyrconnel had committed himself to reliance on French support.

On one of the three days at Chester—Monday 6 September— James performed a symbolic act. Maria Beatrice had heard of the miraculous well of St Winefrede at Holywell, not far from Flint, and had wanted to visit it herself, as Katherine of Aragon had done, and pray for an heir.* James had decided she should stay at Bath, but he himself rode out to the shrine, which was now in the keeping of a Jesuit till recently camouflaged as the keeper of the 'Old Star' Inn. There he knelt in public prayer for a son, and is said to have presented as his offering some fragments of the shift which Mary, his grandmother, had worn at her execution. The significance of the public gesture cannot have been lost on William. During those three days at Chester James had made some of the most important decisions of his reign.

He returned, filled with a sense of mission, by Newport, Lichfield, Coventry, and Banbury, to Oxford, where he arrived on 13 September to deal with the still mutinous fellows of Magdalen. During the summer they had scored a notable success by proving to Jeffreys himself, presiding over the Ecclesiastical Commission, that Anthony Farmer was too raffish a man to be the head of a college. By Sunderland's carelessness the government had been placed in a humiliating position. James had had to drop Farmer, but he was not prepared to overlook the defiance of his instructions, and he had decided to insist on a new candidate who could not be faulted. For this purpose he had pitched

---

* The shrine is a very ancient one, and had remained a centre for the old religion, though its custody was disputed between secular priests and the Jesuits. On 8 May 1687 Maria Beatrice wrote to its proprietor, Sir Roger Mostyn (who was a catholic), indicating that the King had granted her the patronage of the shrine, and that she presented a Jesuit named Thomas Roberts as its custodian (Foley, H., *Records of the English Province of the Society of Jesus*, V, 935). The Jesuit monogram and the date 1687 is carved on a stone inside the well. Some authorities allege that Maria Beatrice accompanied James on his pilgrimage, but this is an error. Father Roberts was ejected at the Revolution, but the Jesuits later returned, and surrendered their custodianship of the shrine only in the present century to the secular priests. It was during the latter part of the Jesuit presence that the 'Welsh Lourdes' was the scene of one of the adventures of Fr. Rolfe, otherwise Baron Corvo.

on Parker, the Bishop of Oxford, and on 14 September he confronted the fellows, headed now by Dr Pudsey, the bursar, in their own hall. They pointed out, of course, that they could not elect a new head, since they already had one. James began in a reproachful tone:

> One would wonder to see so many Church of England men got together on such a thing. I am sorry to see it. I am sorry to see it.

But as he went on he began to lose his temper and his dignity. He changed colour and his words stumbled—

> Go and admit the Bishop of Oxford your head, or Principal, or what you call it—(at this point someone whispered 'President')—*President* of your college.

It was a sorry business, widely reported.* The fellows did not comply, and in due course were ejected. But by this time they were the centres of a *cause célèbre* and Mary of Orange contributed to their fighting fund.

James did not return to Windsor directly from Oxford. He rode westwards again to Bath, and was reunited with Maria Beatrice as he had planned. There can be no doubt that his son was conceived a day or two after the unhappy encounter at Magdalen. The loyal Melfort put up a marble cross in the bath Maria Beatrice had used during her husband's absence, bearing an inscription which has unfortunately been lost, having been expunged after the Revolution. The King returned to London only a week later, leaving his wife to follow in October. In the meantime, no doubt with a wry smile, Stewart's correspondents at the Hague were reading his latest effusion, dashed off on the road to Scotland.† Stewart, who had been sent to propagate the Indulgence policy in the North, was growing impatient at the bad success of his negotiation, and his letter was brusque almost to the point of unfriendliness: 'Mr Carstares has delayed and scruffed things . . . gives only generals.' But he repeated with

---

* The scene has been described in a number of memoirs, of which Bramston's give the mistake about 'President' (Bramston, p. 284) and Bonrepaux (who was present with Sunderland) the changes of colour and stammering.
† Dated from Newark 26 August (O.S.), three days before James's pilgrimage to St. Winefrede's.

plaintive faith that 'His Majesty's sincerity with the certain un-alterableness of the succession will satisfy the Prince'. It was remarkable, his correspondents must have reflected, how sure everyone seemed to be that James would not add to his family now.

The autumn of 1687 was now to open one of the strangest scenes in English history. The Revolution was being preceded by a parliamentary campaign for an election which never took place. The issue, defined with a clarity which no earlier campaign issue had ever achieved, was the repeal of the Test Act; and the two parties were respectively headed by the King and by his heir presumptive, who was the chief executive of a foreign country. William was well informed about the nature of English parliaments. 'The securing of the Commons' House is the chief point' ran a memorandum prepared for him by Hume of Polwarth in February. 'This is not to be done by means of the Peers of England; some choice gentlemen of credite are able to do most in it; then ther ar in this countrey [Holland] very quietly some men of good parts and in clear circumstances who corresponde with them and ar able to influence them as much as any.'[8] Certain features of the electoral pattern which we associate with the next century make their first recognisable appearance in this election manqué. The manifesto of James's party had already been published: it was the Declaration of Indulgence. William's was in great part written too, and written unawares, by James Stewart, and the rest, together with the method of publication, was already under consideration in the Hague.

On 21 September, almost at the moment of James's reunion with Maria Beatrice at Bath, William was approving the outline of a final reply to Stewart, submitted by Fagel. 'It seems to me,' William wrote to Bentinck, 'that when Fagel shall have drafted the answer it would not be a bad idea to communicate it to Dr Burnet. . . . Nobody would be more suitable to translate it into English, print it, and publish it.'[9]

James II's Electoral Campaign

James's return to London was celebrated by a dinner with the Lord Mayor and Corporation,* and four days later messengers were riding into every county of England and Wales with a circular letter to the Lords Lieutenant. Signed by Sunderland, it instructed each Lieutenant to call together the magistrates of his county and put to them 'jointly or separately as he shall think fit', three questions. The answers, whether 'yes', 'no', or 'doubtful' were to be returned in writing to the Privy Council office. In addition the Lieutenants were to report on the state of opinion in each parliamentary constituency, indicate suitable candidates for the next parliament, and suggest additions to the county bench from the ranks of catholics and non-conformists. The three questions were:

If you are elected a member of parliament will you support the repeal of the penal laws and the Test Act?

Will you use your influence to elect a member so pledged?

Will you support the King's Declaration for Liberty of Conscience, by living friendly with those of all persuasions, as subjects of the same Prince, and good Christians ought to do?

Such a poll of opinion had never been attempted before, and

---

* James had recently restored to the corporation the non-conformists of which it had been purged by his brother. On the whole the City was friendly to James's policy.

the novelty of the plan has been very generally underestimated. In a way its originality almost obscures its crudity and folly as a political manoeuvre; for it made a profound contribution to precipitating a truly revolutionary state of affairs. It is true that James did not undertake to publish the returns, most of which have survived to be published in Duckett's *Penal Laws and the Test Act*, or even a summary of them. But merely asking the questions meant throwing away any prospect of carrying his policy with the help of habitual loyalty and anxiety for a quiet life. Each country gentleman was compelled, whether he liked it or not, to consider where he stood. Prevarication, though possible, was in effect opposition. As Penn quickly realised 'the method of questions has angered and united the nation.'[1]

The answers could not be collected quickly. For several months that autumn messages must have been passing from one country house to another. Quiet shoots among the stubble-fields, serious evenings after the fox-hunt, gradually worked out for groups and clans and interests formulae of evasion or de-fiance. The King had started a national debate.

In September Sir John Bramston, the Essex lawyer and land-owner whose ear was always close to the ground, had obtained a copy of Halifax's anonymous contribution to this debate. *A Letter to a Dissenter*, Bramston noted, 'went about in the dark, and sold very deare'.[2] Its strategy was to throw doubt on James's sin-cerity. 'You are to be hugged now, only that you may be better squeezed at another time.' The offer of toleration was too good to be true. It was dangerous to rely on prerogative. The Church of England, by reconciling itself with James, could at any moment replace the dissenters in his good graces. The arguments are clever but, stripped of the brilliance of their language, they are not overwhelming.

After all, the dissenters had not only been persecuted by the Church of England for a quarter of a century: they had been betrayed. In 1660 they had opened the door to the restored monarchy and the restored church, and had been promised tolera-tion in return. Instead they had been hounded by such men as Bishop Compton and Bishop Mews. The measure of support King James was getting from the dissenters in the autumn of 1687 was not insignificant and it was not unthinking. There can have been few warier or more experienced local politicians in England than Ambrose Barnes, of Newcastle on Tyne. He had been through the Commonwealth and the Restoration, and he knew Europe and European politics intimately. And Barnes, like James Stewart, was prepared at this moment to play the King's game. He began to manipulate the inconceivably complicated constitution of his native town 'to make sure the elections went right', and 'began to have no small share in the King's favour'. He intended himself to be the next member for Newcastle, and his philosophy was well summed up by his biographer. 'Some thought the King had found Mr Barnes his weak side. Mr Barnes was sure he had found King James his blind side.'[3] Something stronger than Halifax's intellectual appeals to scepticism and protestant unity was needed to convince the dissenters and their sympathisers that toleration as offered by James was a trap.

On 18 October James Stewart had written once more from Edinburgh to Carstares. Stewart was now a member of the Scottish Privy Council with the responsibility of organising the Indulgence policy in Scotland, and was much cultivated by everybody. Soon, he tells Carstares, he will be returning to London. The tone is far more friendly than the petulant lines dashed off in August; and the reason is clear. Carstares had suggested an approach to Pensionary Fagel, and Stewart rushed eagerly into the opening for which he had worked so long. 'I had certainly long ere now written to Pensionarie Fagel, were it not that I judged you were a better interpreter of anything I could say. I know his real concern for the Prot. religion.'

It seems probable that Stewart never in fact wrote his intended letter to Fagel at all. It hardly mattered, for Fagel's 'reply' was already in draft.* On 15 November, by which time Stewart was back in London, he received a long letter from the Pensionary enclosed in one from Carstares. Fagel's letter, which had been drawn up with the utmost care, elaborately defended William's previously stated position, and was translated into English by Burnet. But as compared with previous statements it seemed to contain a concession, or at any rate a momentous clarification: until now William had been ambiguous about precisely what he meant in

---

* William had approved the lines of the reply on 21 September (Japikse, I. i. 33).

saying he could agree to nothing that endangered the religion which he professed. He now limited this to opposing repeal of the Test Act. He would support—so Fagel said—repeal of the penal laws:

> If his Majesty thought fit to have their concurrence in repealing the Penal Laws, their Highnesses were ready to give it, provided those laws still remained in their full vigour by which the Roman Catholics are shut out of both Houses of Parliament, and out of all public employments, both Civil and Military, as likewise all those laws which confirmed the Protestant religion. [4]

Stewart was overjoyed. He showed the letter to Melfort, the Secretary of State for Scotland, 'who was satisfied with it'; and was so carried away that before showing it to James he scribbled enthusiastically to Carstares in praise of the Pensionary's 'fair and candid reasoning upon the present subject of liberty, beyond what I can express'. That letter too went on to the growing file at the Hague.

Bitter was to be Stewart's disappointment. His next letter was written ten days later, after seeing both Sunderland ('much for the liberty to its full extent') and the King, whom he had tried to persuade into the compromise; 'If he thought it good all Presbyterians should be excluded from public trust, provided they might have the liberty only.' The King was quite clearly of the opposite opinion. 'When the first part of Mr Fagel's letter was read to him, he said the Penall Laws and the Test should stand or fall together.' [5] The letter Stewart was ordered to write to Carstares was as follows:

London 19 (29) November
By my last of the 18th instant, I gave you notice of the receipt of my Lord Pensionary's letter, and what was and is my sense of his extraordinary kindness and concern in that affair. Since that time I have had the opportunity to show them to the King, and at his command did read to him distinctly out of the English copy all the account given of Their Highness' mind touching the Penal Statutes and the Test; and withal signified the Sum of what was subjoyned,

especially the Respect and Deference therein expressed to his Majesty's Person and Government; but to my own Regret, I find that this Answer hath been too long delayed, and that now the King is quite over that Matter, being no ways satisfied with the Distinction made of the Tests from the Penal Laws; and no less positive, that his Highness is neither to be prevailed upon, nor so much as to be further treated with in this matter.*

These were the terms, conveyed in a letter from one Scottish secret agent to another, in which James issued the decision that made the invasion of England inevitable and cost him his throne. William's last offer, perhaps tactical, perhaps genuine, perhaps both at once, was rejected, and James's utter inflexibility made clear. Within a few days the printing presses of Amsterdam were hard at work, and by the end of the year, while the squires were still debating their answers to the King's three questions, contraband consignments of Fagel's letter under the title of *Their Highness The Prince and Princess of Orange's Opinion about a General Liberty of Conscience* began to flood the country.† The squires had their lead: the Prince was for repeal of the Penal Laws but he would stand by anglican monopoly of office; and the dissenters and catholics had theirs: there would be no return to persecution in the next reign. An edition of 50,000 is said to have been printed —one for every hundred inhabitants of England.

The importance of the *Opinion* is that for the first time the position of William was made public. Till now he had manoeuvred in the shadows of diplomacy in apparent friendship with his uncle. It followed that the publication of the *Opinion* and of supporting extracts from Stewart's letters, which soon appeared from the same source, had an influence far beyond the British Isles. It was an international as well as an electoral stroke, and William saw to it that the material was available in Dutch, French, and Latin, as well as English. The Emperor, the King of Spain, and the Pope, the catholic powers on whose support William was depending in the coming struggle with Louis, were now given notice that

* This letter, and this letter alone, is not on the file of copies in the Wodrow MSS. The text is from the printed version of 1689.
† Hoffmann, the Imperial envoy in London, refers to the presence of many thousands of copies in his despatch of 19 January to Vienna. Johnston's letters contain frequent orders for consignments.

there would be no rigorous calvinism, no persecution of catholics, if William gained power in England.

Publication of the unfortunate James Stewart's letters—with all references to Carstares artfully edited out—was necessary in the first place to give an excuse for the Prince's issuing an opinion at this particular time. But the letters, truthfully if misleadingly described as having been 'communicated to Mijn Heer Fagel', served other purposes as well. They made it clear that James had rejected a compromise; and suggested that James, through Stewart, had been secretly negotiating on a basis which was wholly incompatible with the guarantees that the King was publicly giving the Church of England. Worst, perhaps, of all, taken with what Fagel said in his letter, they showed that Stewart himself had hopelessly misinformed James about the religious constitution of the United Provinces, which corresponded exactly to what William was now offering England: no persecution, but a monopoly of office for the adherents of the state church. At a stroke one of James's favourite arguments for his policy—that the Dutch owed their prosperity to the absence of religious discrimination—was shown to be based on a falsehood. In vain the wretched go-between wrote begging Carstares 'that any letters I wrote to you . . . may never be made public' and pleads that they were 'familiarly written and with a quite other design as from me to you'. Extract after extract showed that on the contrary they were written with authority and intended to elicit William's considered opinion; and in later exchanges Fagel made hay with Stewart's feeble attempts to argue that it was unfair to use a private correspondence in connection with a public declaration of policy.

During the first months of 1688 the replies of the country gentlemen to the King's questionnaire came drifting in. Everyone had given an enthusiastic affirmative to the question about living peaceably with other denominations. But the answers to the other two questions were less satisfactory. Many were evasive, often collusively so. Devon, for instance, out of a total of seventy produced fifty-three all in the same words: that the respondent was doubtful until the matter was debated in parliament, and would elect members known to be loyal subjects and true to the protestant religion. A good many magistrates, despite the efforts of the Lords Lieutenant, managed to avoid answering at all, Wales yielding an especially thin crop of replies:

GLAMORGAN SHIRE
Deputy Lieutenants
Sr Edward Mansell of Margam—Absent, not able, as hee
sayes to ride; not having rid 10 miles these 4 yeares
Sr John Aubry—a crasy body; as hee sayes, not able to
undertake the journey
Sr Richard Bassett—Absent
William Herbert Esqr.—Absent
David Jenkins Esqr.—very infirme
David Evans Esqr.—Absent; came part of ye way, and hav-
ing a dangerous fall, forced to return[6]

But the general picture* was very far from that of polite if
hostile evasion drawn by Macaulay: it is one of sharp division,
with a strong majority against the King's policy. More than half
the magistrates listed took a distinct line one way or the other;
excluding absentees, evasions constitute only a third of the
replies. The surviving returns show that repeal would be supported by about a quarter of the magistrates—a not inconsiderable body, even though pressure was used to assemble it. 'With
great intreatys,' wrote the Lord Lieutenant of Wiltshire, 'I prevailed with Mr Chivers to be for the taking off the penal laws
and tests, and will rely solely upon his Majesty; his chiefest
scruple was, that he should be hang'd hereafter for what he does
at present, and desired greater security.'[7] But support was patchy.
It was strong in the non-conformist West Midlands, in the extreme North, and in Kent; and notably weak in Wales and the
South-West. And some thirty per cent of the magistrates consulted entered more or less distinct refusals to part with the
penal laws and the Test Act, their answers ranging from elaborate little essays on the subject to the blunt reply of Richard
Lamplugh, of Ribton in Westmorland, 'I answer, Noe'.[8]

Dorsetshire registered twenty-six clear refusals out of thirty-
three magistrates, Norfolk thirty-seven out of sixty-three,
Hampshire twenty-seven out of forty-seven. Bucks, where
Jeffreys administered the questions, produced twenty-three refusals out of fifty-four magistrates, and the rest of the Eastern

* See Appendix A.

Midlands were much the same. Only in the South and South-West, and in the two southern ridings of Yorkshire, did opposition systematically cloak itself in the polite formula of not being able to make a commitment until the arguments were debated in parliament. It is clear that something like two-thirds of the country gentry were open or potential opponents of repeal—and half of these made no bones about saying so.

Within a very short time the result of the canvass was known. 'All their reports,' wrote the Imperial ambassador in London on 16 January, 'agree on the point that there is neither appearance nor hope of things being carried out in the form or manner the Court had imagined.'[9] And if this was known to Hoffman it was known to other intelligence services too—including William's. Clarendon, indeed, had written to William before Christmas hinting that the majority of answers would not promise well for a compliant parliament.[10] James's position was gravely weakened. But he was now committed. His policy, in all its essentials, had been settled during his autumn progress, and especially during the emotional stay at Chester and the conference with Tyrconnel. One of the decisions that had been reached there was of international importance, and burst like a bomb in the new year. It appears to have been suggested by Tyrconnel; and was to recall the British and Scottish regiments serving with the army of the United Provinces.*

James considered he had power to do this. Indeed he considered he had already exercised this right when the troops had come over to help against Monmouth in 1685; and during 1687 a number of the officers of the Scottish regiments had been induced to return individually by the offer of commissions in James's growing forces. Officers turned out of the Irish forces by Tyrconnel had taken many of their places, and James, not unnaturally, wanted to see a permanent end of this foreign legion which was attracting more and more of his disaffected subjects. But action on the decision was delayed. His finances, already strained, would not run to the expense of paying additional men, and negotiations were set on foot through Barillon

---

* Barillon to Louis XIV, 13 and 16 October and 8 December 1687 (Dalrymple, Book V, pp. 134–8); Lord Falkland's letter of credit 'to make provision for bringing over his Majesty's forces' is dated 16 October (*Cal. Treas. Bks.* 1687, item 2098).

for Louis to pay for some of them to be stationed in France. These discussions were not finished till the end of the year; and they show that James was at least as interested in weakening William as he was in strengthening his own forces, a point the Dutch ambassador was quick to perceive.

All the signs on the other side of the North Sea were of a decision there also. At the turn of the year Albeville, who was spending a good deal of money on spies at the Hague, was reporting increased security precautions: 'Intelligence is got of late with great difficulty because of the dangers those that give it expose themselves to, several having lost their places for giving it, and severely punished.'[11] That October William had received authority from the States to add twenty-four warships to the Dutch navy, ostensibly to strengthen the Mediterranean squadron in dealing with Algerine corsairs: but the ships remained for the time being at Willemstadt, William's personal fortified harbour in Zeeland, until they could be sent on unobtrusive cruises, some to the West Indies, some to the East, and one each to the Mediterranean and Portugal. Even before the preparation of the Fagel letter old Marshal Schomberg was writing from Berlin to Henry Sidney, who commanded the British troops in Holland, and had just returned from unexplained business in southern Europe, urging him to be on hand to advise the Prince. 'You know,' wrote the Marshal, 'that sometimes things in England move very quickly.'[12] By December, in continuation of William's policy of constant surveillance, Sidney was himself in England, informing himself with the aid of the most effective agent William ever sent to England, James Johnston. 'The Prince,' he wrote to Bentinck, 'should take his measures what to do in that case [a parliament willing to repeal the Test Act] for that we must never expect to see a free Parliament here under the present state of affairs.'[13]

For James, with his narrow drive, his passion for organisation, was following up his canvass of the county magistrates with an elaborate and detailed survey of all parliamentary constituencies. He can, again, at least claim to be an innovator. It was the first survey of such scope, combining systematic propaganda with organisation of the government interest in the constituencies themselves. The work of the so-called 'Lords for Regulating the Corporations', over whom, on occasion, James presided in person,* and, still more, of their secretary and their agents in the field, foreshadow later political developments in a very striking way.

The field agents worked in groups of two or three, covering each county borough by borough, establishing a 'correspondent', reminding revenue officers and postmasters of their responsibilities as government voters and propagandists, and distributing pamphlets in support of the Indulgence policy. For each constituency they provided thumb-nail sketches of a kind that were to be familiar for more than a century afterwards:

> ABINGDON The Towne is divided. The presbiterian party for choosing Mr Southby: other Dissenters for Mr Trinder. Mr Tomkins declines to stand. There are five County Justices have votes in this Towne, *viz* Sir John Stonhouse of Radly, James Stonhouse of Tubney, Robert Mayot of Falo, Thomas Read of Appleford, and Sir Edmund Warcup. The four first being contrary minded, may influence the Election to Your Majesty's prejudice; t'is therefore desired they may be put out of Commission.†

Formally the regulators were the responsibility of Sunderland and Jeffreys; but the effective centre and controller of the machine was Robert Brent, a catholic lawyer, to whom the agents were instructed 'to give a full and distinct account of the proceedings by every post, and therein an impartial account of the sentiments of the persons with whom you converse, their inclinations and resolutions, and what expedients are necessary to render the election certain . . . but not to any other person whatever.'[14] This forerunner of national agents seems originally to have made his mark as attorney-general to James when Duke of York, and was related to the catholic Lord Carrington, whom James made Lord Lieutenant of Worcestershire. Brent himself was appointed a magistrate in both Gloucestershire (his native county) and Somerset, and he was clearly of sufficient importance in his heyday to do an unnamed but considerable favour to Gray's Inn, in return for which his son was ordered to be admitted gratis.

---

* 'Mr Kemp' [the code-name for James] goes himself to the Commission for regulating the Corporations (Portland MSS, PWA 2146).

† Duckett, II, 237. Tubney, incidentally, was a Magdalen College living, later to be enjoyed by Dr. Pudsey.

His appearance in history is only fleeting. We shall see him once or twice more, upbraiding no less a person than Jeffreys for not being wholehearted, and writing desperately to Preston when all was lost, urging him to advise the King not to give up. Then, after a brief period in arrest, he vanishes, excepted—not surprisingly—from the Williamite amnesty. But some of his techniques persisted into the age of party; and for about a year he was a man to whom Lord Lieutenants applied, and one who could at a stroke remove a sheriff.[15]

Patronage, above all, was the side of Brent's work that multiplied opposition. Revisions of charters, replacements of officeholders, were ruthlessly used to man positions of influence with the comparatively few who could be depended upon. The effects can be read between the lines of a single example of Brent's work in the memoirs of the Essex magistrate, Bramston:

> Upon the granting of a charter to Maldon, was pleased, by order of Councill, to remove the Mayor and five Aldermen in Maldon; by another severall capital burgesses, and the recorder; and by a third order my selfe from the office of High Steward of the burrough, an office I had held since the return of King Charles the Second.[16]

But James was carried away. He intended to have a parliament that spring though Brent seems already to have been thinking in terms of the autumn.* In mid-November he must have known, though he did not yet announce it, that St Winefrede had answered his prayer, and Maria Beatrice was going to have a child;† which lends a special interest to the interview he had had on 28 November—the day before Stewart's decisive letter to the Hague—with James Earl of Abingdon, head of the great anglican clan of Bertie, in an attempt to persuade him of the need for repeal. Abingdon was Lord Lieutenant of Oxfordshire, and James tested him on the three questions.

* The reason for the date is curious. Sheriffs were appointed in November for the ensuing year, and their main duty was to act as returning officers for the counties. The Test Act gave three months' grace for taking the prescribed oath, so that a catholic sheriff was able to act without infringing the law during the December, January, and February following his appointment. Johnston reports Brent's preference for autumn on 21 December (Portland MSS, P.W.A. 2120).

† The Tuscan envoy, Terriesi, refers to the reported pregnancy of Maria Beatrice in his despatch of 24 November.

'If there was a Parliament now sitting', replied Abingdon warily, 'I should be against those things, but I am not so settled in that opinion, or prejudiced, but if I did see reason, or were convinced upon the debate, I might alter it.' The King at once plied him with reasons: the tests restricted the King's prerogative of appointment, they offended the privilege of peers by excluding catholic peers from the House of Lords, they restricted the people in a free choice of their representatives, and they implied that the King was an idolater. 'He then fell upon his declaration, and the sincerity of his desires, that all persons might live lovingly and quietly.' Abingdon refused to be convinced. He took refuge in the argument that the penal laws were hardly enforced, and then expressed doubts—nearer the mark than he knew—about the certainty of a protestant successor. At last he grew franker still in his lack of confidence and spoke of how the King's neighbour 'on the other side of the water had broke through all laws and promises, so that nobody knew what to trust to'. Suddenly James grew lame and irritable. 'He knew that, but could not tell how to help it.'[17] Three weeks later Abingdon, along with four other Lieutenants, was superseded, making sixteen counties that had changed their Lieutenants since the summer.

That winter peace and war and the future of James's crown lay in the hands of his neighbour across the water, Louis; and it is through his eyes, and the eyes of Louvois, that we must take stock of the European scene as the English country gentlemen considered the answers to James's questions.

At the eastern extremity, in Constantinople, revolt and confusion reigned. Mohammed IV was soon to be replaced by his brother Suleiman II, and although Turkey was to make one more convulsive effort under one more Kiuprili Vizier, the Turkish threat to central Europe was almost spent. On the Danube there was stability and conciliation, with the Imperial armies poised to push further south and east. In the Mediterranean was a rebalancing of naval power, with Louis concentrating his fleet against Algiers in the hope of taking at least some profit from the collapse of Turkish power.

At Berlin the old Elector, his alliance with William cemented, his barren electorate repopulated with refugees, his army headed by Schomberg, was entering the last few months of his reign. Prussia was preparing to enlarge her foothold on the Rhine, whether that was disputed by France, by the Emperor, or by William himself.

Innocent XI was also nearing the end of his life, but he was as intransigent as ever towards France. Relations between the Papacy and Louis had never been so strained. In thirty French dioceses the papal approval for a new bishop had been withheld. In Rome, by way of reprisal, the French ambassador was attempting to enforce with troops a claim to diplomatic immunity extending to the whole quarter surrounding his Embassy. The papal enclave of Avignon had been annexed to France almost simultaneously with the suppression of the last vestiges of independence at neighbouring Orange. Plans were being laid in Versailles for a combined operation against the coast of Italy.

From Spain there were disturbing reports about the health of the idiot King Carlos. Spanish diplomacy moved in step with Imperial diplomacy, and Imperial troops released from the eastern theatre of war were taking up their positions on the Rhenish line that connected the two bastions of Habsburg power in northern Italy and Belgium. The great fortress of Philipsburg on the upper Rhine, which had been half finished when Burnet passed that way in 1686, was now complete and garrisoned. Further north William was now clearly preparing for war. The money for the four-year defence programme, settled to begin in 1687, was being spent in a single year with the help of bank advances—huguenot houses being prominent among the bankers concerned.

This was the context in which Louis considered the problem presented by James. James's navy was already formidable, and his army was growing. The prospect of an heir, and a growing missionary zeal, were making him obstinate. But his internal policy made him an unreliable ally. It might bring about collapse, or it might yet drive him into the arms of William, who, Louis knew, would even now make great sacrifices to secure an English alliance. So, Louis calculated, it would be to his advantage rather than the reverse if James and William persisted in their respective courses, even to the point of William intervening in England. Never has an over-refined calculation proved more disastrously mistaken.

The Tariff War and the Regiments

While the power structure of Europe was generally known and taken into account by everyone concerned with politics, the impact of finance was less studied. The success of the French economy under Colbert had concealed the fact that in default of technological advance there is a limit to the dividends from improved efficiency in the use of existing capital resources. Colbert had reaped those dividends for Louis. But by the time of Colbert's death in 1683 the French treasury was sliding into deficit financing.* The attacks on the huguenots made things worse, with heavy emigration of skill and capital. French domestic industry, so carefully fostered by Colbert, was not holding its own against foreign competition, especially English and Dutch. It was this long-term trend that moved Louis, in the autumn of 1687, to take far-reaching economic measures which struck hard at one of the foundations of the Nijmegen settlement and altered the internal balance of power in the Netherlands.

They began with a decree forbidding the import of herrings into France; and this was followed by a declaration that Louis intended to reintroduce the full rigour of Colbert's tariff of 1667 —the tariff that had once precipitated war between France and

*	1661	1669	1680	1683	million livres Tournois
Net Receipts	84·2	76·5	61·5	93	
Outgoings	93·4	76·3	96·3	109	
+ or −	−9·2	+0·2	−34·9	−16	

(Lavisse, E., *Histoire de France*, 7. ii. 380)

the Netherlands. In vain d'Avaux protested from the Hague that 60,000 Dutchmen depended on the fishing industry for their livelihood; and that irreparable damage would be done to the policy of playing the commercial interest of Amsterdam off against the House of Orange. He was told that the prohibition on herrings was not a tariff but a domestic regulation outside the scope of the Nijmegen provisions guaranteeing free trade between France and the United Provinces; and that the tariff of 1667 was equally in order because it would be applied only to re-exports and not to goods of Dutch origin. 'His Majesty,' wrote Seignelay, 'desires you will confine yourself to the rules prescribed to you by his Majesty's order, whatever should be said or proposed to you.'[1] There were to be no more cheerful dinners with Amsterdam business men, ending with toasts to the joint prosperity of France and the United Provinces. At a crucial moment, and by Louis' agency, the mercantile and Orange interests were consolidated.

Along with herrings and tariffs Louis had that autumn to consider the plan hatched at Chester by James, Tyrconnel, Sunderland, and Barillon concerning the six British regiments in the Netherlands; and partly on the same grounds of financial stringency he found it a difficult proposition. The idea of paying some 4,000 English troops on French soil for the King of England had seemed to Louis a poor bargain. He also, being more wary than James, considered that the presence of English troops in France would imply an open alliance with James and might lead to an untimely breach with William. He fancied, however, that there was some advantage in increasing the tension between William and James, so that after some months' negotiation he agreed to help with the cost of maintaining the troops, but only if they were withdrawn to England.[2]

By the time agreement was reached, as some of James's advisers pointed out, a great change had come over relations between England and the Netherlands. Fagel's letter had been written and answered, and was on the way to publication.* The last chance of a compromise between James and William on religious policy had gone. To demand the return of the regiments in such a context would open a dangerous breach, perhaps even lead to

---

* 'I hear it is printing in Amsterdam.' Johnston to Bentinck, 8 December 1687 (Portland MSS, P.W.A. 2112).

war. Even Sunderland now thought it would be a mistake, though he was too deeply committed to advise against it. He was also trying to screw money out of Louis on the argument that he deserved something to fall back on if James's policy failed.

So it was that in a single fortnight of January 1688 William received the official notification of Maria Beatrice's pregnancy and a peremptory request from James to support the application being made by the British Envoy to the States General for the repatriation of the regiments. He read these, no doubt, bearing in mind what James had said about him, as reported through Johnston on 8 December—'He [William] is inflexible. No man knows him better than I do. He will be at the head of a certain interest, and have a war with France. But without me he can do nothing.'[3]

The pregnancy, of course, William already knew about, and there had been ample time to develop the campaign of rumours about fraud which was to be the counter to it. Incredulity is a good answer to news that suits one's opponent particularly well, but it is not easy to make it serve its purpose very long. Its adoption in this case suggests that William was now thinking in the short term. But there was plenty for the story of fraud to batten on. Terriesi, the Tuscan envoy in London, had noted incredulity and satire in circulation even before the official announcement, and when the gazette appeared Clarendon wrote 'that the news is everwhere ridiculed, as if scarcely anybody believes it to be true'.[4] The shallow, jealous, Anne at this stage seems not to have shared these doubts. 'No words,' wrote Terriesi, 'can express the rage of the Princess of Denmark at the Queen's condition.'[5] But very soon Anne was an enthusiastic doubter of what she did not want to believe. She even wrote to her sister Mary commenting that Maria Beatrice looked extraordinarily well 'which is not usual; for people when they are so far gone, for the most part, look very ill'.[6] So far can self-deception go. But one should not be too hard on Anne. She had miscarried in October, and was to miscarry again in April.

William took no overt action on the request about the regiments. The States General took their time to consider d'Albeville's application, and it was not until 19 February, after 'taking the facts of the case into consideration, with the most wise advice of the Prince of Orange',[7] that they decided 'the present situation of the time and affairs not only does not make adviseable, but cannot allow or permit their High Mightinesses to part with such an important portion of their army, enlisted at so great expense'. They were prepared to allow officers who so wished to resign their commissions and return to England as individuals: a valueless concession, since they were free to do so anyway.

James, as was always his way when frustrated, reacted with furious activity. He called an inconclusive cabinet, consulted the French ambassador, and instructed d'Albeville to protest. But even at this point he does not seem to have thought of appealing specifically to the convention of 1678 between Ossory and William under which the regiments were to be repatriated whenever required. All that d'Albeville's protest elicited, after eleven days, was an immensely long, courteous, involved, and absolute essay in stonewalling, which among much else contained the following passage:

> Their High Mightinesses will make no reply to the instances mentioned by the Envoy Extraordinary, as they do not know what stipulations were made as regards them with his Majesty the King of France, and they could easily show what a bad application was made of what happened in the sad and unfortunate times of King Charles II, did not the veneration which they have for his Majesty's most illustrious house, and the horror of such calamitous times and misfortunes prevent them from touching on such matters.[8]

During the interval between the protest and the reply James discovered the existence of the convention of 1678: the failure to exploit it earlier is a further example of Sunderland's administrative incompetence over vital detail. So with this new ammunition d'Albeville returned to the charge on 5 April; and after a further three weeks of reflection the States produced an even more elaborate and frustrating reply than before. It began with an assertion that the laws of nature and of nations allowed free men to settle and serve where they pleased; observed in passing that 'when their High Mightinesses had the misfortune to be plunged into war with his Majesty the King of Great Britain, Charles II, of glorious memory', they had indeed temporarily dispensed with the services of the British regiments; and at last came to the point that this was the first time they had ever

heard of such an agreement as was now pleaded.* They had
never approved it, nor had their approval ever been sought. They
regarded it as a private transaction between the Prince of Orange
and Ossory, and in no way binding on the employers of the
troops, namely the States. The Dutch constitution and the principle of the separation of powers had never been used to better
political effect.

The month of March had been a bitter one for James. By its
first week enough of the returns from the Lieutenants had been
analysed to show the strength of the opposition among the gentry.
It seemed certain that the spring parliament which he had set his
heart on and repeatedly mentioned in public as the one which
would place the seal of approval on the Indulgence policy,
would in fact be unfavourable. Sunderland had not dared to
change his advice about the regiments; but on the parliamentary
prospects—and probably Brent, whose agents still had much
work to do—he spoke out clearly. It was too risky, and a failure
in parliament could not be retrieved. For almost the only time in
his life James allowed himself to be persuaded to change his mind.
Sunderland's advice was sound enough; but accepting it looked
like, and indeed was, a confession of a domestic and international
defeat. A parliament to approve the Indulgence policy had been
promised, and the gravest possibility William had to fear was that
James would succeed in keeping that promise.

So James tried not to surrender his policy completely. It
would have been most unlike him to do otherwise. He decided
to announce that a parliament would be held in November,
when it might be hoped Brent's electoral machine would have
completed its work of ensuring enough members from the
boroughs to vote down the anglican squires. To tie this firmly
to an absence of any signs of weakness on the Indulgence policy
he republished the Declaration of the previous year together with
an assurance that there would be a Parliament 'In November at
farthest'. This, the so-called 'Second Declaration' was published
on 7 May (N.S.).†

---

* In point of fact van Citters' despatch of 12 March, which reached the
States *before* they answered d'Albeville's first protest, gave notice that James
was going to appeal to the Convention of 1678, the text of which appears
first to have come into his hands on 10 March (Ferguson, 550–1).
† The decision to republish the Declaration can be explained on no other
rational lines. The advice to do so is attributed by Burnet to Penn. 'Pen, and

William was kept in close touch with all these developments in despatches from supporters and agents in England; and the bearer of one such bag, containing Devonshire's letter of 23 March and Shrewsbury's of the 24th, gives a hint of what was really happening in the six regiments behind the smoke-screen put up by their High Mightinesses. This messenger was Emanuel Scrope Howe, one of the four politically active brothers of that family, who appears in the roll of 'Ossory's' Anglo-Dutch regiment of foot for 1689 as 'Captain Emanuel Scroophur'. Nor was he the only recent recruit of whiggish outlook to take up one of William's commissions. John Cutts, formerly a dependant of Monmouth, who after Sedgemoor had taken his sword to the siege of Buda and had been at the storming of 1686, had recently become a captain in the same regiment as Howe. In Balfour's regiment of Scots were serving Henry Erskine, Lord Cardross, a covenanting refugee who had first tried to make a life beyond James's reach in Carolina, and now took the oath to William on 28 March 1688; and more important than any of these, Thomas Talmash, who left England in March to take up a nominal captain's commission in Balfour's regiment of foot.

Talmash, until he was killed in 1694, at the age of only forty-three, was one of the most promising soldiers England had produced since Cromwell's day: there were even stories that he was Cromwell's illegitimate son. His mother, by her second marriage Duchess of Lauderdale, was a Scotswoman, and Talmash's military career had started in an old Cromwellian regiment, the Coldstream Guards. After a spell at Tangier he had become a lieutenant colonel at only thirty-four, and had resigned his commission a year later, soon after James established his dispensing power and the army began to fill up with catholic officers. Before leaving for the Netherlands Talmash was one of the leading figures in a group of youngish opposition parliamentarians and officers who met at the Rose Tavern in Covent Garden: Thomas Wharton and his crony Charles Godfrey (who was married to Marlborough's sister Arabella Churchill); Richard

---

all the tools who were employed by him, had still some hopes of carrying a parliament to agree with the King, if too much time was not lost: whereas the delaying a parliament raised jealousies, as if none were intended, but that it was only talked of to amuse the nation till other designs were ripe.' (Burnet (1838), p. 466.)

Savage, Viscount Colchester, a captain in the Horse Guards; Jack Howe, Emanuel's brother; William Jephson; and Major Thomas Langston of the Duke of St Albans' Regiment of Dragoons, who had, like Cutts, taken part in the storming of Buda.[9] This was one of the nuclei already forming for the purpose of co-operation with an armed intervention by William— their plans covered both disaffection in James's forces and armed support for the invaders. How far these plans had been carried by March, when Talmash left for the Netherlands, can only be guessed, but from what happened subsequently one can suppose they had gone some distance.

Such men as Talmash and Cutts were more than adequate to fill the gaps left by the trickle of officers coming back to England. The number responding to James's final invitation of March 1688 is put variously between forty and sixty—perhaps a quarter of the total officer cadre for the six regiments; but James had been offering inducements ever since 1685, when he had persuaded Colonel Alexander Canon to stay behind after his regiment returned to the Netherlands. Canon was to prove one of James's better officers, but William was only too pleased to see such men go. No doubt one or two agents were included among those repatriated,* but on the whole they were from William's point of view the unreliable elements. So long as William could keep the trained rank and file, a purge of the commissioned ranks, removing such officers as Major Dionysius MacGillicuddy and Captain Maurice Plunkett, suited him very well. Just as James had polarised opinion in the English shires by his questions, so he now helped to create a British force abroad in which every officer was a dependable opponent of his régime.

The only officer William took steps to retain was old Brigadier Hugh Mackay, who commanded the three Scots regiments. He came originally from Scourie in the far north-western highlands

* One such was probably Captain Aeneas Mackay, nephew of Brigadier Hugh Mackay. He returned in March and was posted to one of the new regiments James was raising; but immediately after the Revolution he became a major in the Scots Greys, was lieutenant colonel at Aughrim, and a brigadier in 1695 (*Historical Record of the Fifth Foot, or Northumberland Fusiliers*, 1838). The turnover in the higher ranks of the regiments was especially high as a result of these changes, and must have been stimulating. Of the six colonels only two stayed with William—Balfour and Hugh Mackay. Of the four vacancies one was taken by Talmash, but when the moment of action came the other colonelcies had not been filled.

and had twenty-eight years' service under many colours—British, French, Venetian, and Dutch. He had fought the Turks in Crete and the Dutch in 1673, when he had been in Turenne's invading army. But during that campaign he had married the daughter of the house on which he was billeted, and decided to change sides. In the spring of 1688 the Brigadier, who had hardly been home for nearly twenty years, seems to have thought of accepting repatriation, but a personal interview with William convinced him that it would be Britain for him that year in any case, so he stayed.*

Vital though the six regiments were, they were only a fraction of the force William calculated as necessary for the plans he was now forming. There was defence of the home base to be considered as well as the expeditionary force; and the expeditionary force alone had to be at least a match for what James could put into the field. Whatever conspiracies there might be in England for joining an invader or embarrassing James, they would only come into the open if the invasion looked powerful and professional. Moreover James was the kind of man—and William had measured him well—who might crack without fighting if confronted with the serious possibility of defeat. There was, in fact, the prospect of a bloodless campaign if the expedition was strong enough, and a bloodless campaign was politically most desirable. The possibility of a military intervention so massive that there would be no fighting does not seem to have occurred to Louis, but it was central to the plans of William.

Hence the importance of alliances in William's plans, especially the alliance with Brandenburg. The old Elector Frederick William died on 29 April after, it is said, giving the words 'London : Amsterdam' as the last password and countersign to his palace guard—but contact between Berlin and the Hague was almost continuous. In February General von Spaen, Governor of Frederick William's Rhenish provinces, again visited the Hague. During the first half of 1688 Lord Leven, now a colonel in the Electoral army, was actively employed as a courier between the two courts, and no doubt between William and the aristocratic Scottish exiles in the Netherlands, who included Leven's father,

---

* Mackay paid a brief visit to London in May 1686, when he discussed promotions in the Brigade with James (see his letter to William in Japikse, II. ii. 731). His personal interview with William in spring 1688 is referred to in the *Historical Account*, p. 64.

Lord Melville. The accession in Brandenburg of the new Elector Frederick brought no change of policy. Bentinck was despatched in the second week of May from the Hague to congratulate him and carry the negotiations a stage further.

Simultaneously William was making offers to mediate between the Emperor and the Turks; and his agents in Rome were making an impression on the papal Secretariat of State. If the cloak-and-dagger doings recorded in the reports of Cardinal d'Estrées to Louvois have any basis of fact, Cassoni, Innocent XI's secretary, was in contact with a Dutch agent who masqueraded as a salesman of artificial flowers, and finance was reaching William from the papal treasury on the basis that William would be prepared to take command of an anti-French coalition army on the Rhine.[10] In the strategic north German states of Celle and Hanover another of William's envoys, Simon van Pettekum, was negotiating for troops, and by the summer George William of Celle was also brigaded into the new coalition.[11]

As the network for the invasion of England reached eastwards to Rome, Berlin, and Vienna, it extended itself also into the maritime world of the Atlantic and America. Armies did not move yet; but fleets were already in motion. Here William's entente with the republican authorities in the Netherlands was crucial. Land warfare was his profession, and he could in case of necessity levy or hire troops on his own authority, but for naval power he had to rely on the Dutch politicians.

In the previous summer he had secured from them large votes for naval rearmament. Eighteen ships dating from 1682 were refitted, and more new keels were to be laid down. Authority had been given for nine thousand extra sailors to be levied to man the new vessels—enough to put them on a war footing. Such activity naturally did not go unnoticed by James, who paid an ostentatious visit to his own powerful fleet at Chatham early in May. But to avoid the appearance of a naval concentration a strong Dutch squadron of seven vessels sailed that spring for the West Indies, carrying with it one of the most enthusiastic of the English refugee aristocrats, Charles Mordaunt.* They touched

---

* Mordaunt is one of the most curious figures in the revolutionary epoch. He was at this time still under thirty, had taken the opposite side to his father (who was one of James's Lords of Trade and a roman catholic), and had been a protagonist of Orange intervention since 1686. William regarded him

at Jamaica and Nevis, professing to be on a treasure hunt, and appear to have made some contact with the British squadron on the West Indian station before recrossing the Atlantic. Their presence was duly reported by the suspicious governor of Nevis to the Board of Trade.[12] Whether they went as far as continental America is not clear, but if they had they would have found James's policy making better headway there than in the home country. His great North American design was almost complete. Under James's chosen instrument, Governor Edmund Andros, five formerly independent colonies, Massachusetts, Connecticut, Rhode Island, New Jersey, and New York, now formed the autocratically governed, religiously tolerant 'Dominion of New England'.

It is one of our illusions that until the age of steam America was remote. From London the journey to New York was hardly further or longer than to Constantinople—and a great deal less than the voyage to such places as Bantam and the Straits of Malacca, where English and Dutch interests were at this moment in conflict; or to the Cape of Good Hope, where the first expedition of huguenot settlers arrived in 1688. America was near enough, for instance, to provide James with support in his propaganda struggle at home. Among the many addresses in praise of the toleration policy was one from the dissenting ministers of New England.

Such addresses, which were, of course, vigorously publicised, make an interesting list, which should be pondered by all who think the Revolution had a 'bourgeois' inspiration. They were doubtless stimulated, but they were also thought by their makers to be worth making, and they suggest that whatever impression Halifax's *Letter to a Dissenter* may have made on individuals, large sections of organised dissent and organised business came out publicly for the Indulgence policy. The presbyterians of Canterbury, Tenterden, and Maidstone,* the congregationalists of Hitchin and Hertford, other sectaries in Brighton and Leicestershire, all sent enthusiastic testimonials. The City of London was

as unreliable, but his contacts may well have been important. Arthur Herbert was Mordaunt's maternal uncle.
* The Regulators had great hopes of the dissenting vote in the Kentish boroughs—see their notes on Canterbury, Maidstone, Rochester, and Queenborough in Duckett, I, 361–5.

no less zealous. During the winter and spring there were addresses from many City Companies—Distillers and Cutlers, Goldsmiths and Haberdashers, Bakers and Merchant Taylors—and from the City's own hospital, St Thomas's. In both of the last years of his reign the King could depend on a friendly, nonconformist Lord Mayor.

In spite of all this, and a great deal of activity by government pamphleteers in putting their side of the case,* James was giving ground in the propaganda struggle. A proclamation was issued in the spring against distributing seditious literature, notably Fagel's letter, which had now bred a trail of subsidiary pamphlets. The original letter was now everywhere in England—the Regulators' agents noted it in Wiltshire—but even more serious was the loss of the one great national network that could reach to the people and was now controlled by the gentry. James no longer had access to the pulpit, which in some places was being used openly against him. In April Stillingfleet, Dean of St Paul's and one of the most eloquent preachers in the history of the anglican church, chose a text whose significance cannot have been lost on his hearers: Luke, X. 22:

> But one thing is needful: and *Mary* hath chosen that good part, which shall not be taken away from her.

Yet that spring James still looked strong. It is easy to underestimate the difficulty and boldness of the invasion plan that William had now unquestionably formed. James was formidable on both sea and land. He had the advantage of interior lines, and all the claims of a rightful, recognised title. The use of Dutch troops and ships to force the issue was liable to rouse emotion and unity in the presence of a national and commercial enemy. And as if these obstacles were not deterrent enough, any move against James would leave the whole of William's landward flank exposed to the real enemy, Louis. No more than neutrality could be hoped for from Spain and from the Emperor. They were, after all, catholic monarchs and believers in hereditary right. The invasion plan—not, as yet, perhaps, quite a decision—was therefore one of the most adventurous strokes of war and policy ever to succeed in modern European history. It was bolder

* e.g. *Parliamentum Pacificum*, which came out in January, denying the authenticity of the Fagel letters. Johnston thought it effective.

than Marlborough's march across Europe to Blenheim, and at least as bold as Bismarck's destruction of Louis Napoleon in 1870. No modern operation has so successfully combined force and political judgment to capture a throne.

Such purposiveness is the more astonishing in that the three leading planners were all under severe private stress. William himself had a series of particularly bad attacks of asthma during the spring and summer. While Bentinck was perfecting the alliance with the new Elector of Brandenburg in May little Willem Bentinck, his son and heir, died, and his wife Anne was seriously ill. Gaspar Fagel was already suffering from the cancer that was to kill him before the year was out. Yet these were the men who, with the help of two elderly German generals, an efficient military machine and intelligence service, a cautious section of the English and Scottish aristocracies, and a miscellaneous collection of protestant plotters, were to produce an event that astonished Europe and changed the course of its history.

The Bishops

The spring of 1688 was a wet one, accompanied by an epidemic of influenza. Johnston, William's agent in London, had 'the cold so ill' in February that he could not go out. But by May James was diplomatically isolated and domestically undermined.

The undermining was both deep and widespread, though the various groups at work were not yet fully in contact with one another. The focus of the conspiracy of politicians was Danby, who was already beginning to organise a northern network of potential collaboration with William. Danby's contacts ranged southward into Nottinghamshire, and as far north as Durham, where his ally Lord Lumley was operating in the diocese of one of James's most faithful adherents, Bishop Nathaniel Crewe. Closely associated with Danby was his old ally and contemporary (both men were fifty-three), Compton, the suspended Bishop of London. Also in this group was the young Earl of Shrewsbury, now back in England together with William's principal missionary to the English aristocracy, Sidney. Side by side with this conspiracy of the politicians was the group of young whigs—Wharton, Lovelace, Colchester; and these in turn shaded into the foci of military and naval disaffection whose leaders were at Loo towards the end of April. 'Mr Herbert,' William wrote to Bentinck, 'and the two Russells have been here; I will not tell you what they said to me, since that is better done by word of mouth.'[1] What in fact they said was that in their judgment the moment for intervention in England had arrived; and William had replied that provided he had a specific invitation from leaders of sufficient political weight he could act by the end of September. Whether he would have acted without such an invitation must be uncertain: but he must have been reasonably sure he would get it, and the stipulation, besides adding to his strength, preserved his flexibility down to the latest possible moment. What is certain is that from this point onwards preparations were urgently pressed forward.

All the separate threads led to the Hague. Danby's correspondence was with his son, Lord Dunblane, who was stationed at William's court. Compton had his contact through Mary's chaplain, the Rev. William Stanley. Only the young whigs, strangely enough, have left no trace of their line of communication across the North Sea, though Talmash, Cutts, and Howe were no doubt concerned. All groups had their connection with William's agents in England, of whom the most active, though not the most senior, was James Johnston, who had been in England since October.

This bold and intelligent man was the son of the covenanting Johnston of Warristoun, and had spent more than twenty years in exile on the continent, during which he had become a trusted member of William's intelligence service. It appears to have been Burnet, his cousin, who suggested that he should be sent to England to increase the efficiency of Sidney, who was nominally in charge of William's interests.

Johnston was in his thirties when he undertook this mission: deeply resourceful, clear-sighted to the point of cynicism, well informed on politics and well endowed with access to sources of information. His role was not only to provide intelligence and assessments of the political situation but—as he expressed it—to give 'impressions to rectify false reports'. In other words he was to act as a propagandist as well as an agent, and was to be provided with ample, up-to-date news about attitudes at the Hague. Great care was taken in establishing lines of communication, which led through huguenot accommodation addresses in London to accommodation addresses in the Netherlands and thence to Bentinck. The letters from 'Mr Rivers' were in appearance business correspondence, but when soaked in a solution prepared by Dr Hutton produced a cipher message written in invisible ink. Few men were to know more than Johnston about the inner workings of affairs in the period

immediately preceding the Revolution, whose last important
survivor he was to be.*

A stream of information reached the directors of policy at the
Hague about the state of opinion in England and Scotland
through Johnston. He was a man who did not mince his words—
for instance, he frankly stated that he thought James's policy
would succeed in Scotland, 'though they are sensible of the difference betwixt the state of England, where the body of the People
being the Church of England lose by the taking off of the Lawes
and the Test, and the state of Scotland, where the body of the Nation, nay in a manner all the Nation except the governing part of it,
being dissenters, the nation will gain by the taking off of the Test
and the Lawes'. He followed electoral news closely, reporting in
detail on the government's manipulations in Newcastle, Tewkes-
bury, and Reading; and shrewdly estimated the size of the task
confronting Brent's machine. Jokes and phrases he heard in the
streets were faithfully passed on. And above all he stressed the
need for effective, continuous propaganda. He demanded to be
consulted on every major move over publicity, and devoted much
time to organising the distribution of Williamite literature,
especially Fagel's letter. 'You must have the Printer have correspondents in all the great sea-towns,' he wrote to Bentinck, 'if
they be sent gratis they will be easily dispersed': it was all money
in the bookseller's pocket, he pointed out, since people were
eager to buy political pamphlets. As a pioneer of political propaganda he stands high indeed, launching at one point into theory
on the subject that has a wholly modern ring.

If you intend to keep the nation in humour, you must
entertain it by papers. The Spirit of a People is like that of

* The series of his letters is in Portland MSS 2087–2178 in the Nottingham
University Library. From November 1687 to August 1688 'Mr Rivers'
wrote at least twice a week, sometimes oftener. The correspondence never
seems to have been suspected by the English authorities, though precautions, including the examination of all letters to Holland, were in force
throughout the period. Part of Johnston's remarkable success may be due to
his care never to use a false address as cover. Everything in his cover story
was genuine. His sources included one of Maria Beatrice's bed-chamber
women and someone who could give highly accurate accounts of Privy
Council proceedings. He also had access to Halifax, Lovelace, and, it seems,
Penn. See also Japikse, I. ii. 597–8 on the arrangements for the correspondence, which were most elaborate.

particular persons, often to be entertained by trifles; particularly that of the English, who, like all islanders, seems to ebb and flow like the neighbouring sea. In the late fermentation about the Exclusion, the Excluders never lost ground till they lost the press.[2]

On 14 May King James took two steps which showed simultaneously his sense of danger and his determination not to be deflected. He ordered the Scots Guards to move southwards by sea from Scotland; and issued an order in council that the republished Declaration of Indulgence should be read in all churches after a service a fortnight later. Twice before, in recent years, the pulpit had been used as a national broadcasting system for pronouncements of government—in 1681, following the dissolution of the Oxford Parliament, and in 1683, following the Rye House Plot. One need not look further for a reason behind the order than the importance James attached to reaffirming that his policy was not affected by William's public refusal to support it. The order, however, had an unusual feature: it placed the responsibility for seeing it was carried out on the bishops.

The effect of Compton's training of the London clergy in systematic consultation now became apparent. Compton himself held two meetings with his senior clergy within a few days of James's order, and between 21 and 27 May there followed a period of intense activity, during which at least three assemblies of the London clergy took place, together with much canvassing —'There were near twenty of us,' writes Symon Patrick, 'who were desired to feel the pulse of all the ministers in London.' As so often, an effective minority carried an uncertain majority with them. 'More were for reading than against it,' wrote Johnston of one of these meetings, 'but those who were against it were more active and warm.' One of the opponents of the Declaration (possibly, though not certainly, Fowler, the suspended vicar of St Giles's Cripplegate) challenged the waverers to a vote, but they 'said they would not divide'.*[3] On the 27th a list

---

* Johnston's report of 28 May (Portland MSS., P.W.A. 2161). Macaulay makes this meeting the subject of a celebrated set piece. Johnston does not name Fowler in this connection, though he says elsewhere that Fowler had 'been a great instrument for not reading'. Fowler had begun his career as a presbyterian, and although he had conformed in 1662 he had not forfeited respect in the non-conformist camp. In 1691 he became Bishop of Gloucester.

of all those 'who had promised not to read' was handed in at the Bishop of Peterborough's London lodging, above the shop of a well-known ecclesiastical publisher—for onward transmission to the Archbishop of Canterbury. The clergy were not willing themselves to ask the King to withdraw his order: but they asked their bishops to do so.

Archbishop Sancroft was an old and conscientious man who had cautiously picked his way through dangerous times. He was now past seventy, and during his eleven years as Primate he had made many wise choices of policy. He had professed firm belief in the Popish Plot, and had earnestly tried to reconcile the contradictions of a protestant church headed by a catholic king. The wily Dr Stanley had tried, both in letters and on a personal visit, to extract some useful expression of opinion from the Archbishop on this subject, and had little for his pains:

> And though this (were it much more) cannot in the least shake or alter our steady loyalty to our Sovereign and the Royal Family, yet it embitters the comforts left us, it blasts our present joys, and makes us sit down in dust and ashes. Blessed be God, who hath caused some dawn of light to break from the Eastern shore in the constancy of your Royal Highness and the excellent Prince.'[4]

So the Archbishop had written in the previous November to an overture signed by Mary herself. A letter from Stanley in January urging the Archbishop's intervention in James's attempt to convert his daughter to catholicism had been left unanswered.

On 22 May, while the canvass of the London clergy was still going on, Sancroft held a meeting in Lambeth with the bishops who happened to be in London, the Earl of Clarendon, and Tenison, Vicar of St Martin-in-the-Fields, representing the rank and file. Two of those present—Cartwright, Bishop of Chester, and Watson, Bishop of St David's, who were wholly committed to the Court—left before business seriously began. The decision of the meeting was that a petition should be made provided those bishops within easy reach of London would lend their support. For there was little time. The first day appointed for the reading of the Declaration was now only six days off, and in the early morning of the 23rd mounted messengers set off with brief summonses from Sancroft to seven more bishops to join their brethren in London.

While bishops were spurring to the capital, things were moving fast on the eastern shore of which Sancroft had spoken so tactfully. Bentinck was on his way to Berlin (he arrived on 26 May) to settle the alliance with the new Elector and arrange for an early, secret meeting between Frederick and William. From Amerongen, his envoy in southern Germany, William learned that negotiations for a treaty with Saxony were on the point of success. Most significant of all, William had been in conference with Willem Nieupoort, the official farmer of the admiralty revenue, with the object of negotiating a lump-sum advance on the naval credits recently voted by the States General. Van Citters and Johnston knew well enough what these moves meant, and they cannot have failed to bring them home to Compton and the senior London clergy, whose aim now was to propel the cautious old archbishop into irretrievable opposition to the King.

On 28 May, at about two o'clock, thirteen clergy assembled at Lambeth for the decisive meeting under Sancroft's chairmanship.' Compton was present, with five leading men of his diocese, Grove, Rector of St Andrew Undershaft, Stillingfleet, Dean of St Paul's, Tillotson, then one of his canons, though also Dean of Canterbury, Tenison, and Patrick, a prebendary of Westminster as well as Dean of Peterborough. They were the future flower of the Church.* Every one of these was to be a bishop after the Revolution, and two were future Archbishops of Canterbury. In addition to the suspended Compton, there should also have been ten bishops present as a result of Sancroft's summons, but in fact there were (including Sancroft) only seven: Mews of Winchester, who had taken such a prominent part in the Magdalen

---

* The presence of representatives of the London clergy at this conference is extremely significant. They were more closely organised than any other clerical group in the country, and their corporate spirit had been underlined by Johnston in his intelligence letter of 8 December (Portland MSS, P.W.A. 2112) reporting their anxiety at a rumour that Compton was to be deprived, which 'frightens [them] mightily; for if they had another bishop they could no more carry on jointly the opposition they make to popery; by which they have raised a spirit against it, all over the nation'. Only a week or two later, and still more significantly, he wrote (12 January) that the Bishop of Ely, Patrick, and Sherlock, were willing to contemplate 'a remedy which at another time they would regard as a great evil'. The implication that they would support intervention is obvious (P.W.A. 2126).

affair, was suffering from 'wounds in the hands' but sent a letter of support; the message to Lloyd of Norwich had miscarried; and the energetic Frampton of Gloucester was still on the road.

In the seventeenth century the clerical uniform concealed more than it disclosed about a man's career. These seven bishops had not led secluded lives, and they shared between them much diverse experience of political and religious struggles over half a century. Apart from the most junior, Trelawny of Bristol, who was only thirty-eight, all belonged to the last generation before the Civil War, and even the saintliest among them, the musical Thomas Ken of Bath and Wells, had seen the political and military world as chaplain to Mary in the Hague and to Lord Dartmouth in Tangier. John Lake, of Chichester, had been a soldier in his youth, and had been left for dead after the siege of Basing House. His present see he owed to his services during Monmouth's rebellion. Thomas White of Peterborough had been something of a boxer in his youth, and had served a period as chaplain to another of Compton's pupils, the Princess Anne. Francis Turner of Ely owed his extremely rich bishopric* to James, whose chaplain he had been when the King (then Duke of York) had been High Commissioner in Scotland. It was Turner who, with Ken, had attended Monmouth to the scaffold, urging repentance for treason and adultery. Trelawny, the only representative of the new generation among the seven, had also been active against the Western rebels, and had been deeply dissatisfied at receiving no more in return for his services than the poor see of Bristol. He was at least as much a squire in outlook as he was a clergyman (he had inherited a baronetcy) and assured those who criticised his swearing that when he swore it was as Sir Jonathan Trelawny, not the Bishop of Bristol. His brother was a colonel in James's army, and a protégé of Marlborough.

The seventh bishop (the most senior after Sancroft in point of consecration), was William Lloyd, Bishop of St. Asaph, the diocese which included St Winefrede's well, where James had prayed for the son who was now within a month of being born. Although (like Ken) Lloyd had served at the Hague as Mary's chaplain, and had a pliability that had gained him many preferments, he was almost alone among his colleagues in owing little to the

---

* £2,000 a year. Canterbury was worth £4,000, most of the others about £750. Bristol only commanded £380.

friendship of the House of Stuart. Anti-catholic zeal at the time of the Popish Plot had brought him his bishopric, from which he was constantly on the watch for a better. Through his brother-in-law, the Rev. Jonathan Blagrave, who had remained in the Netherlands as Mary's assistant chaplain, he had maintained his own touch across the North Sea. A month or so before the Lambeth meeting he had formed the belief that Maria Beatrice had already miscarried and that her pregnancy was a fraud kept up for political purposes.*

In the background of this meeting was a recent, and deep, change of opinion in the capital about the Indulgence policy. The support from the dissenters which James had temporarily attracted was washing away—the 'Fagel-Stewart' correspondence and other publicity had done its work. On the previous Sunday Richard Baxter, the most powerful non-conformist preacher in London, had praised the stand taken by the established clergy, to whom some kind of written assurance by the dissenters seems to have been given. Very soon after the Lambeth meeting Johnston, whose shadowy presence is everywhere during this critical period, was enciphering a despatch on the support the bishops were likely to get from the dissenters. Penn had long ago given up hope, and was advocating alternatives—perhaps some distribution of government posts between the religions in fixed proportions, perhaps 'an equivalent' for the anglicans as the price of modest concessions to toleration. 'Look at my nose,' Halifax had said to Johnston in March: 'it is a very ugly one, but I would not take one five hundred times better as an equivalent, because my own is fast to my face.'[5]

Beyond it all was the gathering threat of William's intervention. Precisely what was the degree of knowledge at Lambeth on 28 May is not easy to judge. But within a month Compton's name was to be formally communicated to William as 'one of your principal friends'. In August Tenison was to tell Patrick in strict confidence that invasion was intended; Lloyd of St Asaph had his own sources of information. Johnston makes it abundantly clear that in June the bishops were in direct touch with William.

---

* Lloyd remained obsessed by the subject for the rest of his life, arguing long after the controversy had subsided, against the genuineness of the Prince of Wales. Johnston, however, had no doubt about the authenticity of Maria Beatrice's pregnancy (27 February 1688—P.W.A. 2147).

Sancroft and some of the others may still have hoped in May that a private protest would yet recall James from the brink— though there were now only two days to go. But private protest was not the plan of Compton, Lloyd, Trelawny, or (there is some reason to guess) of the Bishop of Peterborough.

The meeting was a long one, punctuated by dinner, after which, according to his own account, the Archbishop wrote out in his own hand, and from an outline he had himself prepared, the one copy of the request which they intended to hand the King that day. Together with the other bishops present (excluding Compton, who could not ask to be excused from a duty his suspension prevented him from performing) he then signed it; but with the caution of age and experience declined to accompany the party which was to present it, on the ground that for two years past he had been discouraged from appearing at court. Leadership therefore fell to the next in seniority, Lloyd of St Asaph.

It was growing late that May evening as the six bishops glided down the river from Lambeth to Whitehall Stairs in the Archbishop's barge. Only thirty-six hours now remained before the Declaration was due to be read, and that it would not be read they were certain. They were none of them remarkable men, their state of information varied in its completeness, and in some cases their motives were far from pure. But they had embarked on one of the greatest public demonstrations of protest in modern English history. This was the point in the Revolution at which the appeal to the people was made, and James was stripped of his moral authority.

They did not see the King until after darkness had fallen. James had himself been on the river that day, probably on a journey to Chatham to review his growing fleet. But it seems inconceivable that neither Sunderland, to whom the bishops applied for an audience, nor the King himself, to whom Sunderland brought them without, it is said, even looking at the petition, should not have had any inkling of what was going on. The interview opened with an attempt at affability and it is possible that a mere refusal on vague general grounds was what James expected, and might have borne. But the bishops gave a specific reason. It was at these words, towards the end of the petition, that the King exploded:

> . . . among many other considerations, from this especially, because that Declaration is founded upon such a dispensing power, as hath often been declared illegal in Parliament; and . . . your petitioners cannot in prudence, honour, or conscience so far make themselves party to it . . .

The whole ground which he had gained in the decision of *Gooden* v. *Hales* was being threatened. 'What! The Church of England against my dispensing power! The Church of England! They that always preached it!'[6] It was Magdalen over again, but on a national scale. In a famous emotional scene he tried to argue with them, to convince them of their inconsistency. Ken quietly put his finger on the flaw in James's own position: 'Sir, I hope you will give that liberty to us, which you allow to all mankind.' James did not try to answer. He had always ignored the contradiction of treating the state church both as part of the government apparatus and as an independent denomination. He put the petition in his pocket and said he would consider it further, but was careful, before letting the bishops go, to reaffirm his right to the dispensing power.

Sancroft said afterwards that the only copy of the petition was the one handed to the King, but he was mistaken. Printed copies were on the streets within a very short time of the scene at Whitehall. How it happened is not clear; but Lloyd of St Asaph certainly took a copy of his own, and it would have been easy for a trusted agent to carry such a copy by water from Lambeth to a waiting printing press, where the single sheet could be set up and on its way to distribution by midnight. Perhaps the press was Clavell's in St Paul's Churchyard, where the Bishop of Peterborough lodged. Clavell had printed for Lloyd before and probably for Johnston as well.*

* The copy in Lloyd's writing is in the Tanner MSS (Bodleian Library). Agnes Strickland, *The Bishops in the Tower*, (1874) takes the view that Lloyd was responsible for publication, but Mr A. Tindal Hart, *William Lloyd*, (1952) and Canon E. Carpenter, *The Protestant Bishop*, (1956) both consider Compton to have been mainly responsible, largely on the ground that Lloyd was at the palace while the printer must be presumed to have been at work. I have found no contemporary evidence that printed copies were in circulation a few hours after the petition was presented (as most secondary authorities assert), but they were certainly available by 30 May at latest (Luttrell, I. 140, bought one on or before that day). Such evidence as there is seems to implicate both Compton and Lloyd, though the actual agent delivering copy to the printer need not have been either of them, and almost

The boycott on the following Sunday was almost complete. But the fact that in the whole diocese of London only four or five churches complied with the King's order was secondary compared with the news that the chiefs of the established church had defied the King. This was the tide of public excitement on which the Revolution rode. During the week that followed eight more bishops sent in letters of support, and most of their signatures were added to later editions of the petition to show a clear majority of the twenty-five English and Welsh sees that were then filled.* No wonder William wrote, towards the end of a long letter to Bentinck about the progress of the German negotiations, that 'cette affaire des évêques pourroit porter les affaires promptement à des extremités'; and three days later that it was essential to know the sequel—'ce qui pourroit aller loin'.[7] Dr Stanley was directed to convey William's and Mary's approval formally to Sancroft for the stand he had taken.

William might be eager for news from across the North Sea, but his attention was for the moment fixed mainly on another ecclesiastical happening whose scene was on the middle Rhine. On 3 June the Electoral College of the Holy Roman Empire had suffered its third casualty that spring in the death of the aged amateur chemist, Maximilian Henry, Archbishop of Cologne.† So closely do the consequences of this episcopal death tread on the affair of the Seven Bishops that the editor of William's letters, Japikse, mistakenly read the letter just quoted as referring to Cologne.

Maximilian Henry, although he was a Wittelsbach, had always been prepared to oblige Louis XIV, and a few months before his death he had agreed that Wilhelm von Furstenberg, whom

---

certainly would not have been. One copy of the printed petition bearing the date 1688 is listed in the Chetham Library, Manchester, but cannot now be traced. Wing found no other copy. As for Clavell, he was already in trouble with the authorities for publishing copies of the Fagel-Stewart correspondence, and was in touch with Dr Stanley (Portland MSS, P.W.A. 2159).
* Two of the twenty-seven English and Welsh sees (York and Oxford) were vacant, and in four (Durham, Rochester, Chester and St David's) the bishops were committed to James's policy. The eight bishops who proffered their support before the end of May, and took steps to prevent the reading of the Declaration in their dioceses were those of Winchester, Salisbury, Norwich, Carlisle, Worcester, Exeter, Llandaff, and Gloucester. Only five remained uncommitted (Lincoln, Hereford, Bangor, Lichfield, and Sodor and Man).
† The other two being the Elector of Brandenburg and the Elector Palatine.

Louis had made Bishop of Strasbourg in 1683, should be Coadjutor to the Archbishopric while the Elector lived, and his
successor when he died. Maximilian Henry had made only one
condition: that Furstenberg in his turn should designate a
Wittelsbach prince, Clement of Bavaria, as the ultimate successor.
So family duty had been observed, and early in the year the
Chapter of Cologne had endorsed their Archbishop's arrangement by electing von Furstenberg as Coadjutor by a majority of
nineteen votes to five. But the election was canonically dubious,
since von Furstenberg had not vacated his bishopric of Strasbourg; and Pope Innocent, whose approval was required, had
made it quite clear that no approval would be given. He had no
desire to see French influence extended anywhere, least of all on
the Rhine, and he strongly disapproved of pluralities. On 1 April
Louis, whose forward policy in Germany was now centred on
Cologne, had informed the Pope that unless he ratified the election
of von Furstenberg forthwith a general war in western Europe
would ensue. It had been to back this threat that the main French
naval strength had been moved out of the Channel into the
Mediterranean.

So on 3 June, when Maximilian Henry died, Imperial, Papal,
French, and Dutch emissaries had for some months been at
work enlisting support in the Chapter about the arrangements
that were to have preceded, and now were to follow, the vacancy.
As Innocent was quick to point out, Maximilian's death created
a new situation. 'One cannot,' he observed to the French Ambassador, 'appoint a Coadjutor to a dead man.' A new election
was necessary, and in this much more explosive atmosphere
two candidates were proposed—von Furstenberg by the King of
France, and Clement of Bavaria by the Imperial interest. The
situation was odd as well as explosive because there were serious
objections to both candidates. The Pope immediately announced
that he would on no account approve the election of von Furstenberg; and Clement was not only under age, but was not even
in holy orders. Von Furstenberg suffered under the additional
difficulty that, being a bishop already, he could only be elected
by a majority exceeding two-thirds of the Chapter. However, in
the election to the coadjutorship earlier in the year he had shown
that such a majority was within his reach. The election, on which
the peace of Europe depended, was set for 19 July.

Meanwhile James had been pondering the problem set by his bishops, and had decided that in some way or other (he was not quite clear yet how) he must proceed against them. The bishops on their side had been taking energetic steps for their own defence by establishing a fighting fund to which each contributed six per cent of his income.* On 6 June (27 May O.S.) they were given a fortnight's notice to appear before the Privy Council 'to answer to such matters of misdemeanours as may then and there be objected'. The threat was vague, for James, like William, was preoccupied in early June with the developing European situation. On instructions from Paris Barillon had passed on to him the latest French intelligence about William's naval preparations and Seignelay, of the French Admiralty, was now in London with a specific offer from Louis to move fifteen ships back into the Channel and tip the balance there in James's favour. Yet James still clung to his idea of an independent foreign policy. Open identification with France would, he judged, be fatal, and in the continued delusion that isolation and independence were equivalent he rejected the French offer at a conference on 14 June. Four days later, he faced the bishops for the second time, still uncertain what his tactics should be.

The bishops were under no such disability. Three times at least they had been in conference with leading counsel (Pemberton, Sawyer, Finch, and Pollexfen) to decide their stance. They also saw Clarendon, who was suffering agonies between his awareness of the web of conspiracy and his unwillingness to commit himself. Most active of all behind the scenes was Compton, though he neither contributed to the fighting fund nor appeared alongside his brethren. He was already committed to the invitation for which William had asked, and for which Sidney was now collecting the final names. Trelawny, the bishop-baronet, was in direct communication with Johnston. On the day before

---

* The accounts of this fund are preserved (Gutch, *Collecteana Curiosa*, II. p. 368 and ff.) They provide a remarkable insight into the detail of what went on behind the scenes of a state trial of the period. The total raised was £607 7s. 11d. Counsel's fees were to take £240 of this, gratuities and fees to officers amounted to £121 16s. 6d. Mr Ince, the indefatigable solicitor to the bishops, got £48 18s. Somers' fee as Junior Counsel in this, his first great case, came to £32 18s. The degree of pressure on leading members of the Bar to appear on behalf of the bishops can be judged by Johnston (2 July, P.W.A. 2175) where he reports that Cresswell Levinz, who at first was reluctant, was told he would get no more briefs elsewhere if he did not comply.

the bishops were to appear before the Privy Council Johnston recorded a remark by one of them, probably Trelawny—'If we are sent to the Tower, I hope the Prince of Orange will take us out, which two regiments and his authority would do.' Even more significantly he refers to reports William will have had, and will continue to receive, directly from the bishops themselves.[8]

This makes the tactics of the bishops quite clear. Whatever ideas Sancroft may have had on that May evening at Lambeth about a private protest had now given way to a decision to court imprisonment in circumstances of the maximum publicity. When the confrontation took place, at five o'clock on the evening of 18 June, the King, Jeffreys, and the other privy councillors present (among whom James tactlessly allowed his principal catholic adviser, Father Petre, to be included) got much the worst of it. Two weapons were available to the government: the Ecclesiastical Commission or the ordinary courts, and of these two the ordinary courts seemed to James the more reliable. Had they not, in *Gooden* v. *Hales*, decided by eleven voices to one that his dispensing power was lawful? So were they not bound to consider anyone criticising it as guilty of seditious libel? Jeffreys had been uneasy. 'The Judges,' he had said, 'are most of them rogues'—in other words they were extremely sensitive to political climates. Unfortunately also, there was a technical point, of which the bishops took full advantage. For an appearance in the King's Bench they would have to give bail, and this they absolutely refused to do. They undertook to appear on their word of honour, but such was the strength of seventeenth-century formality that this way out was impossible, and the only alternative was remand in custody. In vain Jeffreys cajoled and the King blustered. The bishops were firm: no one had ever heard of a bishop giving bail.

The fever—familiar enough from the days of the Popish Plot—was now in the streets, and not in London streets alone. Disturbances were reported in the provinces, for instance at Lichfield, on 11 June, when there was 'a very great ryot'. Several Sundays had passed, and established and dissenting pulpits alike had been extolling the bishops as anti-catholic heroes to packed congregations. When the bishops emerged on to the Cockpit Steps and embarked on one of the royal barges (hastily made available for the purpose) to be taken to the Tower 'some persons ran into the water to implore a blessing. . . . Both banks of the Thames were lined with multitudes, who, when too distant to be heard, manifested their feelings by falling down on their knees':[9] so van Citters, the Dutch ambassador, providing William with the sequel 'qui pourroit aller loin'. And Van Citters was not the only foreign observer. 'It is as yet impossible,' wrote the imperial ambassador Hoffmann to Vienna, 'to tell what impressions the unexpected imprisonment of these men will make. Time will show what will follow upon it, but this business must be considered as unavoidably leading to a great revolution.'

An irony which nobody overlooked was that the Lieutenant of the Tower, into whose custody the bishops now passed, was the very Sir Edward Hales whose case two years earlier had seemed to establish the dispensing power. The bishops were very distant with Sir Edward, and no sooner were they within the walls than they repaired to chapel. The Second Lesson for the day was peculiarly apt, containing as it did the emphatic text (Corinthians II. vi.):

> Behold now is the accepted time: behold now is the day of salvation.

Yet James too could have found comfort in that text. Two days later his son was born to Maria Beatrice, a few weeks before her time. The audience was numerous but unfortunately did not include either the Princess Anne (who had ostentatiously absented herself by going to Bath) nor the Archbishop of Canterbury. The king himself was in such haste to be present that he had not time to dress or shave.

It is often said that the Revolution of 1688 was not a popular movement, yet it is questionable whether it could have dislodged one source of security and installed a new one without this rising of the popular fever as one dramatic event followed another against the background of probable war. Religious zeal and suspicion of foreigners combined to produce a horror of catholicism. The masses refused to believe that the heir for whom the king was firing salutes and launching firework displays could be anything but a fraud. The tireless Johnston analysed the mood well when he wrote to his masters enclosing a draft pamphlet which, he thought would do much good in England, where even those that believe there is a trick put on the nation, will be glad to know why they themselves think so, and those that only suspect the thing will be glad to find reasons to determine them, and all mankind will see that it is not the spirit of a party that makes men doubt of it.'[10]

The pamphlet made the perfect suggestion for prolonging uncertainty: in moderate language it proposed that the parliament James had promised to call should conduct an impartial inquiry into the rumours surrounding his son's birth.

The trial of the bishops was fixed for 9 July, and the Cologne election for ten days later, so that the last days of June and the first weeks of July were a period of intense political activity throughout Western Europe. There was that sense of great events and great changes impending which in itself helps to dissolve individual bonds and anxieties. Robert Harley's words to his brother, written a few months earlier, must now have recorded the inner feelings of many: 'Every person is now valued according to his interest and what he can do.'[11] In Cologne the agents of the European powers plied the Chapter with presents and pressure in the interests of the Furstenberg and Wittelsbach candidates. In Vienna William's collaborator, Count Waldeck, was negotiating for the Emperor Leopold's neutrality in the impending struggle between William and James. Philipsburg was now bristling with imperialist troops. Gradually the princes of north-west Germany were being manoeuvred by William's diplomatists into providing the indispensable covering forces for the invasion. And in London the imprisoned bishops* continued to be the centre of a whirlwind of popular enthusiasm. Ten leading nonconformists paid them a state visit of sympathy and support, and their dazzling array of counsel came for consultations almost daily.

Meanwhile Sidney, with the help of Johnston, Shrewsbury, and Lumley, was collecting the pledges for which William had stipulated as the condition of armed intervention, and a regular series of messages on the subject was crossing the North Sea by 'the

* Their imprisonment actually lasted only seven days. On the 25th they appeared before the King's Bench and gave bail. The bail document is mainly in Compton's handwriting.

small English vessel no bigger than a packet-boat, but very well rigged and an excellent sailer' which d'Avaux's agents noted continually putting into Maensluys, a modest fishing village at the mouth of the Maas.[12] It had already brought William a list of those Sidney was canvassing, and their code signs.* When Sidney reported on the twenty-eighth he had had to give up his hopes of Halifax (who had refused, though told that the bishops had been led to expect his support), but had secured the acrimonious Earl of Devonshire. Devonshire was a former exclusionist and a link with the whigs, but hardly a major political figure in himself. His adherence to the invitation can in part be attributed to the severe fine (as yet unpaid) which had been imposed on him by the King's Bench for striking the litigious Colonel Colepeper in the bounds of Whitehall palace—an act, Lord Chief Justice Wright had observed, 'next door to pulling the King off his throne'.

But even before receiving this message from Sidney, William had decided he needed a more senior agent of his own in England. Sidney was ill, and Johnston had suggested he should be replaced by 'Dr. Harcourt'. The excuse was ready to hand, and in the very last days of June 'Harcourt'—who proved to be the handsome dragoon officer Zuylestein—arrived for the second time in England, carrying with him not only letters for Sidney but congratulations to James and his Queen on the birth of their son and heir.

The trial of the bishops for seditious libel began on 8 July in Westminster Hall before Lord Chief Justice Wright, three other judges, a carefully selected jury, and an immense crowd, among them the ubiquitous Johnston who was now so weary 'I can scarcely hold the pen'.[13] Chief Justice Wright was considered to be sound on the dispensing power, which he had stoutly defended as a member of the visitatorial team to Magdalen. He owed his advancement to Jeffreys, whose colleague he had been on the Bloody Assize. But the Chief Justice was uneasy. He

* Devonshire—24; Shrewsbury—25; Danby—27; Lumley—29; Compton—31; Sidney—33; Russell—35; Halifax—21; Nottingham—23; Bath—30. The last three were unwilling to risk commitment when it came to the point. Neither Clarendon nor Rochester, whom William had ceased to trust, were in even the preliminary list. Johnston, however, thought Clarendon would join, and adds the Earl of Denbigh as another being canvassed (13 June). This letter suggests the possibility of some thirty signatures.

thought he could depend on two of his colleagues—the catholic Mr Justice Allibone, who had been educated at the Jesuit college of Douai and elevated to the Bench by virtue of the dispensing power, and the aged Mr Justice Holloway, who had sat with Jeffreys at the trial of Algernon Sidney; but he was less sure of the modest Welshman, Mr Justice Powell. Although Powell had allowed his silence to be taken for consent in the case of *Gooden* v. *Hales* he had in fact reserved his opinion, and Chief Justice Herbert, in reporting the opinions of the judges, had strained the truth in respect of Powell—a fact which Chief Justice Wright probably knew. The presiding judge therefore hoped he might get an acquittal on technical grounds, without having to discuss the dispensing power.

Behind the scenes the Government had given a great deal of thought to the line that should be taken, and James had been advised by Jeffreys and Sunderland that an act of amnesty in honour of the new Prince of Wales would dispose of an awkward situation. But James was determined to go on, and ignored this prudent advice. He meant to impose crippling fines on the bishops. Sidney, for his part, writing to William, hoped for precisely this as the dénouement of the campaign.

The trial began as Chief Justice Wright had hoped, in a formal style which avoided the main issue. The actual delivery of the petition was challenged and demands were made for proof that it had been delivered in Middlesex, where the court had jursidiction. Chief Justice Wright was jumping at the chance to direct an acquittal on these grounds when prosecution and defence together prevented him. The prosecution sent out for Sunderland, who alone could prove that the petition had been handed to the King, and the defence obligingly gave them time (though it seems not unanimously). His appearance did not help the Crown's case, though it established their formal point. He was repeatedly interrupted by the audience, and seems to have lost his nerve, changing colour and stumbling in his speech.

In the teeth of repeated rulings against the relevance of the dispensing power, the defence then developed the theme that the petition could not be seditious if the dispensing power was unlawful. Wright's attempt to rule this out of order was interrupted by Powell—'My Lord they must necessarily fall upon this point;

for if the King hath no such power (as clearly he hath not in my judgment) the natural consequence will be that this petition is no diminution of the regal power.' As the trial went on, with occasional interventions from the crowd, which heartily hissed the attorney general when he suggested that a subject asked to perform an illegal act should 'acquiesce', Wright's courage steadily ebbed. In his summing up he tried to avoid venturing any opinion about the dispensing power, while ruling the petition was a libel because it tended to cause public mischief. Holloway hedged also, and Allibone produced a passage which makes James's philosophy and the significance of the Revolution overwhelmingly clear:

> No man can take upon him to write against the actual exercise of Government, unless he have leave from the Government. If he does, he makes a libel, be what he writes true or false; if we once come to impeach the Government by way of argument, it is argument that makes the government or no government. So I lay down, that the Government ought not to be impeached by argument, nor the exercise of Government shaken by argument. Am I to be allowed to discredit the King's ministers because I can manage a proposition, in itself doubtful, with a better pen than another man?

But even Allibone, after this penetrating glance at the power of the press, did not deal with the legality of the dispensing power, which only two years ago Lord Chief Justice Herbert had established in these words, to which James had clung so fast:

> The Kings of England are absolute sovereigns; the laws of England are the King's laws; the King has power to dispense with any of his laws as he sees necessity for it; and the King is sole judge of that necessity.

Such was the doctrine which Powell, the modest and barely honoured hero of the Revolution, now overthrew. He had been a pupil of Jeremy Taylor as a boy in Wales, and there is no reason to suppose that what he said now sprang from any source but his own convictions and a realisation that it had to be said.

He began, unlike his brethren, by refusing to accept that the question of the dispensing power was irrelevant, and continued,

If there be no such dispensing power, there can be no libel in the petition which represented the Declaration founded on such a pretended power to be illegal. Now, gentlemen, this is a dispensation with a vengeance: it amounts to an abrogation and utter repeal of all the laws: for I can see no difference, nor know of any in law, between the King's power to dispense with laws ecclesiastical, and his power to dispense with any other laws whatever. If this be once allowed of, there will need no parliament; all the legislature will be in the King—which is a thing worth considering.

The jury were allowed a concessionary glass of wine before being enclosed for the night. But that was the limit of the Chief Justice's generosity. They were allowed neither light nor heat—not even to light their pipes—and so debated this great constitutional case in almost total darkness. In the end they were reduced to drinking their shaving water. They were narrowly watched by sheriff's officers, who in their turn were kept under observation by the active Mr Ince, the bishops' solicitor, and his assistants. Ince, writing about midnight from outside the jury room, seems to have been reasonably confident of a verdict for his clients, since his letter recommends the sort of scale on which the jury should be tipped if they found for the bishops.[14]

The verdict of Not Guilty, which had actually been reached at six that morning, after the surrender of an isolated recalcitrant juror, was returned when the court reassembled at ten, and the rafters of Westminster Hall rang with cheers. The bishops were virtually carried from court by the enthusiastic crowd and 'when the Archbishop landed at Lambeth the grenadiers of my Lord Litchfield's regiment . . . made a line from the river to his gate, and, kneeling, asked his blessing'. As Johnston wrote, 'The dispensing power is more effectively knocked on the head than if an Act of Parliament had been made against it . . . so it is given up in Westminster Hall. My Lord Chief Justice is much blamed for allowing it to be debated.'[15] James may well have considered removing his Chief Justice. Within a few days he had removed both Powell and the trimmer Holloway. And strangely enough Mr Justice Allibone did not long survive either. Towards the end of August he died at his house in Holborn but not before Johnston had had the last word in the controversy between the

Press and the Bench. 'All will be printed,' he wrote to the Hague, 'without, if not with authority.'

Before James could consider the consequences of his defeat by the Church—indeed on the very day of the acquittal—the invitation for which William had stipulated was ready. It was in Sidney's hand, and signed (in code) by six others—Shrewsbury, Devonshire, Compton, Danby, Lumley and Russell. Contact with Zuylestein had clearly been established by the signatories before the invitation was written. The messenger entrusted with it was Admiral Herbert 'to whom we have communicated our thoughts in many particulars too tedious to have been written, and about which no certain resolutions can be taken, till we have heard again from your highness'.[16] When, exactly, Herbert left London and in what disguise, is as unclear as the precise place at which the document was drawn up.* But he must have made a circuitous journey, for it was over a week before d'Avaux's agents at the Hague noted his arrival on Friday 16 July, and his immediate conference with William, Bentinck, and Dijkvelt. Van Citters, who was fully in touch with what was going on, was recalled at the same time for consultations.

The invitation of the seven was important to William rather as giving him hostages than as adding to his effective strength. The undertaking that 'we who subscribe this will not fail to attend your highness upon your landing' might easily be frustrated by faintness of heart or the intervention of James; and the signatories themselves were not, on the whole, in the first flight of British public life. Even the central judgment made—that 'this is a season in which we may more probably contribute to our own safeties than hereafter'—is made subject to the qualification that some well-informed leaders of opinion do not agree with it. But for all this it is among the most notable of English political documents, the only one in modern English history in which an influential group has called for foreign intervention to end what they regard as an intolerable situation: and intolerable, it is fair

* D'Avaux (20 July) reports that Herbert travelled in the disguise of a seaman. There is nothing but tradition to support the allegation that the invitation was drawn up at Lord Lovelace's house at Hurley, near Marlow. If it were, it is surprising Lovelace did not lend his name to it. There would be every reason to get so compromising a document out of the country as quickly as possible, which suggests hasty completion in London immediately after the acquittal of the bishops was known.

to say, not to themselves alone. 'Your Highness may be assured, there are nineteen parts of twenty of the people throughout the Kingdom, who are desirous of a change.' Such words could hardly have been written until the affair of the bishops had run its course.

Part Three

THE DESCENT ON ENGLAND

The Preparations

The day after Admiral Herbert's arrival at the Hague with his message, Pope Innocent made it clear that he was not to be intimidated by the threats of the King of France. He announced that he considered the youthful Clement of Bavaria an eligible candidate for the archbishopric of Cologne—the election for which was now exactly two days off. On the nineteenth of July the much-canvassed canons held their Chapter and cast twenty-three votes: fourteen for von Furstenberg and nine for Clement of Bavaria. In the absence of either a two-thirds majority for the French candidate or a simple majority for his opponent, the consequence was a deadlock which the Pope alone could resolve.

For King Louis the last weeks of July brought a moment of supreme decision. War before the autumn was already resolved: war before the Emperor Leopold could disentangle himself from the remains of the Turkish conflict and dispute the supremacy of Germany, Italy, and Spain, and what Louis glimpsed beyond them—the Christian Empire that he was not yet too old to grasp. The tactical decision at this point seemed subsidiary to this great plan, yet as things proved, everything was to turn on it. It would be possible for the French northern army under Marshal d'Humières to sweep across the Spanish Netherlands, neutralise if not destroy the Dutch army and its still scattered German allies, and clear the French northern flank once for all. Or should Louis concentrate his entire land force behind the threats he was now issuing about Cologne and the Palatinate—in other words on the Lower and Middle Rhine, with supporting thrusts by shipborne forces against the Pope and the Hapsburg-dominated principalities of Italy?

In making his great decision for the Rhine against the Channel Louis was not ignorant of William's intentions. He had a stream of excellent information from d'Avaux. But until it was too late he never seems to have seen the strategic importance of control over the Channel and the North Atlantic. William's plan seemed far-fetched, perilous, even absurd. And on the personal level Louis found it difficult to take William seriously as an opponent. William might be rich and clever, but he was neither a great soldier nor a great prince. Louis was a great strategist, but he was also a great snob.

William, for his part, though his mind was made up by the end of July, was unable to believe that Louis would allow the invasion of England to take place without interference. As late as September he was still treating Louis' concentration against Cologne as a feint, and saw d'Humières' army as on the point of rolling north-eastwards 'pour empêcher notre dessein'.[1] The need to guard against such interference immensely complicated his preparations; but again, on the personal level it is his steadfastness in holding to his seaborne invasion in face of his own conviction that he might have to fight a holding action on land, which convinces us of his deep faith in predestined success.

During the immensely complicated military, political, and diplomatic transactions that had to be co-ordinated that summer William showed his greatest qualities. His spirits might vary—sometimes he was near despair as this or that bit of the timetable showed signs of lagging—but he remained a supremely gifted delegater. While keeping every important thread in his own hands, he worked through a well-defined and trustworthy command structure, in which the key figure was Bentinck. Fagel, now a very sick man, Dijkvelt, and Bentinck formed the political and diplomatic cabinet; but Bentinck was the staff officer who linked the three armies and two fleets that were now taking shape.

The first of these armies, consisting of the bulk of the Dutch federal forces, but strengthened by contingents hired from Württemberg, Brunswick, and Hanover, was to cover the left flank against the expected intervention by d'Humières. It was to be commanded by William's old associate Waldeck. The second army, consisting mainly of the Brandenburg contingents, was forming under Schomberg, but that aged marshal was already designated to command the seaborne force. He would soon hand over to the Prussian Marshal Schöning, who would take post to the south-east of Waldeck's force, on the Middle Rhine itself. But in August, apart from the German battalions struggling slowly across the great central plain, all these forces, including those destined for the expedition itself, were still quietly encamped in eastern Holland.

The senior Dutch admiral, Cornelius Evertsen, was already riding on the Maas with 21 ships of the Netherlands battle fleet on 1 August. But with a stroke of political genius William now substituted as commander-in-chief, for this operation only, the recently arrived Arthur Herbert. Three Dutch admirals— Evertsen, Almonde, and Bastiaenz—acted respectively as Vice-Admiral and Rear-Admiral of the convoying warships and commodore of the armada of transports that was quietly being assembled on the canals.

The organisation of the armada and its accompanying warships constituted a huge logistical, overshadowed by a very delicate political, problem. Some two hundred transports and nearly twenty thousand men were concerned, and the tasks of co-ordinated movement, purchase of stores, security, and timing, were quite complex enough by themselves. But William had in addition made all planning subject to political considerations, which it was the particular duty of Bentinck to see observed. The success of the whole operation depended on these features of the scheme. Fundamentally they sprang from William's decision that the seaborne army should be at least a match for any force James could put in the field, without having to depend either on support from English sympathisers or on commandeering. Throughout his planning William treated any military help he might get on landing as a purely contingent bonus, and required that everything he needed should either be carried on his ships or paid for in fair hire or purchase. This meant transporting large numbers of horses—some eight thousand—and huge quantities of spare clothing, boots, and comforts in the shape of tobacco and brandy, as well as ammunition on a scale to deal with fortifications if that should prove necessary. It also meant carrying a considerable sum in cash.[2]

Above all William had prescribed that this self-sufficient, self-supporting army should have as British an appearance as possible. The six British regiments would, of course, be its largest single component, and these were supplemented by two somewhat sketchy regiments of emigrés commanded by the Earl of Leven and Sir Robert Peyton. Every Englishman and Scot, of whatever political complexion, from practical or theoretical republicans such as Wildman or Fletcher of Saltoun to alienated tories such as the Earl of Macclesfield, were offered carte blanche and a free passage to swell the numbers. As a result some twenty-five per cent of the army of intervention was British.

After his second German visit, which ended early in August, Bentinck was able to devote himself more or less continuously to collaboration with Herbert and the Dutch admirals in organising the invasion force. Through Herbert ran the main, though probably not the only line to the English conspirators. But now that Sidney had returned to the Hague, accompanied by Johnston,* and Shrewsbury was soon to follow, Herbert was anxious about intelligence. About the end of August he pressed William to allow scouting vessels to visit the English coast and enter into communication with sympathisers; to land a master agent—he suggested Dijkvelt—to co-ordinate intelligence sources; and to designate a special agent to undermine professional hesitations that might be felt by well-wishers in James's forces about changing sides in the presence of the enemy.

William was unresponsive to all this. Security, with its hope of achieving at any rate a tactical surprise, was at this point more important than intelligence, and it was essential not to drop the formal mask of correct relations with James too soon. Against Herbert's proposal for a special subversive agent he wrote: 'Il faut que les amis en Angleterre prenne des mesures la-dessus, ne le pouvant prescrire d'icy.'³ He preferred that intelligence reports should be routed through the Dutch embassy, to which a fully briefed van Citters (recalled in mid-July for consultations) would shortly return; and it seems likely that William did not choose to disclose the full extent of his network in England, even

---

* 'Mr Sidney goes through Flanders to the waters of Aix next week'. 'Mr Rivers [Johnston] bid me tell you to write no more to him for he is going to the country'. Johnston 3/13 August, P.W.A. 2177.

to Herbert. Colonel Sir Henry Bellasise,* for instance, who had resigned his colonelcy in the Anglo-Dutch Brigade under obscure circumstances a year or two before, was now living quietly in Yorkshire, and there are indications that Zuylestein either never genuinely came back from his mission of compliment in July or returned to England incognito before the invasion as William's principal agent.

Carefully worded letters of support from England continued to come in during July and August: the Earl of Carlisle; Lord Lovelace. Sidney had brought with him some oral assurances from John Churchill, the future Duke of Marlborough, which amounted, like so much of the rest of this material, to a promise of support if William looked like succeeding. Churchill had every reason for knowing what was afoot, and many contacts that would be useful to William. Apart from his own rank in James's army, one of his closest followers was Colonel Trelawny, brother of the protesting Bishop of Bristol; and his brother commanded one of James's men-of-war. Yet the major political figures still hesitated, and were to hesitate until the end. William now distrusted both the Hyde brothers—especially Rochester—and Halifax,† and had made his feelings clear, at any rate as regards Rochester. William did not mean to hand himself over to the men of the centre whom his father-in-law had rejected, to be another Charles II.

The main spade-work of diplomacy in Germany had been accomplished by August, its crowning act being the signature on 5 August by Bentinck and Fuchs of the detailed protocol for the hire of Brandenburg troops. Within a fortnight William was writing to the Elector as the most intimate of his allies, urgently pressing him to get his remoter contingents on the move for Cleves. The slow movement of land forces controlled by half a dozen different princes across the German plain was already behindhand. The Dutch troops they were intended to relieve

---

* Bellasis had served in the Anglo-Dutch brigade since 1674, and had fought at Grave, Maastricht, and Mont-Cassell. He had taken his regiment to England in 1685 and resigned his commission in 1687. He was promoted colonel after the Revolution, however. For his activity in Yorkshire see Reresby, p. 413.

† Largely, it may be supposed, on the strength of Johnston's reports, which stress Rochester's willingness to support the Indulgence policy. Johnston also considered Halifax unreliable.

could not be moved without frightening the Regenten about possible French intervention and undoing all the good work being put in by Fagel in the political world of Amsterdam. Fortunately, they could be moved more quickly than their German reliefs when the time came. The canals could carry a regiment across the breadth of the Netherlands in two days.

At the end of August William almost lost heart. The arrival of Sidney and Johnston on 27 August by a secret route, followed soon afterwards by Shrewsbury, did not raise his spirits. On the contrary in two separate letters, one in French to Bentinck and the other in Dutch to Fagel, written on the same day, soon after Sidney's arrival, he admits to being almost in despair. 'Ick ben in de uyterste verlegentheyt ende bekommerung';* 'j'advoue que cela [the increasing breakdown of security] me mest en des pienes et incertitudes épouvantables, et que j'ay plus que jamais besoin de la Direction divine'.[4] The most important paper in Sidney's bag was a draft manifesto prepared by Danby for William's approval; but it was accompanied by a memorandum from Danby himself venturing the opinion that perhaps the whole operation would be best deferred until the following spring.[5] William liked neither the evidence of timidity nor the draft manifesto, with its emphasis on the role of the politicians and a free parliament, and ordered it to be rewritten by Fagel and Dijkvelt: 'It needs considerable changes. You will see that by the conclusion I throw myself entirely at the mercy of a parliament. Although I am afraid it cannot be otherwise, nevertheless handing over one's fate to them is not without hazard.'[6] Significantly the only non-Dutch adviser he asked to be consulted on the manifesto was to be the Scot, Melville—William always trusted the Scots more than the English.

The care William took about publications was shown only two days later when Bentinck referred to him on the layout of the proposed manifesto. Twin portraits of himself and Mary should appear at the mast-head. The heraldry should be referred to an expert. Mary was to come with him politically: a lesser man would have brought her to England physically, in the hope of exploiting her Englishness and her protestantism. But, as at the meeting with the Elector at Mook two years earlier, William was not the

* 'I am in the utmost uncertainty and affliction.'

man to share the centre of the stage at any major crisis of his career.

It was not so much the despatches from England as the despatches from Paris that caused William's despair at the end of August. Van Wassanaer-Starremberg, the Dutch ambassador, reported large bodies of French troops on the move, and associated them with Cologne. The ambassador was right—Louis' decision to move on the Rhine was made on 27 August—but William refused to believe it. He felt that security had broken down so seriously that Louis could not possibly be ignoring the danger to himself posed by the probable destruction of James.[7]

William's anxiety was widely shared. Dutch East India stock fell on the Amsterdam bourse by eighty points, from 580 to 500, on 25 August. There was still strong resistance in the States General to the military credits William was seeking, for seven thousand extra soldiers and nine thousand additional seamen. Even though the men had already been recruited and paid from cash in hand (including a large subvention brought from England by van Citters in July) the money was badly needed for this enormously costly operation. Money was pouring out, for it was the commodity William never stinted, but even the seven and a half million guilders already disposed of, together with his private resources, was to be barely enough.*

On 6 September, with secret orders already issued to his armies, Louis despatched a letter to the Pope informing him that no further delay in the installation of von Furstenberg could be tolerated, and that the war now about to break out was entirely Innocent's responsibility. This, of course, was accompanied by vigorous reassertion of the exaggerated claims of diplomatic privilege for the French ambassador in Rome; and, behind the scenes, by warning orders for a naval descent on the coast of Italy and the seizure of the papal enclave of Avignon, which were issued on 13 September. On 18 September Innocent sent for the leading French cardinal in Rome, d'Estrées, to issue a formal repudiation of Louis' ultimatum. 'Though the world should collapse,' declared this military old man, 'a just God will punish

---

* D'Avaux reported substantial shipments of money from England to William, right down to October, e.g. his despatches of 30 September, 7 October. He also noted the arrival (30 September) in Holland from London of the important Huguenot business man Papin. See Appendix B.

the guilty.'[8] He went on to announce his decision on the Cologne dispute. Von Furstenberg, not having received the required two-thirds of the votes, was not elected. It followed that the papal approval and confirmation should be extended to Clement of Bavaria. Three days later Schomberg, at the head of 3,000 Brandenburgers, occupied Cologne, and Louis ordered the arrest of all Austrian subjects residing in Paris.

In the midst of these critical moves Louis did not wholly neglect his northern flank, though the gesture was hardly effectual. He sent Bonrepaux to London on 4 September with a renewed offer of naval help in the Channel, and planned a diplomatic démarche in the Hague with the aim of frightening the Regenten. Unfortunately James and Sunderland, though they also had ample information by this time about William's intentions, were temporarily in a mood of disbelief about them. A naval convention between England and France was drawn up at Windsor on 13 September, but was left incomplete and unpursued by the staff conversations that alone could make it effective. James was still possessed by the idea that a military entanglement with France would hopelessly compromise him in his domestic policy. So when, on Louis' instructions, d'Avaux informed the States General that France would regard any attack on England as a casus belli with the Netherlands, a frantic denial of any arrangement between England and France rapidly issued from London. The absence of any such arrangement could not be more effectively demonstrated than by this incident itself. Only a few days before d'Avaux's démarche the British ambassador at the Hague had, on James's instructions, delivered a polite enquiry to the States General about the military preparations which were now obvious. Louis's un-coordinated menace on James's behalf provided the States with the perfect reply to the British ambassador that they were anxious about joint aggression from England and France.

William was not in the Netherlands to enjoy this comedy. He was putting the finishing touches to his arrangements with his German allies. On 7 September he was at Minden for a conference with the Elector of Brandenburg, and a little later he was at Rintelen to see the Landgrave of Hesse. He must have returned to Loo on the very day Innocent settled the Cologne election. His letter to Bentinck from Minden shows that his anxieties had now shifted from German alliances to the readiness of the fleet. 'If the fleet is not soon ready all will be ruined. It is absolutely necessary to give more to the sailors if that will engage them more.'[9]

Soon after returning to the Hague he had his last letter from James. The tone was gruffer even than usual. 'I intend,' it concluded, 'to go tomorrow to London, and the next day to Chatham, to see the condition of the new batteries I have made in the Medway, and my ships which are there.'[10] But King James still could not quite drop the idea that he discussed international politics with William in an avuncular way. Writing from Windsor on 27 September, he said how sorry he was 'there is so much likelihood of war upon the Reyn, nobody wishing more the peace of Christendom than myself'.[11] He was perhaps more than usually ill-informed since the British ambassador in Paris had been recalled for what James considered indiscreet encouragement of the French demonstration at the Hague. The war on the Rhine had already broken out. On Friday 24 September, after a manifesto placing his pacific intentions on record, and an appeal to a general council of the Church, Louis had launched four armies—some seventy thousand men—into Germany on a front stretching from Philipsburg in the south to Liège in the north. The army of Marshal d'Humières wheeled south-eastwards in obedience to Louvois' orders, and James's fate was sealed.

The Invasion

James reacted slowly to the invasion of the Rhineland, and for more than a fortnight after it he continued on the course he had already started. The threat from William, to which he had first woken up early in September, he assessed as a further round in the Dutch wars of his youth, rather than a bid to deprive him of his throne, and he seems never to have grasped the difference made by Louis' commitment on the Rhine.[1] Still, the English battle fleet was moved out of harbour into the outer roadstead of the Downs, whence it could either operate in the North Sea or block the Straits of Dover if William should head south. James half expected a thrust at the Thames itself, on the pattern of 1667, and therefore took particular pains with the landward defences on the Medway, where he committed substantial garrisons. This anxiety to cover every contingency was a basic weakness in James's strategy, for although he disposed of something like forty thousand men, garrisons ate seriously into his mobile reserve. After Portsmouth, Plymouth, Hull, Bristol, Sheerness, Yarmouth, and the rest had been provided for, James's field army was hardly stronger than William's.*

But James did not consider William was likely to get ashore in any force. The English strategy was based on the idea that before any landings could be attempted William would have to fight a traditional naval battle. Since the opposing fleets were not so very

---

* The official abstract of land forces (H.M.C. Dartmouth MSS, V, 171) gives a total of 40,117, of which 2,291 were Scots and 2,816 Irish. The 'Irish' figure relates only to regiments on the Irish establishment, and excludes the large Irish component in the English regiments.

different in strength the result should be a stalemate of naval power in the Narrow Seas into which it would be madness for a transport flotilla to venture. In any case, winter was approaching, and it would soon be too late in the season for the flat-bottomed boats and other such passenger craft as William was hiring at every seaport in Holland.

James read the situation as a professional naval officer: but with William politics always came uppermost, and by basing his plans primarily on political considerations he produced a strategy for which James was totally unprepared. William wished to avoid fighting—particularly fighting at sea—since he foresaw that a naval battle would produce exactly the national confrontation between British and Dutch which would damage the political basis of his intervention. He also wished, with his eye on the ultimate objective of war against France, to preserve British naval and military strength as far as possible. He had therefore decided on a massive convoy operation in which the fighting fleet would ride close to the precious transports, and only engage in action if they were directly threatened. It was a most perilous decision, since a handful of fighting ships could do terrible damage if they once came within range of the helpless transports, and the war-ships would be hampered in both speed and movement. William's naval experts, both British and Dutch, were strongly against the idea, and he had great difficulty not only in getting them to accept it, but in keeping them to their acceptance. As late as 26 September Bentinck was told by William to repeat to Admiral Herbert that 'he must avoid fighting as much as he can, for, since the result is always uncertain, though we are stronger, this is no time to show his bravery'.[2] William never had much confidence in this violent and temperamental man, with his one eye and his mistresses; and Burnet 'often reflected', when Herbert came into his mind, 'on the Providence of God, that makes some men instruments in great things to which they themselves have no sort of affection or disposition'.[3]

For similar reasons to those underlying his strategy, William was far more interested in the internal conspiracy as it affected James's navy, and in propaganda to back it, than in the conspiratorial landsmen who were now moving towards their posts of action, mainly in Yorkshire. A special broadsheet addressed to James's fleet was prepared (in extremely Dutch English) and sent

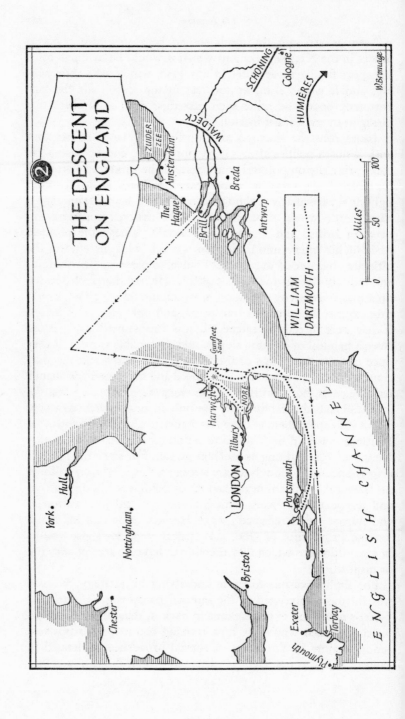

THE DESCENT
ON ENGLAND

WILLIAM ——→
DARTMOUTH ········

Miles
0   50   100

ENGLISH CHANNEL

ZUIDER ZEE
Amsterdam
The Hague
Brill
Breda
Antwerp
WALDECK
SCHONING
Cologne
HUMIÈRES

York
Hull
Chester
Nottingham
LONDON
Tilbury
Harwich
Gunfleet Sand
NORE
Bristol
Portsmouth
Exeter
Torbay
Plymouth

W.Bromage

to Bentinck for polishing and printing on 29 September. And there were better lines through which to work. In Herbert and Russell, who seems to have arrived in Holland early in October and was the third of the seven signatories of the invitation to do so, he had not only deprived James of two of the most effective English sea officers but had opened communication to commanders still serving in the English fleet now hovering uneasily off Sheerness.

That fleet was growing stronger in ships, but the spirit was bad. Even as late as 27 October men were still being pressed to make up the crews, and officers were showing a reluctance to join their ships. 'Gentlemen,' complained Pepys, who was carrying most of the burden at the Admiralty, 'are not above being jealous of any censure, or else they would not appeare to the King every day at Court, complaining that their shipps are not ready, when nothing is wanting towards making them ready but their own attendance on board.'⁴ Some of these laggard officers were doing worse than grumble.

In James's armed forces one of the closest knit groups was the 'Tangerines'—the officers who had served, first under Herbert, then under Kirk, in the hard-living garrison of Tangier until it was evacuated in 1684 for reasons of economy.* Mordaunt, who for a long time had been among William's most enthusiastic adherents, had served there for a time; so had Colonel Charles Trelawny, brother of the baronet-bishop of Bristol and now with his regiment at Portsmouth; Captain Churchill of the *Newcastle* (John Churchill's younger brother); and Captain Matthew Aylmer of the *Swallow*. This was the group with which Herbert, their old commander, was now in touch, and plans were being laid in London during mid-September at meetings in which Kirk and Aylmer took a leading part. The man selected as the agent of the group was another Tangerine, Lieutenant George Byng, shortly to be appointed to the *Defiance*.⁵ Byng held commissions in both the army and the navy, but although he was over thirty his merits had not yet been recognised by authorities such as Lord

* Dartmouth had been sent out to supervise the evacuation, and this could well have contributed to his unpopularity with the 'Tangerines'. Dartmouth, in his most despairing moment, seems to compare it to his experience at Tangier: 'Sir,' he wrote to Pepys on 13/23 November, 'I can never enough acknowledge your share in my sufferings even from Tangier to the Long Sands Head.' (Dartmouth MSS, V, 269.)

Dartmouth, who in the early days of October took charge of the fleet off Sheerness, and with unconscious irony hoisted his flag on the *Resolution*. Dartmouth was a loyal anglican, but firmness was not the strongest streak in his character. Byng's role was imparted to him by Captain Aylmer as they travelled down to join the fleet; and in a fairly short time they had enlisted the captain of Byng's ship, John Ashby, and another captain, Wolfran Cornwall.*

All this was under careful observation by Johnston's successor as William's principal agent in England. Jacob van Leeuwen was Bentinck's private secretary, and had travelled to England on 11 September as secretary to the returning Dutch ambassador, van Citters. Another leading agent had been sent about the same time to Scotland with the help of Melville. Very soon after arriving van Leeuwen made contact with Russell, Danby, and Lumley, who, as Herbert had expected, were growing anxious about the lack of communication. He then concentrated on gathering military intelligence, and by the end of the month, in a report which may have been carried by Russell, he provided the Hague with a copious report on James's naval and military dispositions. He somewhat overestimated the strength of James's fleet, putting it at 44 fighting ships with 10 more fitting out.† But he furnished full particulars of the main garrisons, from which it would be possible to infer with some accuracy the size of James's field army. He also provided the names of the garrison commanders.⁶

On the other side of the North Sea things moved with much greater efficiency. On 19 September Admiral Herbert held a meeting of those concerned with the convoy operation: Bastiaenz, the Dutch commodore, Captain Callenberg, naval secretary de Wilde, and Bentinck. Their calculations showed that they would have to carry eighteen battalions of infantry (of about 600 men each), 3,280 cavalry, 4,000 horses, and large stocks of provisions furnished by de Wilde, which included nearly 300 tons of hay: ten days' rations for each horse at 16 lbs per animal. In addition there were the English and Scottish emigrés, the baggage of senior officers (about which William had issued a special re-

* High promotion came to all these officers after the Revolution. Byng, Aylmer, and Ashby all became admirals. Churchill transferred to the land service and became a general, as did Kirk and Trelawny.

† The actual state of the fleet on 1 October was twenty-one fighting ships and eleven fireships at sea, and twenty-six (of which seven were fireships) fitting out; a total of forty fighting ships and eighteen fireships.

minder), the portable bridge, of a pattern developed during the Hungarian campaigns, a mobile smithy, William's personal coach and horses, four tons of tobacco, 1,600 hogsheads of beer (and 50 of brandy), 10,000 pairs of spare boots, moulds for striking money, and, most important of all, a printing press.* They made the requirement for moving all this, 196 'smacken, roeyers, galioots, boots, and fluyten', the hire for which came to 157,000 guilders. The actual number of transports proved to be slightly more than this—225; but the logistics were good for the period. All transports were to be ready by 22 September, three days after the conference; and Captain Callenberg was to arrange for a sloop to take station off the Nore and send back daily reports on the English fleet to Admiral Evertsen by pinnace.[7]

The troops for the expedition were already chosen, and William was at Mook on 26 September personally supervising their departure. It is typical of his continued care for security that the marching orders he issued did not disclose the ultimate destination of the troops, who were told for the time being that they were for Flanders; and minute instructions were given to Bentinck that the truth should not be disclosed until the moment for embarkation arrived. Of the eighteen infantry battalions six were, of course, the Anglo-Dutch Brigade under Mackay,† and four more (the regiments of Hagedorn, Fagel, Birkenfeld and Wijnbergen) were federal regulars. Particular security about the movement of all these troops was needed because William had not yet got formal authority from the Republic to use them against England. But no such restriction applied to the personal troops of the House of Orange which provided the rest of the

* And, of course, money. This did not go on board until 25 October, when d'Avaux's agents noted 'sixty to eighty sleds carrying little chests' containing bullion being shipped. William strained his own resources to the utmost, deposits being called up as far afield as Spain.

† On the actual expedition the six regiments were commanded as follows: 'Bellasyse's' by Lieutenant-Colonel Philip Babington (Colonel Sir Henry Bellasis being on what proved to be detached duty in Yorkshire); 'Late Ossory's' by Lieutenant-Colonel Pierson (acting for Colonel Canon, who had been repatriated and was commanding a regiment in James's army); 'Talmash's' by the recently promoted Colonel Thomas Talmash; 'Mackay's' by Lieutenant-Colonel Colyear, later Earl of Portmore; 'Balfour's' by Colonel Bartholt Balfour, who was to fall at Killiekrankie; and 'Wauchope's' by Major George Ramsay (both Colonel Wauchope and Lieutenant-Colonel Middleton having returned to England). Thus only one regiment (Balfour's) had its regular colonel in charge.

infantry in the shape of five battalions including one belonging to
cousin Nassau-Odijk. Thus all but three of the foot battalions
were British or Dutch, the three exceptions being a Brandenburg
battalion commanded by Prince Albert Frederick of Brandenburg,
and two hired Scandinavian regiments, Holstein's and Carelsen's.
To these had to be added the two refugee regiments referred to
rather scornfully in the logistic chart as 'people of Lord Levin
and Lord Pieton' (Lord Leven and the whiggish Sir Robert
Peyton). They were assigned only three vessels by the planners.

The cavalry—fifteen regiments with a paper strength of 3,660—
was almost entirely Dutch. Three were guards regiments from
William's household forces; five more—Waldeck's, Ginckel's,
Mompellion's, Van der Lippe's, and Zuylestein's—were established units of the main Dutch army. Those of 'Sgravemoer,
Sapbroek, Seyde and Oyé seem to have been newer Dutch forma-
tions. Only Fioddorp's cavalry and Marrewis's dragoons suggest
Scandinavian or German mercenaries. A regiment of refugee
huguenot officers mounted at William's expense made up the
fifteenth. Together with the artillery, which needed at least a
dozen vessels, and the three ship-loads of 'English Lords' the
nominal muster was over 15,000 fighting men.*

The embarkation began on 22 September at a number of different points on the Dutch coast, and was complete by 6 October—
an uncomfortable period of heaving barges, struggling horses,
and argumentative commissaries. In the middle of it all, on board
his flagship the *Leyden* the one-eyed Lieutenant-Admiral-General
was working out his strategy in a memorandum spattered with
seamanlike spelling.[8] He judged that the fighting ships under his
command were 'more than sufficient' to deal with anything Lord
Dartmouth could do, though it would be desirable to have a
few extra ships as a precaution against the appearance of a French
squadron. Spare masts and rigging would have to be shipped in
order to refit after an engagement without having to put back into
harbour; large numbers of rowing boats would be needed for
the disembarkation, but the transports themselves, besides being

---

* Burnet (Somers Tracts, ix, 276) gives a total paper strength of 14,352
(10,692 infantry and 3,600 cavalry) and an actual muster of about 12,000.
But this excludes artillerymen. Bentinck's logistical calculation of 19 September, which can be taken as more reliable but also excludes artillery per-
sonnel, budgets for a total of 15,160 (11,880 foot and 3,280 horse) (Japikse,
I. ii. 606).

well ventilated, should be as shallow in the draught as possible so as to be capable of coming well in shore. But that brought the vital question: where to land?

The Thames and the Medway, despite James's suspicions, were never seriously considered. The choice lay between the York-shire coast, where the land-based conspirators were strongest and the sea crossing was the shortest; and the south-west. After a careful balancing of the arguments Herbert came down strongly in favour of the south-west. The north 'I hold soe dangerex that I hardly thinck it practicable'. The comprehensiveness of Herbert's strategic thinking is shown by the argument he thought decisive: given risings in both the south-west and the north-east, it would be easier to support a northern rising from bridge-heads in the south than the reverse. The experience of Monmouth had shown how unsupported irregular forces could be bottled up and des-troyed in the peninsula. To this argument William was quick to add another. Once a landing in the south-west had been made good, it would be possible to use part of the fleet to cut James's communications, for reinforcement or retreat, with Ireland.

On 29 September James had been down to visit his fleet for the second time in a week, chatting as amiably as he could with his officers. He was now beginning to realise that support must be wooed, and to contemplate a political retreat. Early in Sep-tember, when he and Sunderland had still been pooh-poohing the possibility of an invasion, the writs for the parliament prom-ised in his little-read Declaration had been issued. But a procla-mation which speedily followed on 21 September had shown the first hints of concession. James had reiterated his intention to propose 'liberty of conscience for all his subjects', but added that 'he was willing Roman Catholics should remain incapable of being members of the House of Commons, to remove those fears and apprehensions, lest the legislative power should be en-grossed by them'. It was the first conciliatory gesture of his reign, and marked the abandonment of a principle he had con-sidered indispensable in the past. On 4 October, in continuance of his hope of making peace with Anglicanism, he requested the attendance of the opposition bishops.*

* The summons went to six of the celebrated seven (all but Lloyd of St. Asaph), and to Mews of Winchester, Compton of London, and Sprat of Rochester.

William's operational orders to Herbert were issued two days later on 6 October.[9] The fleet was to drop down the Hollander Diep and lie off Helvoetsluys. No officer or seaman was now to go ashore without leave, and the fleet was to be ready:

> Tot maintien van de Protestantse religie ende de Vryheyt van het Coninckrijk van Groot Brittagne, gebruickende dairtoe alle bequaeme middelen van inductie, sooverre de tijd ende gelegentheijt van saecken sal willen lyden.*

In addition to these general instructions Herbert's powerful force of fifty-two fighting ships was empowered to clear the North Sea and the Channel of all ships carrying contraband of war 'on what pretext soever'. If there was to be French intervention William was prepared to face it.

But by what authority did William issue these far-ranging orders? He so far had none from the Dutch state. Juridically, like his ancestor William the Silent in the days of the rebellion against Spain, he was using the authority of the sovereign Princes of Orange to launch the expedition. But more authority than this was needed to employ regiments and ships in the pay of the States General against a foreign power.

It was the triumph of the last weeks of Fagel's life to provide this. On 29 September the Grand Pensionary had obtained the essential decision in the form of a secret resolution of the States of Holland, without which the expedition could never have sailed. He used flimsy materials—notably d'Avaux's unfortunate reference to an 'alliance' between Louis and James—to convince his colleagues that there was indeed a repetition of the bitterly remembered Anglo-French coalition against the Republic which had been so damaging in 1678. Louis' measures against Dutch shipping had put his audience in a responsive mood. With all this he combined his own burning conviction that France was in the long term Holland's most dangerous enemy, and the States had voted:

> To thank his Highness for his communication, also for his decision, on his own responsibility, though with the assistance of the States; to make all possible and the strongest

* 'For the maintenance of the Protestant religion and the freedom of the Kingdom of Great Britain, using for that object all suitable methods of proceeding, to the extent that time and circumstances may dictate.' (Japikse, I. ii. 613.)

efforts to secure the consent of other Provinces; that all members present shall not divulge this communication to anybody, only absent members excepted; further, to earnestly request his Highness to take all possible precautions for his personal safety. . . .*

It was with this resolution in his pocket that William had felt able to issue operational orders to Herbert; but it was not until 8 October—two days after those orders were issued, that the States General themselves approved the expedition on this curious basis of an undertaking on William's own responsibility 'with the support of the Republic'.

8 October was also the day James had appointed for his meeting with the bishops, and he had important news for them. He had decided that day to cancel the writs for his proposed parliament. To him this meant the abandonment, at least for the time being, of the whole cherished policy of toleration blessed by parliamentary sanction. But the bishops, it seems, were unimpressed. One of them complained that they might as well not have come at all. It was only the intervention of Sancroft, who had not been at the interview, but saw the King privately two days later, that persuaded the rest to attend a further conference, fixed for 13 October, at which they would tender their formal advice—in other words their terms for a reconciliation.[10]

The pattern of the European war was now rapidly unrolling. Louis was formally at war with the Pope and had seized Avignon. His troops had, under the direction of Vauban, completed the investment of Philipsburg, and French battalions and squadrons were erupting over the Palatinate, Baden, and the three ecclesiastical Electorates. At Magdeburg, on 15 October, Brandenburg, Saxony, and Brunswick completed a defensive alliance. 'Vous avez veu les imprimés,' wrote William to Waldeck, who was now commanding the covering army—now some 16,000 strong —in the south-east holding a line between Hertogenbosch and Deventer:† France, William considered, must be deemed to have

* Ferguson, p. 566. The resolution was sent the very next day by William to his cousin, the Stadhouder of Friesland, with a request for good offices in getting approval from the States of Friesland (*Archives of the House of Orange Nassau*, II. v. 592).

† By the end of the year Waldeck's army had been raised to a strength of over 20,000. It included contingents from Brandenburg, Hesse, Luneburg and Würtemberg, as well as Dutch troops.

declared war on the Empire as well as on the Emperor, and it was essential to strengthen the troops on the Rhine before the inevitable fall of Philipsburg; but it would unfortunately be inexpedient to respond in any way to the Elector Palatine's cry for help.[11] On 10 October William finally committed himself. The manifesto justifying the invasion of England—drafted by Danby, improved by Dijkvelt and Bentinck, polished by Burnet and Melville, was published.

The northern conspirators, in the meantime, were on the move. Early in October there had been consultations in London between Danby and Devonshire, which had included Thomas Wharton, leader of the whig group that was to make contact with William if he landed in the south-west. Devonshire left for Yorkshire on the thirteenth and Danby, after making his will, soon followed. He professed to be taking the sulphur waters at Ribston near Knaresborough. Very soon afterwards, with an irony that can hardly not have been deliberate, Charles Bertie was writing to James's naval commander, Lord Dartmouth, describing the delightful house party at Ribston, and how one of their whig neighbours 'is environing his gardens with a kind of fortification'.[12]

The terms presented to James by the bishops on 13 October were not the less humiliating for being expressed in the most humble language. Dispensations from the Test were to cease, and those already granted were to be cancelled; the fellows of Magdalen were to be restored; the four Roman Catholic vicars apostolical were to stop exercising ecclesiastical jurisdiction; vacancies on the episcopal bench were to be filled at once—especially the archbishopric of York 'for which', observed Sancroft, '(pardon me, Sir, if I am bold to say) you have now before you a very fair choice'; the electoral machinery under Brent was to be dismantled, and a parliament should be convened 'in which the Church of England may be secured', and 'provision may be made for due liberty of conscience'. Finally, and most humiliating of all, the King should agree to listen to arguments in favour of Anglicanism 'such as may by God's grace be effectual to persuade your Majesty to return to the communion of the Church of England'.[13] In return for all this the bishops promised nothing. James expected a bargain. What he got was a programme.*

* Sancroft's original draft of the document (Gutch, I. 405) was couched in

And all through October the wind beat steadily against the coast of Holland from the west. On every rational calculation this fortune of war favoured James. William's men and horses were on board and the last details for sailing had been settled on 11 October. Every day that passed with the wind against the invasion fleet would weaken its sense of purpose, deplete William's reserves of cash, and give James time to prepare a warmer reception. If the west wind lasted into November winter storms would make the North Sea impassable to transports, and by the spring the whole balance of Europe would probably be altered. Nor was this all. The breathing space would give James the chance to retrieve himself on the domestic front by the concessions to which he was now almost reconciled. A stream of decrees reversing the policy of the last three years poured out of Whitehall in October. Lord Lieutenants were restored, the fellows of Magdalen were re-installed, charters were granted in the old form. And in spite of the frosty attitude of the bishops James still hoped for a formal reconciliation with the Church, in which the bishops could be persuaded publicly to condemn the invasion.

Yet the advantages were not wholly on James's side. The interval also allowed fresh showers of propaganda time to sink in and conspiracy time to spread. At least one pamphlet—*Le Royaume Usurpé*—which d'Avaux had detected in August being seen through the press by Zuylestein, made its appearance in England to sustain the doubts thrown on the birth of James's heir.[14] But the chance given to Byng and his allies in the fleet was more important, and may have been decisive. James's fleet was certainly less reliable at the end of October than it had been at the beginning.

Consciousness that his captains were 'caballing' too much while the fleet lay in the Nore, was one of the reasons that decided Lord Dartmouth to set out on a cruise and shift his station. He even contemplated taking advantage of the wind and making a descent on the Dutch coast, but both the King and his captains dissuaded

---

conditional terms, leading up to a passage, which seems never to have been drafted, setting out what the bishops would be prepared to do if their advice was accepted. The document finally submitted is purely in the form of advice —a most significant difference. (Gutch I. 410). These discussions were all relayed back to William (Burnet to Herbert, 2 November 1688).

him. The new station was the buoy of Gunfleet, off Harwich, from which Dartmouth reckoned he would have a better start when the Dutch sailed than if he had had to pick his way through the shoals and shallows at the mouth of the Thames estuary. There was an adequate roadstead between the coast and the long narrow Gunfleet sandbank which stretches for some twenty miles, protecting Suffolk from the open sea. In that station, Dartmouth hoped, he would have 'more sea room' and his caballing captains would be out of the way of 'dayley pamphlets and newes letters'.[15]

As Dartmouth was reaching this resolution James was having a further interview with Archbishop Sancroft. The summons had been abrupt, but the King was conciliatory. He went through the concessions of the last few days, laying particular stress on the restoration of Magdalen and the corporations, and then came to the point. He had undoubted intelligence of William's intended invasion. Would the bishops formally and publicly condemn it? Such action, James said, 'would be very much for his service, and a thing very well becoming the bishops'. Sancroft hedged. Hardly any bishops, he said, were in town; there were grievances (particularly in Ireland) still outstanding. But he doubted, when he was asked to speak frankly, whether there was any need for such a declaration. It seemed to him most unlikely that William had any such intention.[16] Sancroft was a conscientious man: after the Revolution he was to sacrifice his office and his income to his conscience. But here he was acting as a politician. It is inconceivable that on 26 October, when this interview took place, he should not have known of the invasion threat.

Three days later the wind had shifted enough for William to sail. The Prince took solemn leave of the States General, and said farewell to Fagel, whose political skill had made the whole design possible. He had also found time to add a codicil to his will, making a substantial legacy to Bentinck; to write once more urging the laggard Elector of Brandenburg (whose observer, Kron, was to travel on the expedition) to hasten his advance; and to apologise to the Governor of the Spanish Netherlands, the Marquis de Gastañaga, for not allowing him to accompany the invasion. One must, William explained, take account of English anti-catholic prejudice. Then the whole armada debouched from the mouth of the Maas, passed the low-lying island of Goree, and made north-westwards into the choppy grey open sea. First came the fighting fleet in its two divisions—more than fifty warships—then the long line of transports, making altogether nearly three hundred vessels. No larger invasion has ever been mounted against the British Isles. As the last transport cleared the coastline a watching pinnace, with two protecting frigates, fired four guns to signal that the manoeuvre was complete, and then hurried alongside the Prince's headquarter ship, the *Brill*, to report.[17]

It was not until the following morning that the huge fleet, with its protecting warships, was marshalled for the voyage. The *Brill*, a modest frigate of thirty guns, in which William was accompanied by his personal staff and two senior Dutch naval advisers, led the inner convoy, followed by a line of vessels carrying Schomberg and the military staff, the English gentry, and the Prince's baggage. Well ahead sailed Herbert's big flagship, the *Leyden*; while heaving and wallowing to the rear came the troop-carriers—the *Blaeuwe Pot*, the *Juffrow Hester*, the *Jonge Ruyter* and the *Barley-Mill*, the *Concord* and the *Fidelity*, that had been hired in every dockyard in the United Provinces. The whole convoy was estimated to cover some twenty miles.[18]

The shift in the wind had only been just enough to make the impatient Prince, conscious that time was against him, venture out. The change had been from due west to south west by south, which would make Yorkshire—Herbert's 'dangerex' alternative—possible. But as Albeville, James's ambassador at the Hague, who had watched their departure, wrote to Whitehall the following day, the wind was veering back to the west, 'which,' the ambassador thought, 'may do them some damage', and he was quite right.* During the day of Saturday 30 October, as they struggled northwards against the changing gale, the sea grew choppier, and the night brought a storm so violent that the armada was completely scattered—'on ne pouvait pas voir deux ensemble' wrote Rapin, who was with the huguenot cavalry. There was nothing for it but to signal that every ship should make for the nearest friendly port. And so the fleet limped back in two's and three's to harbours up and down the Dutch coast.[19]

The material damage was not great, the worst being the loss

* On the whole Albeville's intelligence was good, though slow, and he certainly worked hard. He claimed, over the period, for eleven special messengers, and employed two fishing-boats full-time to watch William's fleet. (Calendar of Treasury Books, 2 January 1689.)

of several hundred horses which had been suffocated when the hatches had been battened down for the storm. No ship had been lost, and the fleet was gathered together again with surprising speed at its original starting-point, though the warships could not gain the shelter of the estuary, and had to ride in the open sea. But the next ten days must have been the worst of William's career. Surrounded by his dampened army and his battered fleet, he had to fight bitterly against the fatal but plausible change of plan that was now urged upon him—to send the fighting fleet across to engage Dartmouth, and hold the transports in reserve. 'There were few among us,' wrote Burnet, 'that did not conclude . . . that the whole design was lost. . . . Many that have passed for heroes, yet showed then the agonies of fear.' He himself cannot have improved morale by writing a long letter to Admiral Herbert suggesting that the bad weather was a judgment on the admiral's evil habits of life. Bad news came in from every side. Philipsburg had surrendered. Waldeck, from the covering army, wrote almost hysterically for orders. He was suffering from gout, was short of troops, unable to travel. And all the time the gales pelted furiously from the north-west—so furiously that for some days it was impossible to communicate with the battle-fleet at all. William's steadiness at this moment is a most conspicuous evidence of his greatness. 'The worst loss,' he wrote to Waldeck the day after his humiliating return, 'is the time and the horses'; and signed himself 'Yours passionately'.[20]

Ensconced behind his sandbanks off Harwich, where he had taken station on 3 November, Lord Dartmouth was feeling steadily more confident. The King had given him a free hand. His force was growing stronger, and now mustered some fifty vessels. The bad spirit of which he had been conscious back at the Nore seemed to have dispersed. He had been troubled by the ease of communication with London, and James's reluctance to make enough political concessions. 'I feare,' he had written to James just before sailing, 'they [his officers] have other advices, and still thinke all our mischiefs spring directly or indirectly from the old conduit of Whitehall.' But once at the Gunfleet he was sure 'there was nothing but a readiness in all the commanders to do their duty to your Majestie' . . . 'Sir, we are now at sea before the Dutch with all their boasting, and I cannot see much sense in their attempt with the hazard of such a fleet and army at the latter end of October.'[21] And this was written before the news of William's set-back reached him—it travelled so slowly that it was 8 November before Dartmouth had this fresh ground for increased confidence.

It was otherwise on the political front in Whitehall. Most of the principal political figures were conspicuously out of town; and Sunderland, who had gone so deep with James, was in a growing state of panic.* He had advised the October concessions, and had told the King that even greater sacrifices would be necessary. Especially, he urged, the machinery for regulating the corporations —Brent's political agency—should be abandoned, but this James would not relinquish. Sunderland was a politician, not a fighting man, and he had little to contribute to this phase of affairs, where fleets and armies were superseding negotiations. James, on whom the main burden of higher command was falling, had noticed the demoralisation of his chief minister, yet hesitated for some time before getting rid of him, until the news of William's false start gave a burst of renewed confidence from which to act. On 8 November he deprived Sunderland of all his offices.

So even William's misfortune, by imparting unjustified confidence to James and his admiral, had some compensation. It also accentuated the already tense state of feeling in England, and it was into this that William, in the middle of all his other preoccupations, found time to direct the one blow which he was at that moment in a position to strike. On 3 November two ships were despatched from Amsterdam carrying fifty thousand copies of William's manifesto announcing his decision to respond to an invitation from English temporal and spiritual peers to intervene in English affairs by force. Time was even found to add a postscript dealing with James's recent concessions, and imply that they were inadequate and fraudulent. One ship sailed for the English east coast, and the other for the south. Elaborate arrangements had already been made for their cargoes to be distributed; and both clearly completed their mission.† On 10 November

---

* Already, in the middle of September, his wife was writing to Henry Sidney, asking for advice on 'what place you'd advise my lord to go to'. (13 and 21 September 1688. Blencowe, II, pp. 272 and 275.)

† See Japikse, II. ii, pp. 618–19 for a specimen of instructions on the distribution of leaflets. Packets (in this particular case containing copies of the Prince's appeal to the British fleet) were to be consigned to 'some trusty person in London who is usually entrusted with the receiving and dispersing

copies of the declaration were picked up in Yorkshire, and on 11 November a certain Captain Langham, from one of the Anglo-Dutch regiments, was arrested in Kent with a parcel of copies in his luggage.

Intercepted copies reached King James as early as the tenth, and from them he seems to have learned for the first time of his opponent's claim to possess an invitation. He seems genuinely to have believed the claim was no more than propaganda, but it was obviously far too damaging to be allowed to go uncontradicted—especially in its reference to spiritual peers. With his usual impetuosity, but rather more than his usual insight, he immediately summoned Compton, whose signature to the letter of July was in fact the sole basis of William's claim. The bishop, according to his own account of the interview, met the King's challenge with the masterly equivocation that he 'was confident the rest of the bishops would as readily answer in the negative as myself'. When James asked him for a public denial and a repudiation of the invasion, Compton naturally said he would have to consult his colleagues.[22]

That very Thursday, 11 November, while Compton was playing out time with James, William's reassembled fleet was again sailing from the Maas. Once clear of the estuary they remained hove-to all night, and the morning found them with sails still furled. William was waiting for the last in the long series of intelligence agents through whom he had kept James under constant observation. It was Zuylestein, returning 'from some creek or place upon the coasts of England, where he was to meet somebody'.[23] It is possible that Zuylestein's outward journey had been with one of the leaflet ships, and the up-to-date information he brought with him was clearly most important, including as it did a remarkably good estimate of the size of James's field army. His advice to a council of war hastily convened on board the *Brill* (Dijkvelt and other Dutch officials were summoned to it from the shore) was that the most promising objective was not the coast of Yorkshire but Dorset or Devon. Very shortly afterwards the whole armada sailed with the prevailing wind north-westwards

---

of such secrett papers as ar frequently sent thither from Holland'. The code word for release was 'I come from Exeter'. The usual method of dispersal was very simple. Copies were put in the Penny Post addressed to a suitable circulation list.

into the squalls and darkness. Simultaneously the Scheveling fishing fleet set out due west as a decoy to the French privateers, who were on the watch from Dunkirk.

Lord Dartmouth, though he was under the impression that his own was slightly the weaker fleet, considered he was well informed. 'I have sent out three good sailing frigates and brisk men to attend their motion,' he was writing to James three days before William sailed; and on the ninth, judging correctly that William would soon be at sea again, he was even more reassuring: 'I have my scouts abroad, and I believe it is impossible for us to miss such a fleet'. Besides the three frigates he had the *Katherine* yacht hovering off the coast of Friesland, the *Sandados* cruising near Heligoland, the *Kitchen* somewhere to the east of the Goodwins, and the *Kingfisher* ketch collecting despatches from an English firm of wine-merchants at Ostend who were also spies.[24]

But on that night of the 12/13 November he was blinded by bad weather. The scouting frigates, battered by the eastern gale, had staggered back to the main fleet on the eleventh, dismasted and without information. The other 'advice vessels' were still at sea.* And as day broke on Saturday, 13 November, Dartmouth could see on the horizon thirteen warships scudding with almost bare masts, southwards. They were the most easterly guardships of Herbert's fleet. What had happened was that, soon after midnight, at a point perhaps eighty miles off Spurn Head, William had changed the course of the whole armada from north-west to south-west. The wind had veered to give him the chance of seizing the alternative Zuylestein had so strongly advised.† Nevertheless it was a marvellously bold decision, since it meant taking the convoy within fifteen miles of the main English fleet, whose position William undoubtedly knew. What made the risk worth taking was that he knew also that the only way from behind the Gunfleet to the open sea lay round the northern tip of the long sandbank.

* Pepys, whose devotion to the innumerable details of his duty as Secretary of the Admiralty at this time has an almost touching quality, was better informed than the fleet commander. Writing 'past midnight' on the thirteenth he passed on two despatches that had just reached him reporting that William had sailed.

† William's note to Bentinck, written at 1 a.m. on board the *Brill*, records the decision 'I hold course to West, and hope to pass the Straits of Dover tomorrow'. It is odd that Bentinck was not with the Prince at this critical moment.

Lord Dartmouth did his best, though one may wonder whether all his captains did theirs. It took his fleet a long time to get clear. The north wind, that was carrying William merrily towards the coast of Essex, blew in their teeth as they tacked northwards for hours through the shallows. Three frigates lying outside the sandbank were quicker, and scraped the rear of the transport fleet to capture an enemy fly-boat that had lost its rudder: a valuable prize, for it contained Major Ventris Columbine* and 200 men from one of the Anglo-Dutch regiments. But wind and tide were against the main English fleet, and the pursuit could not begin until the day was almost over. Even then Dartmouth felt obliged to keep as close inshore as he could in case William was aiming for the Thames.

Meanwhile James was still pursuing his desperate negotiation with the bishops. He could not bring himself to believe that men so deeply committed to obedience could possibly refuse to help him now. He saw a group of five on the Friday William sailed north-westwards—Sancroft, Compton, Crewe of Durham, Cartwright of Chester, and Watson of St David's. The last three had been among the most compliant of the whole bench. They all denied any part in the invitation (Compton passing the question off by saying he had already given his answer), and an inconclusive discussion followed about a possible public statement to this effect, coupled with James's proposal for a public 'abhorrence' of the invasion by the bishops. They parted in mutual misunderstanding—the bishops confident that they had given no commitment even to consider the King's request, and the King believing they had agreed to produce the public statement he wanted.

In this manner James wasted his time while his adversary's fleet ploughed southwards, with Dartmouth in a pursuit that grew ever fainter. The wretched admiral considered himself 'the most unfortunate man living', and was now openly terrified of engaging the Dutch if he should catch up with them. About 11 in the morning Captain Tennant of the *Tiger* frigate saw them pass 'on the backside of the Goodwin', and thought them 'too many for our fleet'.[25] Off the North Foreland, which was reached about midday, Herbert came on board the *Brill* for a council of

---

* Major Columbine became lieutenant colonel of the 6th Foot in 1689 and its colonel in 1695—the year of his death. His son was an even more successful soldier; colonel of the 10th Foot and (1739) lieutenant general.

war, and the possibility of a direct stroke at London seems to have been considered and rejected. The wind was still from the north and fine weather gave the opportunity for a demonstration. The remarshalled fleet steered for the Straits of Dover, and at one o'clock passed, almost in review order, under the eyes of large crowds gathered on either shore, from the North Sea into the Channel. 'Ce n'est pas une chose commune,' wrote Rapin, who was on board William's fleet, 'que de voir ensemble cinq ou six cents vaisseaux.'[26] 'They are about halfe seas over,' said Mr Bastick, who was watching from Dover, 'and are soe thick there is noe telling of them.'[27]* Music was struck up on some of the ships, salutes were fired, and from the mast-head of the *Brill* and other ships flew huge streamers carefully prepared in advance bearing the Orange motto 'I will maintain', and the slogan 'the Liberty of England and the Protestant Religion'.†

They were now something like a hundred miles ahead of Dartmouth's fleet, and moved more slowly, no doubt in order to maintain formation. By dawn next morning they were cruising off the Isle of Wight and James's strongest southern fortress, Portsmouth. Here again their moral effect was considerable, and Sir Robert Holms, the governor of Yarmouth Castle, grew anxious about his troops. Next day he was writing under confidential cover to Secretary Preston that 'part of the Melitia is growne mutinous already, refusing to follow their Commanders' orders, as I am afraid they will do everywhere where his Majestie has occasion to call for them . . . God knowes how I shall be dealt withall by this Melitia.'[28]

William toyed with the idea of a landing that day. It was his thirty-eighth birthday and the anniversary of his marriage, all of which could have been turned to heartening use. But another brief pause for consultation decided him to press on. Portsmouth, where James's illegitimate son the Duke of Berwick was in command, might resist, and the chance of a bloodless campaign be lost.

* And yet, at almost the same time, back in Delft, Antony van Leeuwenhoek, who five years earlier had been the first human being to see bacteria, was observing the tail of a tadpole through his microscope—'a sight . . . more delightful than any mine eyes have ever beheld'.
† D'Avaux had noted the preparation of the streamers as early as 8 October. The slogans were in letters three feet high, and mostly in Latin—'pro libertate et libero parliamento'; 'pro libertate et religione'; and 'pro religione protestante'.

He sailed slowly on westwards, and it took twenty-four hours to reach Torbay, where a convenient shift in the wind to the south made for a perfect landfall at about dawn. They had been at sea for nearly four days. Far to the eastward Dartmouth was just rounding Beachy Head.

Fog and drizzle greeted them, but the weather gradually cleared and the landing began in autumnal sunshine while the warships stood out to sea watching for any sign of the English fleet. The first ashore was Count Solms, commander of William's foot-guards, with a party of his grenadiers. The English and Scottish regiments followed to establish the bridgehead. Last of all came the cavalry, whose horses, after their uncomfortable journey, were thrown overboard to swim to the beach. The whole disembarkation was completed—a great tribute to Bentinck's gifts as a staff officer—in not much more than twenty-four hours.

William himself landed at the fishing village of Brixham only a few hours after the first party had gone ashore, and in the afternoon a brief service of thanksgiving was offered on the sands. The Prince did not select the bustling Gilbert Burnet to officiate, though he was already, rather thankfully one suspects, on dry land. It was the broad, blond, calvinist intelligence agent William Carstares, who had worked so long and so hard for this day, who now led the troops in the 118th Psalm—'They came about me like bees, and are extinct even as the fire among the thorns; for in the name of the Lord I will destroy them.' An hour or so beforehand the Prince had passed off Burnet's eager compliments with the only joke he is recorded as ever having made—and like his other remarks it was very much to the point. 'Well, Doctor,' said the calvinist William as the assiduous anglican hurried up to him with congratulations, 'what do you think of predestination now?'

The Advance from the West

The invaders, after an uncomfortable night spent in pouring rain, struggled painfully inland through the Devonshire mire in three columns of march. As they trudged through Paignton, Newton Bushell, Chudleigh, making only a few miles a day towards Exeter, they were greeted with respect rather than enthusiasm. But the country people were pleased with their behaviour. The soldiers asked for eggs and chickens, but paid for them; and a good many of the troops were English, carried English colours, and marched to English tunes, including, no doubt, the catchy, anti-Irish *Lilliburlero*. If William attracted few recruits, there was no resistance whatever. Nevertheless, for the leaders of the expedition these days were among the most perilous in the adventure. There was no turning back now, and what was worse, no effective communication with the fleet, the home base, or sympathisers in England. For the time being the director of the huge combined operation stretching from the Rhine to the Atlantic was silenced, and without information.

During this period of four days—15–19 November—in which William could do nothing except concentrate on getting to Exeter, events took a decisive turn both on the Rhine and in London. Louis' forces virtually completed the occupation of the 'Country of the Four Electors' by capturing Mannheim, and James's negotiations with the Church of England came to an end.

The French conquest of the Rhineland had been a rapid, brutal business. Almost at the last moment the Archbishop-Elector of Trier had hesitated about opening his territory to Louis' troops,

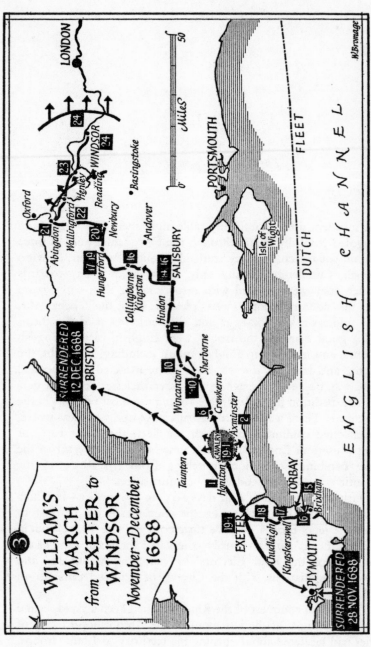

The dates in November and December (new style) show the principal halts of William's personal headquarters and the positions of his cavalry thrusts along the Thames Valley and in reprisal Coblentz, his principal town, had been pounded by Marshal Boufflers' heavy mortars. The French soldiers lived off the country, and collected heavy contributions in money. Far worse was to follow, and decisions about it were already being taken. Louvois had always thought of the Rhenish invasion as primarily a defensive move, a clearing of the French field of fire whereby the Emperor and his German allies could be permanently prevented from interfering with French plans in Spain and the Mediterranean. And now William's initial success was beginning to make Louvois and his master look less confidently towards the Channel. It would be necessary to reduce the French commitment by withdrawing from some of these easily won conquests on the Rhine. Louvois' calculation, on the eve of the surrender of Mannheim, was that whether the Emperor now sued for peace or persisted in war (and the Empire, as distinct from the Emperor, had not yet decided on war, so slow was the procedure of the Diet), the French would do well to cash their winnings at once by making sure the fortifications they now occupied would never be available to a potential enemy. By the kind of shift in thought which often overtakes centralised governments, an ambiguity led on to unspeakably ruthless actions. 'Demolition' of strong points, it was held, was an indisputable right of international law: and silently, in the mind of Louvois and his advisers, 'demolition of fortifications' became 'destruction of towns'. The fact that some of the doomed towns lay in one of the most tolerant states in Europe, the Palatinate, which was not only the haven of thousands of huguenots but the home of a large Jewish population, no doubt helped in the decision towards ruthlessness. The day after Mannheim surrendered, the 17th of November, Louvois gave the first indications of how policy was developing at Versailles. 'I see the King inclined,' he wrote, 'to demolish entirely the town and castle of Mannheim, and, if such a decision be taken, to carry out a complete destruction of the inhabited area in such a manner that not one stone shall rest upon another which might tempt an Elector, to whom the territory might be returned in a peace treaty, to make another establishment there. His Majesty considers that this proposal should not be disclosed to anybody.'[1]

While William was coming ashore at Torbay the English bishops had been meeting at Lambeth to consider their plans for the meeting with the King which had been fixed for the following day; and at ten o'clock on 16 November they voyaged once more down the river to Whitehall and a waiting crowd. There were four prelates this time—Sancroft, Compton, White of Peterborough and Sprat of Rochester—but they represented a wider coalition than the seven of the previous May, for Sprat had then still been fervently supporting the Indulgence policy. At this moment, in the shadow of the Revolution that was to begin the Church of England's decline as a political force, its leaders held the key of public opinion in their hands and were negotiating on equal terms with the King himself. For James, in his isolation, had come to the conclusion that neither lay politicians nor military force could be of use to him if he lost the battle for public confidence.

James did not yet know of William's successful landing, and it is probable that the bishops did not know either when they were ushered in: but they were as firm as if they had known. They absolutely refused to make any public denial of complicity in inviting William's intervention. They had never, they explained, given any promise to draw up such a declaration: their undertaking had been limited to consultation about it, and the consultation had led them to the conclusion that such a paper was unnecessary. The declaration by William which the King had shown them at the last interview might be a forgery, and was not generally credited. In any case the bishops ought not to be singled out as the only people publicly to condemn it: it would look as if they were particularly suspect. As a last, unkind, thrust Sancroft observed that the bishops had learned from their experience a few months ago that it was dangerous and unwelcome for them to meddle in politics. The King struggled helplessly in the toils of these and similar sophisticated arguments: 'Must I not be believed?' he burst out at one point, when the bishops questioned the genuineness of William's declaration. But confidence, as he had unwillingly to confess, was the issue. The admission was wrung from him by a bland suggestion that since he already had their formal denials, he was perfectly free to say so in a declaration of his own. 'No,' said the wretched King. 'If I should publish it, the people would not believe me.' After two hours of this James gave up and dismissed the bishops, saying he would 'stand on my own legs and trust to myself and my own arms'.* The bishops had scarcely gone before news of William's disembarkation arrived in Whitehall.

James might talk of fighting, but he had no very clear plan of campaign. Dartmouth, who had given up the pursuit and been blown back to anchorage in the Downs, was ordered to deal with a new situation in which the enemy fleet was now free to fight 'with the least exposure of the King's fleet'.² He needed no encouragement for a policy of inaction. Even before William landed he had decided, after a council of war on board the *Resolution*, 'not to fight them if in honour it could be avoided'.³ Herbert's orders from William perfectly complemented this decision. A small squadron was to escort the empty transports back to Holland as quickly as possible (to curtail the hiring charges) and the rest of the fleet was to cover the seaward flank of the invading army in its advance on London. If the English fleet was encountered Herbert was to offer the usual courtesies and invite discussion. Only if this was refused was battle to be joined. 'Gouverne yourself as you shall judge best.'⁴ A little later, on 23 November, Herbert was to learn from Russell, who was acting as naval liaison officer at William's headquarters, that at least eight of Dartmouth's captains were not prepared to fight.

News of the landing at Torbay travelled fairly slowly across England, and was not known in the North until two days later. Beacons were not used by the government of a disunited nation. But by 18 November the whole island knew, and a number of conspiratorial squadrons were on the move for William. On the morning of the 17th a party of some sixty Buckinghamshire gentlemen was seen passing through Oxford under the command of the redoubtable Thomas Wharton, who had been one of the leaders of the whig minority in the Parliament of 1685 and was the reputed author of *Lilliburlero*. On the 18th another of the Wharton brothers, Henry, passed through Oxford on a similar errand, accompanied by one of the Wharton group's closest collaborators, William Jephson. Jephson, besides being a whig professional soldier, was brother-in-law to Simon Patrick, the Dean of Peterborough, who had played so notable a part in organising resistance to the reading of James's declaration in

* Two separate accounts of this interview, one by White, and the other by Sprat, are preserved in the Tanner MSS and printed in Gutch, I. pp. 431–45.

London. Nor were these the only parties in motion headed by former exclusionists and dabblers in the Rye House Plot. Lord Lovelace was making his way from Hurley in the Thames Valley towards Gloucester together with two other professional soldiers, Lord Colchester and Charles Godfrey. Colchester brought with him part of the guards troop he commanded. Godfrey was Thomas Wharton's closest companion, and was also allied closely to the only soldier who, at this stage, could perhaps still have saved James; for Arabella Godfrey was John Churchill's sister.* The future Duke of Marlborough had a difficult hand to play, and it is significant that while continuing to protest his loyalty to James he had this connection in the whig groups who were the first to break cover, and another—his brother George—with Dartmouth's fleet, in command of the man-of-war *Newcastle*.

William's communications, as he approached Exeter, were even more precarious than he had supposed. On landing at Torbay one of his first acts had been to despatch a fast-sailing advice boat for the Hague with intelligence reports and instructions for his allies and field commanders on the mainland. Indeed his chief ally, the Elector of Brandenburg, was so anxious to know the outcome of the expedition that he had sent a special observer with it, and himself lingered on at the Hague. Waldeck, anxiously watching the French, was no less in need of news and orders. But the advice boat never reached its destination. It was intercepted by one of Dartmouth's cruisers, the *Pearl*, and brought into the Downs with its precious load of papers, which included Burnet's letter to his wife, William's plans for an advance on London, private despatches for the Elector and, most important of all operationally, an exact account of the strength of William's fleet. Dartmouth, who had no facilities for translating out of Dutch and German, passed this priceless mine of intelligence on to London after gathering from it that, contrary to his suppositions, the enemy fleet was slightly weaker than his own; so he plucked up courage and began to think in terms of a raid on the coast of Devonshire.†

* As well as being James's former mistress and (by him) mother of the Duke of Berwick, now, at the age of eighteen, in command at James's main southern bastion, Portsmouth. For Godfrey and Jephson see Carswell, *Old Cause*, pp. 45 and 53.

† The faithful Pepys speedily had the information evaluated and passed back to Dartmouth; but it all took time, and Dartmouth's officers were not slow

For a man in such peril James's movements were extremely slow. His army was not to begin marching westwards from Hounslow until the 20th, partly because some regiments had been prematurely ordered north, and had to be recalled. James himself did not plan to set out for his field headquarters at Salisbury until Tuesday, 23rd November, so that he was allowing a whole week to pass between his announcement that he would stand 'on his own legs' and any visible attempt to do so. The interval enabled him to make the last important appointment of his reign. On the 21st, the Bishop of Exeter, Lamplugh, arrived in Whitehall exhausted by a breakneck journey from his cathedral city, and protesting his loyalty. He had refused to stay in his diocese, he explained, when it had fallen into the hands of rebels. Lamplugh was an undistinguished bishop, but at least he had not taken part in the painful negotiations of the past few days. With a sudden gesture that was meant to be both generous in itself and conciliatory to the anglicans, James promoted him on the spot to the long-vacant throne of York.

William had established himself at Exeter on the 19th with a comparatively small part of his army—four battalions of infantry,* two regiments of cavalry, and the English contingent of refugees. The rest were quartered in outlying villages to the south. But this force was quite enough to make the entry to Exeter an impressive occasion which immediately provided matter for the Prince's printing press in the shape of *A letter from Exon to a Gentleman in London*. The pamphlet, which no doubt exaggerates the good order of the 200 English gentlemen headed by the Earl of Macclesfield and each accompanied by a negro servant, forms the basis of Macaulay's celebrated description of the event. Particular stress was laid on the formidable appearance of Marrewis's Scandinavian dragoons, with their black armour, bearskin caps, and 'flaming swords'.† But allowing for all

---

to express doubts about whether Pepys had carried out his task properly; one of many incidents demonstrating their lack of enthusiasm.
* Two battalions of his personal foot-guards, two English regiments (Talmash's and Babington's), the Garde du Corps and Marrewis's dragoons. Burnet describes the Prince's guard regiments as 'Switzers with fuzees', and it is quite possible that they were predominantly Swiss and German, rather than Dutch.
† 'He entered the city in as pompous a manner as the time and people would permit; which solemn entry was extolled and magnified at London, and a

hyperbole, the show was more striking than anything the capital of the west had seen for many years, and brought home to all who saw it that they were in the presence of seasoned troops and one of the greatest soldier-politicians of his own or any other time.

William stayed at Exeter for the better part of a fortnight, but in his case there were a number of sound reasons for apparent sluggishness at a time when thrust might have been expected. Probably the least of these was the comparative reluctance of English supporters to join his colours. Within a day or so of his arrival he was joined by the two Wharton contingents, which included the first elements of James's armed forces to desert, and by some senior officers of the Portsmouth garrison. And between the 22nd and the 24th elements of three of James's cavalry regiments came in under the command of Major Thomas Langston of the Rose Tavern group, Sir Francis Compton, and Lord Cornbury, whom William had snubbed so heartily a year or so before. These were accompanied by the leader of the powerful anglican clan of Bertie, the Earl of Abingdon. Abingdon was a most important acquisition, for in wealth and influence he stood head and shoulders above most of the peers William had brought with him; but Cornbury's desertion, for the moment, had the greatest moral effect.

Cornbury was Clarendon's son, and so, as nephew of James's first wife, virtually a member of the royal family. Although only twenty-eight, and a man of no particular ability, he was a full colonel, had sat for Wiltshire in James's parliament, and made a figure in his cousin Anne's circle, where he was Master of the Horse to her husband, George of Denmark. He must, therefore, be regarded as a catspaw of those who dominated Anne—namely the Churchills. The news of Cornbury's defection caused consternation in London where James was still lingering, despite his announced intention to set out for Salisbury on the 23rd. So shaken was he by the news that he put off his departure for another week; and the Austrian ambassador reported to Vienna

---

paper published with an account of the magnificence of it; adding such a terrible description of the Findland and Swiss Guards as made a strong impression on the vulgar'. Echard, L., *History of the Revolution and the Establishment of England in the Year 1688* (1725), p. 166.

that Cornbury's desertion 'has destroyed all hopes of the King's success'.*

These recruits may not have brought William much additional strength, but they provided what was much more important: information. It seems highly probably that very soon after arriving at Exeter William had assurances that he could depend on even more important desertions and insurrections than Cornbury's. One such, indeed, had broken out on the day of Cornbury's arrival at Exeter. Henry Booth, Lord Delamere, had risen in Cheshire and it is possible, though there is no direct evidence, that some of William's cruisers had now penetrated the Irish Sea to make contact with the Cheshire insurgents. The effect of Delamere's rising was to block the main port for Ireland, Chester.† William never committed himself unless he was confident and well informed, and on 26 November he wrote to Waldeck:

> The state of affairs here is as it was represented to me before my departure from Holland, and so I have grounds for hoping that, with the blessing of God, I shall succeed in this great affair.[5]

The conclusive reasons for William's long stay in Exeter were

---

* The moving spirit in the desertion, which was represented to the troops taking part as a raid, appears to have been Langston, who had been in touch during the spring with the Whartons and Talmash. Cornbury seems to have hesitated after setting out (at one point he 'hung an arse and sneaked away to Salisbury') and only joined William on the 24th. He played no further important part in the Revolution or subsequent politics. Langston became a colonel in 1693 and a brigadier general in 1704; and died in 1723. (See *Macphersons' Original Papers*, I, pp. 287 *et seq.*)

† Booth had not been a signatory of the invitation of the seven, nor was he an ally of Danby. His family, one of the most powerful in Cheshire, had a long tradition of non-conformity and armed intervention in politics. They had fought for the Parliament against Charles I, and Booth's father had sat in Cromwell's House of Commons before attempting an insurrection on behalf of Charles II in 1659—which earned him a peerage after the Restoration. But the Booths had become thoroughly involved in the opposition politics of 1679–83. Henry Booth was in many respects the archetype of a whig. He considered that there was a contract between King and people, and that the mixed constitution of King, Lords, and Commons was best so long as it guaranteed his liberty and property. But if this 'shall become precarious I will then be for any other form of government under which my liberty and property may be more secure, and until then I don't desire to change.' Since the head of the Gerard family—Charles, Earl of Macclesfield— was the senior nobleman accompanying William from Holland, two of the major interests in Cheshire were combined in support of William.

strictly operational. He had to assemble a transport column—the journey from the coast had been terribly hampered by the lack of wheels. But although the infantry and artillery were for the time being immobilised, the rest of the Orangist army had not been idle while the Prince held court in Exeter. The cavalry rapidly swept forward across the borders of Somerset and Dorset on to a line from Membury to Chard, with the advanced headquarters at Honiton, so that only about forty miles separated them and James's forward elements at Warminster. Here they were in a position to parry the manoeuvre that had been fatal to Monmouth—a bottling-up operation against the isthmus joining Devon to the mainland.

A halt was also necessary to eliminate any threat from the rear, where Plymouth was an important garrison for King James. This was dealt with by Edward Russell and Lord Leven's scratch regiment of refugees, who took the decorously reluctant surrender of James's commander, the Earl of Bath, on 28 November.* Plymouth promptly became William's principal naval base. By that date, therefore, William was effective master of the two southwestern counties; had established communication with the continent and with the main foci of support in England; had his army in a strong defensive position; and had blocked James's chief port for reinforcements from Ireland.

Simultaneously the basis of a formal political organisation for the Orangist party was being laid. This was the work of Edward Seymour, one of the most potent and experienced parliamentarians of the south-west, who had joined the Prince the day after Cornbury with his cousin, Portman. He had sat in every parliament since the Restoration and had twice been Speaker. His family pride was such that he corrected the Prince's welcome to him as a member of the Duke of Somerset's family with the grand observation that 'the Duke of Somerset belongs to my family'. Seymour was horrified to find that no formal association in support of the Prince yet existed, and promptly started one with the programme that it should not be dissolved until constitutional guarantees had been restored.†

---

* Bath is mentioned by Johnston as a possible signatory of the invitation. (Portland MSS, P.W.A. 2167).
† Johnston, who had accompanied William, subsequently appears as chief canvasser for the Association (*Clarendon Diary*, 5/15 December 1688).

Even now James might have turned the tables on William by convening a parliament. The bishops had urged it on him, and so did Clarendon and Rochester during the strange lull while William was gathering the threads together at Exeter and James was still hesitating in Whitehall. But a parliament, so long as William was in the country, meant negotiation, and the French ambassador was at this point remarkably successful in gaining the King's ear for the policy of active resistance that suited Louis' plans. The proposal for a parliament was finally made to James by an assembly of peers, in which Clarendon was conspicuous, on the day the King had resolved to leave for Salisbury. 'What you ask,' James told them, 'is what I passionately desire. I promise on the word of a King to call a legal and free parliament the moment the Prince of Orange shall depart. But how can you have a free parliament now that a foreign Prince at the head of a foreign force has it in his power to return a hundred members?'[6]

William had no intention of departing. He was considering memoranda from Burnet on the ecclesiastical promotions that should be made in the hour of victory, and the problem of whether it would be better to depose James or merely suspend him. Although William had been careful to wrap his public statements in language about the redress of grievances, and had assured his European allies that his intervention was entirely selfless, his objectives were clear to him. It was the policy of Louis that he should fight; it was the policy of the bulk of English politicians that he should negotiate, so that they might extract the maximum concessions from James and discard William when they had done so. To rational observers these seemed to be the alternatives. William's greatness as a politician is shown by his perception that the best road to power lay in neither fighting James nor negotiating with him. Nothing in William's conduct is more conspicuous than his avoidance of any meeting with his uncle. Such a meeting would inevitably have strengthened the hands of the compromising grandees, whom William already regarded as a more serious obstacle to his plans than the King.

James left for Salisbury at last on Sunday, 28 November, half-resolved to fight, and accompanied not only by his principal commanders but by the French ambassador. Before leaving he had ordered Dartmouth, who was still harbouring in the Downs, to take a more active role against Herbert, and on the 26th, after

several days' delay, the dithering English admiral had sailed
westwards to make his base at Spithead and perhaps seek out the
Dutch. But at once his misfortunes began all over again, his squadron was battered by contrary gales, his captains showed decreas-
ing enthusiasm, and altogether, as he put it, 'the Channell is
harder working than any battle'.[7] At one moment he had another
glimpse of the opposing fleet, which had been demonstrating
against Portsmouth, and 'sure I shall have some luck at last, for I
shall struggle all I can'.[8] The King showed extraordinary patience
with his admiral, assuring him repeatedly that he still had confidence in him; but the most significant news in the fleet was a
certificate from Captain George Churchill of the *Newcastle* that
his ship was unseaworthy. Churchill put into Plymouth and declared for the Prince while his brother, James's Lieutenant General, was travelling with his master to Salisbury.

Yet James still had an appearance of strength. He had a powerful fleet in being, and on land, even after allowing for the garrisons and the contingents still on the march to join him, his field
force of over 20,000 outnumbered William. Unfortunately,
apart from its French commander, Louis Duras, Earl of Feversham, there were very few senior officers in it who had not decided
to betray the King as soon as the right moment arrived. Kirk,
Trelawny, Grafton, Ormonde, George of Denmark, and Churchill
himself all had their plans completed and (in all likelihood) their
farewell letters written, before they left London. It was necessary
that this should be so, for certain events had to take place simultaneously in London and Salisbury. The assurances about what
would happen were contained in a letter from Anne to William
on the day the King took the Portsmouth Road, and it must have
reached William before he left Exeter.

James's mind seems to have revolved uselessly from the idea of
fighting to the idea of negotiation, and then always to have
returned to the need to preserve his son. Nothing had damaged his
self-confidence so much as the temporarily successful attack on
the genuineness of the Prince of Wales. All his attempts to answer
the doubters with affidavits and eye-witnesses (such as Jeffreys,
who cheerfully said he had seen the child 'piping hot') had simply
raised louder hoots of disbelief. He was being driven into a
position like that of a sane man trying to prove his sanity. And
similar disbelief greeted his repeated denials of an alliance with

Louis. For this he had only himself to blame: his constant inter-
views with Barillon, his appointment of a French general to command his army, the fact that Tyrconnel actually was in league
with France—all this made it impossible for people not to believe
he had not made an alliance which would clearly have been so
much in his interest. As if finally to confirm both these themes of
William's propaganda, he chose this moment to make arrangements for the five-month-old Prince of Wales to escape to France,
by sending him to Portsmouth and the custody of the Duke of
Berwick.

He had meant to hold a series of inspiriting reviews at Salisbury, but soon after his arrival he was overcome by an irre-
pressible bleeding from the nose which confined him to his room
for most of the four days he spent there. They were the days on
which the main trap was sprung beneath him. He had arrived
at Salisbury on Monday. On Wednesday, 1 December, the Earl
of Devonshire seized Nottingham, and on Thursday Danby
made himself master of York. A day or two later Hull and Carlisle, the other two main northern garrisons, were taken over by
insurgents. Simultaneously, on the Wednesday, William moved
his headquarters forward from Exeter to Honiton, and thence on
Thursday to Axminster, where he detached a powerful body of
cavalry under Bentinck to reconnoitre the crossings of the Stour
north-eastwards towards Wincanton. These were the troops that
on Friday morning ran into some of Sarsfield's Irish horse, and
the skirmish that followed produced almost the only casualties of
the campaign.

In the midst of all these blows James had discovered the trail
of treason in his own camp. It had led him to Kirk, who was
placed under arrest, and on the Friday evening he assembled
his chief officers having, in all probability, already resolved on
retreat. Withdrawal to a new defensive position on the Thames
was the advice of his commander in chief, Feversham: Churchill
and his confederates gave their votes for an aggressive strategy,
but their advice was solely for the record, and it was not accepted.
That night Churchill, Grafton, and a number of other officers
deserted to the Prince of Orange, leaving behind letters which
carefully blended affectionate loyalty with the dictates of their
consciences. George of Denmark, who had greeted each hammer-
blow with the cry of 'Est-ce possible?' did the same on the

following night when the retreat had reached Andover. William greeted Churchill cordially, and James, who mustered a wry joke on the disappearance of George, sent his son-in-law's carriages after him, observing that 'the loss of a good trooper would have been of more consequence'. But old Marshal Schomberg, who had served with professional loyalty in almost every army in Europe, was heard to say that Churchill was the first lieutenant-general he had ever known run from his colours. Schomberg had often changed masters, but never when he was in the field.

Anne had left her part until it was almost too late. The King was only a few hours' march from London when, accompanied by Sarah Churchill, she escaped from Whitehall through the door used for emptying her lavatory and was taken by Bishop Compton, the Earl of Dorset, and a party of dragoons by way of Epping to Nottingham, which was now the northern headquarters of the rising.

This massive movement of grandees, which is always made so prominent a feature of any account of the Revolution, may be thought to demonstrate that it was at bottom an aristocratic movement. But the consequences went far beyond the grandees, whether those who had taken the plunge or those who, like Clarendon, were now hesitating on the brink. For the most part the aristocratic officers of James's army did not take their men over with them, and James's regiments, many of them now now leaderless, began to dissolve. During December the south-east of England was covered with roving bands of deserters. Mob violence, directed principally at catholics or supposed catholics, broke out in London on 2 December, in Dover on 8 December, at Bury, and in Shropshire. Credit collapsed, and James's government was no longer able to borrow for immediate needs. William's army, now broadening its front from Bristol to Sherborne, was the one effective force in the country.

With James's retreat from Salisbury and the flight of Anne political manoeuvre once more takes over from military force. It was no longer a question of whether William's intervention would succeed: it had succeeded. The two great issues for which William stood—the alignment of Britain against France in the European struggle, and the check to James's centralising policy—were now both guaranteed. That much had been finally settled by James's incapacity at Salisbury and the brief crackle of carbines at Wincanton. In many ways the most effective decision James made on arriving back in London was his withdrawal of any attempt to control communications between London and the West, which had been imposed as soon as William's landing was known. Clarendon was one of those who decided to take early advantage of the changed situation and visit Wiltshire, partly to make a political reconnaissance of William's camp, but partly also to do some canvassing for his son Lord Cornbury among the Wiltshire gentry against what he foresaw would be an early general election.

William and the Politicians

The day James returned to London and almost burst into tears on the news of his daughter's desertion, William advanced gently to Crewkerne, where he found waiting for him the Vice-Chancellor of Oxford, offering the university's welcome and the use of college plate for the cause. But it would be a gross oversimplification to say that the greater part of anglican England had declared for William. The Lords who had risen with Danby and Devonshire had been careful not to place themselves under William's orders, and had left the way open for a compromise. They were, Danby explained to the Governor of York, 'in arms for a free Parliament, and for the preservation of the Protestant religion and government as by law established, which the King had very near destroyed, and which the Prince of Orange was come to *assist* them to defend'. When Reresby replied that he too was a parliamentarian and a protestant 'but I was also for the King', Danby said they were for the King too.[1] This was not mere constitutional juggling with words. For the temporarily militant anglican politicians the most satisfactory outcome of the whole business would have been a James reduced to docility, or his resignation in favour of one of his daughters. There were denizens of William's camp who were most unwelcome. 'I met Wildman in the street,' noted Clarendon distastefully during his visit to Salisbury; and soon afterwards he and the Earl of Abingdon were shaking their heads over the Wildmans and Fergusons 'and several other persons, who, he found, were of their principles'.[2]

Clarendon and Abingdon need not have been so anxious about the relics of commonwealth fanaticism and democracy. William had little use for them (though he had a good deal for the champions of the Exclusionist movement of nine years earlier). But the success of the invasion necessarily raised the expectations of those who had worked so hard and risked so much to mount it. A large share of the rewards had been earned by Bentinck, Zuylestein, and Schomberg, by Johnston, Carstares, Hutton, and Burnet; and above all, by William himself. The struggle of November between William and James was over: that of December and January was between William and the politicians, with James's future as one of the issues.

On returning to London James had made almost every concession the politicians could ask. In the afternoon of 7 December, the morrow of Anne's disappearance, he held a meeting of some forty peers in his dining room at Whitehall and announced that on reflection he had abandoned his objections to a parliament while William was in the country, and would summon one for 25 January. He would also issue a free pardon to all William's supporters, and would open negotiations with William about the arrangements under which the proposed parliament should be held. He even promised to consider the removal of all catholics from office. The writs for the new parliament were prepared, though not issued, by Jeffreys in the next few days, and on 10 December the negotiations with William were entrusted to Halifax, Nottingham, and Godolphin. But so confused was the situation that they did not set out on their mission for nearly a week.

Between the time these concessions were decided and the commissioners appointed an event occurred which has never been fully explained, but had a marked effect at a critical moment. On 8 December there appeared in the streets of London a 'Third Declaration of the Prince of Orange', which, unlike its restrained and dignified predecessors, bitterly denounced the catholics and gave notice that catholics captured in arms by William's forces would receive no quarter. The language was harsh and clearly implied that the country was menaced by a catholic conspiracy. William promptly repudiated it, but this is no proof that it did not emanate from his mobile printing press. It struck just the note that was needed to release the passions of the mob and frighten James's last reliable supporters into flight. Petre, Jeffreys, and Brent all prepared for escape. There are signs that it was from this moment that James himself turned away from compromise, just as he had turned away from armed resistance.*

While James was announcing his concessions to the peers in London, William, now at Sherborne, was opening communication with James's fleet, in the person of Lieutenant Byng, who had obtained leave from Lord Dartmouth to go ashore at Gosport 'on pretence of going into Huntingdonshire upon affairs that very much concerned him'.³ Byng reached Sherborne on the 9th after an adventurous journey disguised as a farmer, and delivered letters from the Orangist officers in Dartmouth's fleet. William sent him back the same day to Portsmouth with an invitation to the admiral to place his fleet under William's command and an assurance that this would be 'an act so commendable that it will not only oblidge me for ever to be your friend, but even to study which way I may show my kindness to you in the most particular manner'.⁴ Byng somewhat exaggerates in saying that this was a promise not to promote Herbert over Dartmouth's head in a new order of things, but it was as near such a commitment as William usually came in such circumstances.

Dartmouth did not receive this letter for some time: its delivery presented a problem which was only solved by leaving it anonymously in his cabin. He certainly had not read it when he received two letters from James, both dated on the day William wrote from Sherborne. One of these in effect told Dartmouth to avoid any further hostilities and 'preserve his squadron'. The other, which showed only too plainly the pitiful indecision into which James had fallen, instructed him to transport the Prince of Wales to the nearest French port and then cancelled the instruction in a postscript. Dartmouth, who comes so badly out of the Revolution as an admiral, emerges at this point quite well as an adviser. His reply to James refusing to be 'the unhappie instrument of so apparent ruine to your Majestie, and my country as an act of this kinde will be' was clearly written from both heart and head. 'Pray, Sir, consider farther on this weightie point, for can the Prince's being sent to France have other prospect than the entaileing a perpetuall warre upon your nation and posterity, and

---

* Credit for this Declaration was later claimed by Hugh Speke, a double agent whom James had planted in the Orangist camp at Exeter. He then, at the behest of William, fed his original employer with exaggerated accounts of the strength and success of the invaders.

giving France a temptation to molest, invade, nay hazard the conquest of England, which I hope in God never to see.'⁵ But James was already resolved on flight. Those who were too closely identified with the old policy to hope for anything under the new were already vanishing. While Dartmouth was writing his appeal to the King, Jeffreys was surrendering the great seal and Rizzini, the Modenese envoy, was urging the Queen's flight. On 12 December James completed the arrangements for her to leave. The delay of five days before she did so was due to the need to get the Prince of Wales back from Portsmouth.

With the King committed to concessions and contemplating flight; and the whole political world trying to get its bearings on a new régime, the three commissioners appointed to deal with William were acting only nominally on behalf of James. So far as they represented anyone but themselves, Halifax, Godolphin, and Nottingham spoke for the uncommitted part of the nation, and in their minds James's personal future was a matter of no more than tactical interest.

William had stayed at Sherborne for three days—longer than at any stopping-place since Exeter—and had then moved forward again by way of James's deserted headquarters at Salisbury to Hungerford, which he reached on 17 December. He was acting with much greater confidence now. The assurances brought by Byng had allowed him to issue definite orders for the return of the transport fleet to Holland. The army was far ahead, brigaded now, and no longer deployed for possible battle. The main body was streaming over the Berkshire Downs into the Thames Valley. Von Birckenfeldt's infantry were quartered in Great and Little Bedwin, and Marrewis's black-armoured horsemen were at Newbury. Ginckel's heavy dragoons had pushed as far ahead as Abingdon on the road for Oxford, where William was planning to make his next major halt. At Reading, on the southern flank of the advance, Nassau met some resistance from Irish and Scottish troops who disputed the Thames crossing at Caversham; but it was soon over. The Irish fell back, and the Scots, after deposing their officers, went over to the other side under the command of a sergeant and two corporals who had formerly served in one of William's Scottish regiments. William's promptness in reward was shown by his order that the three should be given immediate commissions, and the whole battalion a month's pay in advance.

The commissioners met William at Hungerford on 18 December, ostensibly to discuss the arrangements under which a free parliament could be held. But the more significant transaction at Hungerford was William's reference to an assembly of his principal English followers for advice, and the debate which followed on whether it was desirable at this moment to convene a parliament at all. The emigré element were for putting it off until they had time to accumulate some parliamentary interest, while the home-based magnates who had joined William were for assembling it at once. In deciding between them William made the first purely English political decision of his career. He knew, because Halifax had disclosed it to Burnet, that James was thinking about flight: it followed that to oppose the parliament James had now agreed to call would be the one move that might enable James to recover. As William put it—deleting the proposal that the calling of a parliament should be postponed—'We may drive away the King, but perhaps we may not know how easily to come by a Parliament.'[6] They were words which a few days later came back to Clarendon with overwhelming force.

James had perhaps genuinely been in the mood to fight, and if need be die, at the head of his troops when he set out for Salisbury three weeks before. He had made his will, and it had been witnessed by the nine men on whom the functioning of his government depended—Jeffreys, the Lord Chancellor, Melfort and Preston, the two Secretaries of State, two leading catholic peers (Arundell and Belasis); and four men who were essentially senior officials: Pepys, Godolphin, Bridgeman, and Blathwayte. This core of central government had begun to crumble soon after the retreat from Salisbury. Melfort had disappeared; catholic advisers were clearly no longer to be acceptable; Jeffreys began to pack and send his furniture to the country on 8 December—the day of the 'Third Declaration' and Clarendon's quiet departure for the other side. Petre had vanished, so had Brent. The papal nuncio, d'Adda, was already on the wing. From the time of his return to London James's closest advisers were the French ambassador and the representatives of the small Italian states attached to Maria Beatrice's interest.

On their advice, and while the Hungerford conference was still in progress, he sent the Queen and the Prince of Wales to France, and probably decided that he himself would soon follow them. 'I am at ease,' he wrote feelingly to Dartmouth on 20 December, 'now I have sent them away.'[7] A new role—the last of the self-deceptions by which he concealed his personal inadequacies—was now stealing over him. The far-sighted, strong-minded man of affairs was becoming the saintly monarch who has discarded an ungrateful nation, a second royal martyr, who, this time, would live to reproach his enemies. The Jesuit father Con, writing to his superior in Rome, took an unkinder, and truer view of the reasons for the collapse: the imprudence, avarice, and ambition of James's catholic advisers; the weakness, dishonesty, and corruption of the ministers; and the inadequacy of the hier-archy, especially the Nuncio, whom he describes as 'un Giovan-etto, un bel *coram vobis* per far l'amore alle donne'.*

From the point of view of his new character James made the immediate mistake of commenting publicly that William's terms were better than he had expected. They provided that Portsmouth, the Tower of London, and Tilbury (James's sole remaining strong points) should be put in neutral hands; release of all prisoners held by James; disbanding of all catholic troops in James's army;† financial support for William's forces; and either joint occupation or mutual absence by Prince and King from London during the holding of parliament. On the afternoon of 20 December James presided over a meeting of peers and notables assembled to consider these conditions, and managed to prolong the discussion until evening required an adjournment. Late that night he wrote anguished letters to his naval and military com-manders declaring his intention to withdraw from the kingdom. Such of his ships as remained loyal should, he directed, report to Tyrconnel. The rest of his forces should cease all resistance, though he expressed the hope that they would not actively sup-port William. He then ordered the destruction of all the parlia-mentary writs except the fifteen which had already issued, and having done everything a chief executive could do to make

* 'A trivial young man, a fine fop for making love to ladies' (*Clarendon Diary*, Appendix, Vol. II, p. 470).
† Not, of course, in William's. Quite a number of his troops were catholics, but as one of them said, 'though his soul was God's, his sword was the Prince of Orange's'.

matters difficult for his successors he retired, partly by water and
partly by post-horse, to Emley Ferry, a small harbour on the
north coast of Kent, where he had arranged for a yacht to take
him to the Continent.

It was only two years since he had exclaimed with such passion
against the idea of being a vassal of France. Now he was passing
into the mechanical grip of Louis. Maria Beatrice was to feel it
first. 'His Majesty commanded me,' wrote Louvois shortly after
her arrival at Boulogne to his agent there, 'to tell you that even
if the King of England were to write to the Queen to return,
either alone or with the Prince of Wales, to England . . . his intention would still be that you should bring the Queen and the
Prince of Wales to Vincennes.'[8]

Yet William, dictating his terms from Hungerford, was by no
means in so strong a position as showed on the surface. His war-
chest, depleted by the policy of paying for his supplies, was beginning to run low—whence the demand for support payments
in the Hungerford terms. And the news from the Continent, which
was now just beginning to reach him, was disturbing. Fagel, on
whom he depended to keep the republic firmly in hand, was
dying (he died on the day Halifax and his fellow-commissioners
arrived), and William, writing to Waldeck, was 'so étourdi that
I do not know what to say'. Political affairs in the Netherlands
were being badly managed, and 'if they can't find a better method
while I'm away, I'm afraid they'll do very badly'.[9] It was clear
that the Continent was very soon going to need his undivided
attention. He must have carried on with his plan of campaign in
England, which now meant turning northwards towards Oxford
to make junction with the insurrection in the Midlands, with an
anxious heart.

Just as Pope Innocent's war with the Turks can be called the
last of the Crusades, so the gatherings of noblemen and notables
as the magic monarchy dissolves are reminiscent of a pattern two
and a half centuries earlier. Two loose assemblies of notables, one
advising William on his progress towards Oxford, the other abandoned by James at Whitehall, constituted at this moment the
political leadership of the nation. They were far from constituting
two parties. The distribution of political views between the two
was almost random: traditionalist anglicans were strongly represented in William's camp, and former exclusionists (the nearest

test one can apply for whiggery) were among the notables who assembled in London on 21 December to learn that the King had vanished.*

Most of the politically active notables at this moment were peers, and those who were not (with the exception of the Lord Mayor and Aldermen of London, who were treated as a national authority in this moment of crisis) were important landowners, such as Seymour among the tories and Wharton among the whigs. But the peerage had begun to acquire a certain senatorial character. The bishops were certainly senatorial, and there were also many temporal peers who had been raised to the House of Lords by Charles and James for military or political services. The brief interval following the disappearance of James was the supreme moment in modern English history for a peerage which was itself in process of transformation; and this momentary predominance, perhaps, helped to prolong the vigour and political importance of the peerage into the two succeeding centuries. Alone among hereditary peerages it was to be able to turn its back on its feudal origins without sinking into dependence on a centralised monarchy.†

The notables whose meeting James had adjourned before his flight assembled that morning at the Guildhall and put Sancroft in the chair: they were to meet daily for the rest of the week. There was no question now of considering William's terms or of maintaining the semblance of a negotiation with him. The political conclusion of that day was a declaration by the self-constituted committee of peers condemning James's flight (which they termed 'desertion') and resolving 'to apply themselves to the Prince of

* Old Lord Wharton, for instance, remained in London throughout the crisis, while his two sons were with William. The same was true of the Earl of Bedford and the Marquess of Winchester.

† The membership of the London gathering may be taken as the twenty-three who signed the letter of 11/21 December to Dartmouth ordering the cessation of hostilities. Five were bishops (Canterbury, York, Winchester, Rochester and Peterborough). Echard (195) implies a few more members of this gathering, making them twenty-seven (22 temporal peers and 5 bishops). There were at this stage at least a dozen peers in William's camp. Disregarding catholics and peers regarded as wholly compromised with the regime (e.g. Sunderland, Jeffreys) the effective peerage mustered about 100 (see K. H. D. Haley, *English Historical Review*, April 1954, which analyses the survey of the peerage made for Dijkvelt's visit in 1687). The three nuclei—London, those with William, and those with Danby at Nottingham—must have amounted to about half this number, currently providing national leadership

Orange, who had with great kindness, vast expense, and much hazard' undertaken the delivery of the nation from popery and arbitrary power. In the meantime they would work for a free parliament, security for the Church of England, due liberty for protestant dissenters, and 'the support of the Protestant Religion and Interest over the whole world'.[10] They also took a number of urgent executive measures. A letter was sent to Dartmouth ordering him to cease hostilities; catholics were ordered to be removed from the armed forces and disarmed; Lord Ranelagh, the Paymaster-General, was despatched to William with instructions to take his pleasure about the payment of his troops. Hales, the catholic commander of the Tower, was replaced.* At a separate meeting of military commanders it was decided that all the troops in London should place themselves under William's orders.

William was at Abingdon when he received the news that James had fled. He turned at once away from the consolidating movement on Oxford which was the logical completion of securing the line of the Thames. Clarendon saw him that day dining at Wallingford, and noted that even William was unable to conceal his delight. The decision of the Lords merely 'to apply' to him was not entirely satisfactory, but apart from that it must at that moment have seemed to him that the struggle was all but over. What must have been almost his first act on hearing the news was to write to Danby, whom he was to have joined at Oxford, telling him to disband his irregular forces. William was thinking of the sort of 'rusty ruffians' whom Clarendon was to see a day or two later, controlling the traffic over Magdalen Bridge. But the Prince made a significant addition to his letter. The gentlemen to whom he owed so much should now use their parliamentary influence, 'keeping their inclination for me'.[11]

The messages from James and from the Lords of the Guildhall were not the only letters received on 23 December by Lord Dartmouth. He also had one from his wife, who vividly paints the chaos into which things in London were now falling:

> I knowe my deare hart this juncture of time is very amaseing to everybody throughout this nation and must be so pertickelery to you upon all accounts . . . Lord Chandseler is prisoner in the Tower . . . indeed this town as bin mighty

* He had in fact fled with James, as his sole companion.

unquiat since the King's departure, by pulling the chappels
down and houses of papists and imbassadors, so that everybody is in great frights, and wish for the Prince of Oringe's
coming to quiat things.[12]

There had been ugly pillaging and hooliganism on the night of
the 21st, directed against the property of anyone whom the mob
of roughs and apprentices took to be catholic. The Spanish embassy had been a particular sufferer, in spite of Spain's alliance
with William. William had shown his insight into English politics
when he had refused the well-meant offer of the Governor of the
Spanish Netherlands to accompany the invasion. The ambassador
had to be rescued from his wrecked embassy by troops and lodged
in Whitehall free of charge by the committee of peers, while a
profuse apology was sent to Madrid. It was said privately that
indignation about unpaid bills had as much to do with the attack
on the Spanish embassy as the tradition of the Armada.

But worse was to follow. On the 22nd James's military commander, Lord Feversham, whose headquarters were now at
Uxbridge, had decided the King's valedictory letter required him
to disband as many of his troops as he could reach, in order to
avoid their being added to William's strength; and then to lay
down his command. After writing William his personal surrender he discharged about 4,000 men, mostly Irish, who joined
the already numerous bands of leaderless soldiery roving the
south-east corner of England. To Londoners this was equivalent
to the release of a band of savages, and the news bred the panic—
not only in London but in many other towns—known as the
'Irish night'. All night the streets were ablaze with light and
crowded with people in momentary expectation of massacre.
On the following day the shaken committee of Lords at the Guildhall authorised the local militia to fire on rioters if necessary,
the guards were ordered to stand to arms in St James's Park, and
the artillery which had so recently made the journey to Salisbury
and back was dragged out from the Tower and mounted at Hyde
Park Corner and Charing Cross.

William had been very angry with Feversham. 'I am not to be
thus dealt with' was his curt way of expressing it, and Churchill
was at once commissioned to round up and remarshal as many of
the disbanded troops as he could.[13] William was by now at

Henley, and it was there, in the middle of the night, that a lawyer named Nappleton arrived with the information that James was still in the country. His stranded boat had been seized by a party of self-appointed frontier guards, and he was now the prisoner of a mob of fishermen at Faversham, on the Dover Road.

It was the same kind of situation as the false start from the Texel, and William showed the same cool, adaptable persistence as the canal boatman he had watched long ago and described to Sir William Temple. He pressed on towards London, sending word ahead of him to the Lords of the Guildhall that although they had not invited him to occupy the capital the City Corporation had done so, and he was complying with their wishes. On Christmas Eve by continental reckoning, and 14 December by the insular calendar,* he established himself in Windsor Castle, where the whig portion of his retinue still talked eagerly about James's 'abdication' and the possibility that a new parliament would now be summoned 'on Cromwell's model', sending shudders down the spines of such magnates as Clarendon.[14]

The 15/25 December—William's first full day at Windsor— was a Sunday, and it was towards the evening of that day that a thoroughly exhausted Lord Feversham arrived at the castle with a message from James. Feversham had been indefatigable since disbanding his forces at Uxbridge four days earlier. In that time he had made and revoked a decision to retire into private life, and accepted a commission from the Lords at the Guildhall to ride with a body of guards three-quarters of the way to Dover and rescue James. The letter he now brought from James had been written at Rochester, and said that he proposed to return to London where, he suggested, he and William should meet on Monday to reach an agreement. It was almost the first sensible thing James had done during his reign. William countered it with a pair of decisions which once more cleared his way to the throne. He committed Feversham to prison; and sent Zuylestein, the resourceful dragoon, to London with a letter acknowledging James's suggestion, requesting time to consider it, but saying he could not come to London until it was clear of James's forces. In the meantime he suggested James should remain at Rochester. The letter did not mention that Feversham had been detained.

* From this point onwards dates are given in the combined Old and New Styles, instead of in the New Style.

One thought was still uppermost in William's mind: he must not have a personal meeting with his uncle.

James received this letter on Sunday evening, once more in his old palace of Whitehall. He had been through a most extraordinary week since setting out for exile on Monday night. He can have had little sleep. Monday night had been spent riding to the coast of the Swale, Tuesday night cooped up in the customs hoy while amateur coastguards searched his pockets and accused him of being a Jesuit in disguise. Throughout Wednesday he had been imploring his captors to let him continue his journey. He seems to have been convinced that William would have him executed, and preached what was virtually a sermon, lasting half an hour, on the text that 'he who is not with me is against me'. To one of his audience, more sympathetic than the rest, he protested his good intentions and asked 'What have I done? What are the errors of my reign?' to which 'you may be sure I answered nothing'. But later his spirits seemed to revive. He managed to communicate with London, and was better lodged. He chatted, unwisely, with those present about the wonders of St Winefrede's Well and a fragment of the True Cross which he had unfortunately lost.[15] But he had momentarily regained his nerve, and when he returned to London on Sunday morning he was surprised and delighted to be met by cheering bystanders. Once in his palace he began to take up the threads of government, and held a privy council, which sanctioned a proclamation against riots. This was the situation when Zuylestein arrived at Whitehall.

James was conciliatory. He would retire to Rochester if that would suit William, but in the meantime he hoped William would come to London where St James's would be made ready for him, and a conference could take place. Zuylestein made no attempt to negotiate—his mission was one of reconnaissance: he only said, with a darkness that was no doubt deliberate, that he did not think William would come to London until all James's troops had been withdrawn. Then, accepting a letter from James to William, he withdrew to leave the King to learn, a few minutes later, that the earlier envoy, Feversham, had been made a prisoner.

William held a meeting at Windsor on the following morning to decide what should be done next. The situation was a disturbing one: the willingness of the Guildhall junta to rescue James and bring him back to London after they had 'applied' to William; the refusal of Sancroft to act as chairman of the junta as soon as he learned James was still in England; the friendly welcome given to James by the London crowd: all this pointed to the possibility of a negotiated settlement in which James would be able to balance his unquestionable rights against William's military strength. He must avoid meeting James, and he must also, if he could, implicate the English politicians in that refusal and in the pressure which must now be exerted to cause James's final withdrawal from the political scene.

The arrest of Feversham on Saturday 15/25 December and the Windsor meeting two days later demonstrate William's tactical skill at its very highest; and during the intervening day he was already carrying himself as a king, in supreme control of events. He ordered Dartmouth back to the Nore, kept the satrap of Wales, the great Duke of Beaufort, kicking his heels for more than an hour before he would receive him, snubbed the Earl of Rochester, and gave an audience, in his most frigid manner, to a deputation of Irish peers. He also had a long, private interview with two of the most experienced House of Commons parliamentarians in England, Henry Powle and Sir Robert Howard. In view of what happened later, this interview assumes great significance.

Neither Powle nor Howard had sat in James's parliament of 1685; but apart from that their parliamentary experience went back to the Cavalier Parliament, which Howard had entered at the Restoration, and Powle in 1671. Both had played a prominent part in the Exclusion controversy against James; and both were political opponents of Danby. Powle was a barrister, a master of parliamentary procedure, and a skilled debater. Barillon, in the days when he was subsidising the opposition to Charles II, had thought him fit for the highest offices, and had arranged a substantial payment for him from French secret service funds. But both Powle and Howard were extremely well off and well connected in their own rights. Powle, as his second wife, had married the widow of the Earl of Dorset—herself the daughter of the great Lionel Cranfield of James I's reign.* Howard, under the

* And so stepfather to the reigning Earl of Dorset, Charles Sackville. Dorset had been Bishop Compton's partner in organising the escape of Anne from Whitehall—he was in fact married to Compton's niece.

Restoration régime, had been for some years Secretary of the Treasury, and held the valuable life office of Auditor of the Exchequer, besides being a substantial landed proprietor in Norfolk, and a son of Thomas Howard, Earl of Berkshire. The political activity of both men, during the last two or three years, had been obscure, though there is no evidence that they were concerned in the Revolutionary conspiracy itself. It is reasonable to infer that William's business with these two veteran whigs was concerned with the arrangements for the forthcoming parliament.

One may suspect, therefore, that when William met the peers at Windsor on 27 December, he had some inklings of a possible parliamentary plan. We do not know the exact composition of the meeting, but it included Halifax, who had come from London the previous day, Clarendon, who attended at William's special invitation but arrived late, Mordaunt, Delamere, Shrewsbury, and, probably, Bishop Lloyd of St Asaph. They were told that Zuylestein had failed to make contact with James, that James had invited William to London, and that William considered the King would not be safe there. The advice they gave was that James should be advised to leave London and stay at Ham House, in Richmond. This direction, Halifax suggested, should be transmitted by the commander of William's household troops, Count Solms. William thought otherwise. He would sign the letter containing the message, but 'by your favour my lord, it is the advice of the peers here, and some of yourselves shall carry it'.[16] Without giving them time to recover, he nominated Shrewsbury, Halifax, and Delamere as the emissaries; and so it was that the Trimmer who had set out ten days before as James's ambassador to William, found himself returning, with three battalions of William's guards, as the agent for what was in effect the deposition of James. Count Solms was also of the party, carrying orders to take over the guard posts in Whitehall.

It was raining heavily when they reached Westminster late on Monday night. The Imperial ambassador, Hoffmann, watching from his window, saw Solms's guards marching through St James's Park about ten o'clock. The English sentries, after a brief parley, during which Solms made it clear that his orders were to use force if need be,* were quietly withdrawn, and William's

---

* Rapin graphically describes how the Dutch guards, with matches burning, were drawn up fifteen paces from James's guard (Vol. X, p. 149).

commissioners entered the palace about midnight, where they woke the King up with their message. At almost the same moment, and a few hundred yards away, Dr Tenison and Dr Symon Patrick were 'discoursing' in Patrick's parlour in Westminster cloisters, when 'one knocked at the door, and in came the Bishop of St Asaph', dripping with rain.[17] He announced that he had already been at Lambeth, where a meeting under Sancroft had commissioned him to arrange an early interview between the bishops and the Prince, who was now on his way to London. He probably also related, though Patrick does not record it, that James was now virtually a prisoner. The King had, in fact, been told that he was to be ready to leave by nine o'clock the following morning, since William intended to be in London by midday.

So James at last departed, and with rather more dignity on the second occasion than on the first. Halifax, embarrassed for perhaps the only time in his life, had behaved almost rudely at the bedside interview, but Delamere, who regarded James as having already abdicated, was more considerate, and Shrewsbury seems to have exhibited his usual extraordinary talent for taking the emotion out of great constitutional moments. Punctually at nine next morning, accompanied by a company of picked Dutch guards, James made his way once more by barge towards Rochester. The guards were all catholics, but they also had their orders, which were to let James slip away to France as soon as he could do so with certainty: which, after a few days, he did. William, who had spent the critical night a few miles away at Sion House, Chiswick, entered the capital towards evening on Tuesday, 18/28 December. The bells were rung, and there were excited crowds in the streets waving oranges impaled on sticks. But they did not see William, who made his way inconspicuously across the Park to St. James's.

The Revolution

It is easy to feel that the politically creative phase of the Revolution, which now began, followed a natural—almost a predestined path. William's deliberate unobtrusiveness during the two months following his victory has enabled a picture to be drawn of a nation solemnly resettling its affairs in freedom from all external pressures. The great constitutional debate of the early months of 1689 appears to turn on legal issues: but underlying these legal issues were immediate political realities, domestic and external. However uncommunicative William might appear to the English public, he was as much preoccupied with these realities as anyone. There was the question of internal order and of the continuity of legal authority, even if only provisional; there were the two other kingdoms over which James had ruled, and his dominions in America, which Louis was already planning to invade from Canada; and all this had to be settled against the background of the developing continental war, and the question of what part England should play in it.

In the problem of restoring order one urgent need was to stem the tide of anti-romanism that had been whipped up by the folly of James and the propaganda of his opponents. William's personal tolerance was here strengthened by political motives. Anti-catholic excesses would be most unpleasing to some of his most important allies—notably the Emperor, and Spain. On 28 December Waldeck was relaying to William Dijkvelt's warning about how the catholic powers were watching the situation: 'I hope your Highness will have enough power to prevent the anxieties against the Papists.'¹ The papal nuncio, d'Adda, who had been caught, much as James had been, trying to slip out of the country disguised as a footman in the suite of the Modenese envoy, was released on William's orders and provided with a diplomatic passport on which to retire respectably. Two catholic peers who had been imprisoned, Langdale and Montgomery, were set at liberty. Very soon after arriving in London William made a well-publicised visit to Charles II's widow, Catherine of Braganza, to pay his respects; and on her saying how much she missed her Lord Chamberlain, Feversham, James's old commander-in-chief was also released, his imprisonment having served its purpose. Even the two catholic vicars-general, Leyburn and Bonaventure Giffard, and Robert Brent, all of whom had fallen into the net during the days of chaos, were allowed quietly to disappear abroad after a few months of imprisonment, and if Jeffreys himself had not conveniently died during January, he too might have been permitted to slip into obscurity so far as William was concerned.

All the more striking is it, therefore, that William's unobtrusive empiricism succeeded in preserving the notion of 'the protestant interest' as essentially synonymous with opposition to France in the continental struggle. George of Denmark (in the farewell letter to James which can scarcely have been of his own composition) had used the phrase to describe the grounds on which he was going over to William; and it appears again in the cautious 'application' of the Guildhall Lords on 21 December, where they specifically refer to the need to support and encourage 'the Protestant Religion and Interest over the whole world'. It is likely that William had read those words with more satisfaction than any others in the message.²

The revulsion against France was not merely a matter of abstract ideology. It was in the minds of all literate Englishmen. Throughout the constitutional debates of January and February news of the French devastations in the Rhineland was reinforcing the impression made by the revocation of the Edict of Nantes:

'Vous pouvez compter,' wrote the Comte de Tessé to Louvois in February, 'que rien du tout n'est resté du superbe château d'Heidelberg. Il y avait, hier à midi, outre le château, quatre cent trente-deux maisons brûlées . . .'³

In coming years the 'poor palatines' were to displace the huguenots as the Englishman's most favoured refugees.

Legitimate authority was cobbled up by skilful recourse to the precedents of 1660—in itself a decision of far-reaching consequence, since it pointed to continuity of form, as against novelty. There was no more talk of a reversion to Cromwell's electoral system. On 21/31 December, four days after William's arrival in London, the Lords, to the number of about ninety, assembled in their own House 'at the Prince's request' and two days later passed a resolution asking him to take over the administration until a Convention could be assembled. The Lords were in a touchy mood over this, as Halifax, their chairman, recorded. Having tasted executive power in their own right, they were disposed to vote only a grudging tribute to William for having convened them: they felt they could have convened themselves, and summons by anyone but a King reflected on their 'birthright which might be prejudiced'. Halifax also noted, with weary cynicism, that 'the words "lives and fortunes" were so worn out that they were not fit to be used in the Thanks &c'. But with an even greater indifference the Lords refused to receive James's second farewell letter, which was bravely produced by the Earl of Middleton. Godolphin, that far-sighted official who had avoided any overt breach with James, assured his fellow-peers that he had read it, and it contained nothing of interest.[4]

The peers' invitation was presented to William on Christmas Day, and he received it rather coolly. He would not, he said, give his reply, until he had heard the views of the Commons, which he was contriving to get by another Restoration precedent. Just as Monk had reassembled those who had sat in the Long Parliament, William had summoned, for Boxing Day, all those who had sat in the House of Commons under Charles II—membership of James II's Parliament, significantly, did not qualify. One cannot avoid detecting the hands of Powle and Howard. The result was an assembly of about a hundred and sixty, to which a contingent of City aldermen and councillors was added. Powle took the chair. This body addressed William in the same sense as the Lords, adding the interesting rider that William's 'circular letters' for elections to the Convention should, so far as counties were concerned, be addressed to coroners. The sheriffs were regarded as tainted by James's manipulations.*

William punctiliously avoided any act that could be described as governmental until these formalities had been completed; but before the end of the year he had constituted a kind of provisional government and made some notable uses of his new authority. His new foreign office was in effect provided from Holland, whence Dijkvelt, Odijk, and Witsen arrived on Boxing Day—a sure sign that William had decided to establish the headquarters of the coalition against Louis in London. Two Secretaries were also appointed, one for English, the other for Irish affairs. The Secretary for England was William Jephson, the colonel who had been among the first to join William at Exeter, and who, through his brother-in-law Symon Patrick, had a direct link with the whiggish wing of the Anglican Church. The Secretary for Ireland was William Harbord, an exile and former Exclusionist, who had accompanied William from Holland. Scottish affairs, one may guess, were already in the hands of Carstares and Johnston. The rest of the government machine was restored to life by an immediate proclamation confirming all officials (including even Pepys) in their posts until further order. Immediate steps, however, were taken to replace unreliable or catholic officers in the armed forces, and on 30 December a lengthy list of military promotions was issued.

In only one respect can it be said that William anticipated his new authority, but it could hardly have been a more emphatic step in British foreign policy. On 21/31 December he broke off diplomatic relations with France by requesting Barillon to leave the country within twenty-four hours. It was none too soon, for the unwearying French ambassador was already applying himself to the manipulation of political opinion. He was seen on board ship by a huguenot of William's entourage, who could not resist asking, as they rode together towards Dover, whether Barillon could have believed he would be travelling in such company. By his departure one of the most important figures in the London political word was eliminated.

It is one of the paradoxes of the election which now took place

* This assembly, after prescribing the form of the election it had ordered, and enabling its members to subscribe to the Association of Exeter, dispersed on 28 December/7 January.

that much of the work of James's electoral agents survived him to assist his opponent. In so far as Brent's regulators had encouraged dissenting interests in the constituencies, those interests were now at the service of whiggish candidates favouring toleration for all protestants and the establishment of William at the head of affairs.* This surviving, and to some extent artificial, strength of the dissenters helped to counterbalance the absence of the usual exertion of government influence, for which the machinery was temporarily clogged. Nevertheless, it was an advantage for a candidate to have been associated with William, and a disadvantage to have been too closely identified with James. Officials of the old régime, such as Pepys and Gwyn, were not returned; and failure to subscribe to the Exeter Association was a grave handicap to a candidate.† The loyalist Musgraves of Westmorland and Cumberland retained only two of the six seats in their sphere of influence. But the political exiles who had come over with William did well. Wildman was returned, and so was Harbord—Harbord, indeed, for three different places.

William himself, however, certainly did not put himself at the head of an electoral machine. He had other matters to occupy him. Clarendon found that when he applied to see the Prince it was one of William's 'writing days' which he devoted to European affairs. But he was also preoccupied with Ireland and Scotland.[5]

Even before arriving in London William had been beset by deputations from the Anglo-Irish, and Whitehall was thronged with Irish protestant landlords and politicians. Their personal and financial anxieties were reflected in the determination of the

* An interesting example is Abingdon, where the recorder, Thomas Medlicot, who had dissenting sympathies, defeated the anglican Sir John Stonhouse, whose family had held the seat since the Restoration. Medlicot had been dismissed from his recordership in 1686, and had been restored to it again in furtherance of the Indulgence policy. He survived as M.P. only till 6 May 1689, when Stonhouse managed to unseat him on petition, and defeated a new dissenting candidate, Southby, in the subsequent election. (Plumb, 'Elections to the Convention Parliament', *Cambridge Historical Journal*, Vol. V, p. 253.) In Yorkshire 13 out of 28 candidates listed by James's agents were returned, and all but one of these subsequently voted that the throne was vacant. Six had been listed by James's agents as probable supporters of the Indulgence policy, and two were dissenters. In Suffolk the only two candidates forecast by James's agents as likely to be elected, and who were actually returned, were dissenters. Both voted for the vacancy. (Plumb, p. 242.)
† Ironically, the non-return of Pepys for Harwich was attributed to 'a conventicle set up here since this unhappy liberty of conscience.' (Letters and Second Diary (1932), p. 200.)

anglican establishment to see their form of episcopacy firmly
restored in Ireland. But what made the Irish question most
urgent was that Ireland provided a back door through which
James and Louis were already intending to deliver their counterattack. The ground was prepared, for Tyrconnel had kept up relations with Versailles through all the meanderings of James's
policy.

William's name is so closely identified with the protestant
ascendancy in Ireland that it comes almost as a shock to find that
his initial approach to the Irish question was the reverse of
protestant. Yet it fits very well with his essentially empirical, non-
ideological approach to politics. He had carefully avoided any
commitment to the Anglo-Irish. In response to feelers from
Tyrconnel, which appear to have reached William through the
Temples, a negotiation was begun which could have ended in a
submission by Tyrconnel in return for toleration of catholicism
in Ireland. The agent chosen by William to pursue this, who was
despatched to Ireland early in January, was the catholic Richard
Hamilton,* who had commanded one of the regiments sent over
by Tyrconnel to help James. The exact terms that Hamilton was
authorised to offer are not known, but they must have included
discontinuance of the episcopalian régime which Clarendon—
who was on tenterhooks throughout January on this subject—
had always stood for. Hamilton seems to have returned to England at least once, but the negotiation eventually broke down,
and he remained in Ireland to fight in James's army on the Boyne.
One of William's objectives was undoubtedly to avoid the diversion of strength from the Continent that an Irish war would
demand: the fact remains that the gesture of compromise was
made, and that if it had succeeded many tragic chapters in the
history of the British Isles might never have been written. In the
end it was anglican pressure and French intervention that drove
William to war in Ireland.

Anglicanism was as much a veneer in Scotland as it was in

* Hamilton was peculiarly well chosen for his task, being the brother-in-
law (by her first marriage) of the Countess of Tyrconnel, otherwise Frances
Jennings, sister of Marlborough's Sarah. It is usually said that Hamilton
never returned from his mission in Ireland, but 'Colonel Hambleton sent
from the Prince to Tyrconnel is upon his return and daily expected from the
Prince' (News letter of 24 January 1689 in HMC Portland, III, 422) suggests
the reverse.

Ireland, and the Scottish bishops had further weakened their position by agreeing (unlike their English brethren) to issue a public condemnation of William's invasion. Scottish episcopalianism had therefore no credit balance, in the shape of resistance to James, on which to draw now that William had triumphed. The collapse of organised government had been more serious in Scotland than in England, and most Scottish noblemen, instead of trying to restore order, applied themselves to the new seat of power after taking suitable steps to insure themselves with James as well. As early as 7/17 January it was possible to assemble in London thirty Scottish peers and eighty leading gentry as a kind of ad hoc Scottish parliament. This body, like its earlier English counterpart, made a tender of provisional power to William, who, as soon as he received it, sent the veteran Mackay northwards by sea to Edinburgh, accompanied by the three Scottish regiments that had come from Holland. The Scottish politicians found it less easy to return to Scotland since the roads were now closed except to the holders of special passes. William found Scotland an even more troublesome problem than Ireland: 'The Scotchmen,' he told Halifax, 'by their severall stories distracted his mind more than anything.'

William's silence during January and February therefore did not imply inactivity. He was quietly feeling his way towards pragmatic solutions in all three kingdoms. Assent out of self-interest rather than imposition of a pattern; plurality of power and patronage so long as there was unity of foreign policy; continuity rather than change; the practical rather than the consistent; these were the principles on which he was working, and they are principles best worked out in privacy. Between the Declarations he published at the beginning of the expedition, and his message to the Convention when it met on 22 January/1 February, William did not make a single personal public declaration of policy.

*   *   *

With the Convention begins the continuous series of parliaments that have sat at Westminster for nearly three hundred years. The lords taking part numbered one hundred and fifteen; and of the five hundred and thirteen members of the Commons one hundred and eighty-three—one in three—had never sat in

parliament before. Such a shift was well beyond the usual experience, and it is noteworthy that these new men included not only
such a veteran commonwealthsman as Wildman, who came
in for Wootton Basset, but the future leadership of the whigs—
Somers, Montagu, and Harley. The parliamentary experience of
the remaining three hundred and thirty went, for the most part,
back to Charles II's parliaments—notably the Exclusionist houses
of 1678–81: fewer than a hundred had sat for the first time in
James's loyal parliament of 1685. There was, undoubtedly a core
of traditionalist anglicans—perhaps a quarter of the whole
House*—but they were equalled, if not outnumbered by those
who at last saw the opportunity of establishing a balance between
the elected House and the hereditary traditional executive. As
a whole the assembly was ready for the strong leadership which
the trend of events and a powerful whig phalanx was able to
provide. Each House elected the same Speaker as the ad hoc
assemblies of December. Halifax, who divided the Lords against
Danby, took the Chair of the Lords, and the veteran Henry Powle
presided over the Commons.

William's message to the Houses congratulated them on being
'a full and fair representative of the Nation' and urged immediate
work for 'a happy and lasting settlement'. But it dwelt most
strongly on external affairs, beginning with the state of Ireland,
and going on to some very plain speaking about the Continent.
The United Provinces, said the message, had enabled William
'to rescue this Nation' and they now expected 'the returns of
Friendship and Assistance which may be expected from you as
Protestants and Englishmen'.[6] There must be no delay, therefore
over the niceties of constitutional discussion. The theme was
etched in stronger language by Speaker Powle as soon as the
message had been read. After dwelling on the fatal consequences
of anarchy, and the threat of the possible loss of Ireland—both

---

* Dr Plumb (*op. cit.*) estimates the traditional anglicans at about 160. Even
if the 183 new members are disregarded altogether, this leaves 170 who were
either whigs or, in the words of a later politician 'would go with a going
game'. But the 183 were predominantly whiggish, so that at this stage of the
Convention there was a powerful majority against the traditional order. The
only vote on the constitutional issue against which it is possible to measure
this calculation (on agreeing with the Lords' amendment on the 'vacancy' of
the throne) confirms this assessment. In this exceptionally full division 433
votes were cast, 151 for the Lords' amendment, 282 against: majority 131.

these points were designed to impress the traditionalists—he went on to emphasise 'more particularly the Growth of the Exorbitant Power of France, and the vast Designs of that Turbulent and Aspiring Monarch, not only the open Persecutor of the Protestant Religion, but likewise the sworn Enemy of the English Nation'. The Commons then adjourned for a week, while the Lords, in a kind of farewell to their fifteenth-century past, plunged energetically into argument about the responsibility for the death of the Earl of Essex in 1683.

The most notable fact about the constitutional discussions of February is that the celebrated resolution that James had abdicated and the throne was thereby vacant* was passed by the Commons on a single day without a division on 28 January/ 7 February 1689. Symbolically (the House being in Committee) Richard Hampden, son of the Civil War hero, and himself a man whose parliamentary experience had begun under the Protectorate, was in the Chair. Formally it was a triumph of political theory over the logic of the traditional constitution. In practice it guaranteed William's succession to the crown: and on the face of it it could have meant that England was now to be a republic. It was proposed by Sir Robert Howard, the other participant, with Powle, in the long interview William had had at Windsor on 16/26 December.†

The Commons went on to pass a series of conciliatory motions intended to soothe the old order. They thanked the armed forces for their behaviour during the Revolution, and the clergy who had resisted James's Indulgence policy. Finally, to drive home their view of what ought to happen next, they registered the opinion that 'it hath been found by experience inconsistent with this Protestant Kindom to be governed by a Popish Prince'.

The struggles of the traditionalists in the Lords, led by the

---

* 'That King James the Second having endeavoured to subvert the Constitution of the Kingdom, by breaking the original Contract between King and People; and by the Advice of Jesuits and other wicked Persons, having violated the Fundamental Laws, and withdrawn himself out of the Kingdom, hath Abdicated the Government, and that the Throne is thereby vacant.'
† It is quite clear that 'abdication' represented the official policy of William's own advisers, as well as the whig leadership (see Dijkvelt's interview with Clarendon on 14/24 January (*Clarendon Diary*, pp. 296–8)). William's contact with Howard was not confined to the Windsor interview—he dined with him on 26 January (*ibid.* p. 308); and also had a long interview with Pollexfen (*ibid.* p. 276).

Hyde brothers, against the inspired inconsistency of the Commons resolution, lasted for nearly a fortnight—from 29 January until 12 February. On narrow votes the Lords rejected the concept of a regency, accepted the doctrine of an original contract between King and People which James had broken, and then boggled at the stern whig doctrine embodied in the words 'abdicate' and 'vacant'. Two conferences with the Commons followed, in which there was much theoretical discussion, with Somers, now the leading light among the whig lawyers, quoting Grotius, Calvin, Brisonius, and Budaeus in support of the Commons' choice of language. Behind the scenes Danby opened up a channel to Mary with a suggestion that she should assume the throne in her own right, and have William as consort.

These debates were not conducted without pressure from outside parliament. There were strong signs of popular impatience and a petition was published in the name of 'great numbers of citizens and other inhabitants of London and Westminster' calling on the Lords to hasten their deliberations and settle William and Mary forthwith on the throne. Lord Lovelace produced it in the House on 2/12 February, and a large mob appeared in the street outside to reinforce the demand for an immediate settlement.

Simultaneously William had a carefully regulated interview with his leading supporters in the Lords together with Danby, whose intrigue on the subject of Mary William had taken speedy steps to frustrate. With characteristic economy he confined himself to three points. If a regency was decided on, he said, he would not be regent; nor would he accept the crown in dependence on the life of another (i.e. during Mary's lifetime only). Thus he rejected the expedients of both the Hydes and Danby. In compensation he held out a modest offering to the enthusiasts for hereditary right: he was prepared to see the crown descend to Anne and her issue in preference to any children he might have by a wife other than Mary.[7]

The date of this interview is uncertain, though it must have been between the second and fifth of February. Unquestionably, at this point, William had decided he must be king if it could be managed; yet one can well believe it was with reluctance, and that the resolution had been reached very recently indeed. Between the offer of provisional power by the Lords, and the similar offer by the Commons, he had written to Waldeck, and there was no reason why he should not have written sincerely words which ring with sincerity:

> Je suis passif en tout cett affaire sans avoir parle a qui que ce soit quoy que j'eu esté extremement tourmente. Et mesme si j'avois voulu donne le moindre encouragement je suis persuade qu'ils m'auroient declare Roy ce que je n'ambitione point n'estant pas venu pour cela icy.[8]

On the other hand Schomberg, writing on William's behalf to Berlin as early as 28 December, made it quite clear that William had no intention whatever of relinquishing the authority he now possessed over the British armed forces.

The result of William's intervention was electric. On 6/16 February the abdication resolution was forced through the Lords. Halifax stretched the authority of the Chair to the utmost. Several peers who had till then voted with the traditionalists failed to attend (Godolphin, for instance, pleaded urgent business at the Treasury). A few—a decisive few—were whipped up to vote down the Clarendonians. Among these were Crewe, the Bishop of Durham, who, as one of James's most zealous supporters, had not till then dared to appear in the House; the Earl of Carlisle, who came on crutches; and the Earl of Lincoln, who was said to be half mad. Above all, Danby and his group were resigned to the failure of their particular compromise. The day was carried by sixty-two votes to forty-seven.

Then, and not till then, did William consider the way was clear for Mary to join him in England. In no respect, perhaps, did he show his foresight more clearly than in his decision to insulate from politics this wife whom lesser men would have treated as a popular and dynastic asset. On 10/20 February she embarked, and arrived in London two days later.

Ash Wednesday, the 13/23 February was a pouring wet day, like the days of William's landing and of his arrival in London. The rain sluiced down outside the Inigo Jones Banqueting Hall where forty years ago, almost to the day, the crowds had waited to see the death of King Charles I and now assembled to see a new King and Queen made. William looked pale and ill. His cough had grown worse, and his wife had noticed, as soon as she arrived, how much weight he had lost. The House of Commons was present in force, but there was only a thin attendance of peers as the Clerk of the Crown read Somers's truncated masterpiece, the Bill of Rights, containing the terms on which William and Mary were offered the throne. Somers's committee had been told quietly to modify the elaborate constitutional document which they had at first contemplated. Then Halifax, the embodiment of compromise, and Speaker Powle advanced with the crown itself towards the two chairs on which William and Mary were seated, and offered it to them in the name of both Houses 'the Representative of the Nation'. William was called upon for only the briefest of acknowledgments. Then Lords and Commons retreated backwards before the throne; and, preceded by trumpeters and heralds, went in procession through the streets proclaiming William and Mary King and Queen.

Conclusion

The Revolution installed a great master of patronage on the throne. Patronage was certainly not a new thing in British politics, but had never before been used with such generosity or such sense of purpose. The new King's long experience of controlling patronage in the Netherlands, superimposed on his own businesslike character, had given him a pronounced policy on political rewards and punishments. Loyal and efficient support he rewarded without stint; and past opposition, provided it was genuinely abandoned, he was willing to overlook. But although he was willing to live and let live, and was careful to avoid anything that could be called proscription, he had no mercy on the inveterate opponent and the man who continued to try to deal with two masters. Sunderland, in consequence, was to fare better in the new reign than the Hyde brothers.

The rewards of those who had taken leading parts in the great adventure and its preparation make a spectacular catalogue.* Schomberg received the dukedom, the Garter, and the immense sum of money for which he had stipulated. William was heard to express doubts whether he had fully earned so much, but the old man was soon to pay for them in full on the Boyne, with his life. Bentinck and Zuylestein became respectively Earls of Portland and of Rochford, and Ginckel, after his successes in Ireland, Earl of Athlone—all with substantial grants of money and land. Ruvigny became in due course a viscount and later an earl—Earl

---

* Nor did William neglect those who had given service in much humbler ranks. One of his earliest requests to Parliament was for a special 'donative' to all ranks that had taken part in the invasion.

of Galway; the services of the Earl of Macclesfield were rewarded with the Presidency of Wales; and those of the Powlett family with yet another dukedom: that of Bolton.*

Of the 'immortal seven' who had signed the invitation of June six received high honours within a few years of the Revolution. Shrewsbury and Devonshire received dukedoms, Danby became Marquis of Carmarthen, and Lumley and Russell both received earldoms—one of Scarbrough and the other of Orford. Admiral Herbert was raised to the Lords as Earl of Torrington and the long, if obscure, services of Sidney were recognised by yet another earldom—Romney. Only Compton, for the second time in his career, was denied the one promotion that could have raised him higher. His contribution had been great, perhaps indispensable, but it had been such as to disqualify him from being Archbishop of Canterbury.

Another of William's earldoms went to Marlborough, and it would be possible to trace the whole British command structure during the wars of the next twenty years in the promotions in the armed forces that followed in the wake of the Revolution. Officers of the Anglo-Dutch Brigade were conspicuous in these promotions. Consider, for instance, the careers of the commanding officers of the regiments during the invasion operation. George Ramsay was thirty-six, and a lieutenant-colonel with twelve years service behind him in 1688. In 1690 he was made colonel of the Scots Guards and a brigadier, and three years later became a major-general. In 1702 he reached the summit of his career as commander-in-chief in Scotland and a lieutenant-general. Thomas Livingstone was one of those promoted colonel in the last days of 1688, and took his new regiment, the Scots Greys, to fight its old commander Claverhouse, and then on to defeat his own old comrades in arms, Canon and Buchan. In 1696 he became a major-general, and, like Ramsay, ended his service as commander-in-chief in Scotland, having 'purchased a greater estate than any other soldier in the King's reign'.

Colonel Barthold Balfour would have risen as high as Livingstone or Ramsay if he had not been killed as a brigadier, acting as second-in-command to Mackay at Killiekrankie. David Colyear did better than any of them. He was only thirty-two when he be-

---

* The reign of William is richer in ordinary dukedoms than any other. He conferred no fewer than seven.

came a colonel on the same list as Livingstone, and went to serve in Ireland, where he had the strange fortune to attract the attention of James II's former mistress, Catherine Sedley, whom he married. William raised him first to a barony, then to the Irish earldom of Portmore. Later, like so many of his colleagues, he commanded in Scotland and then served in high ranks in Flanders and Gibraltar, to retire with the reputation of 'one of the best foot officers in the world'. But of the whole group, the most distinguished was Talmash, with his Tangerine background. He was only thirty-eight when William made him colonel of the second Foot Guards in May 1689; within a year he was a major-general, and was a lieutenant-general in three. He was at Aughrim and Limerick, Steinkirk and Neerwinden, and his mortal wound on the expedition to Brest removed Marlborough's most formidable military competitor. The typical British senior commander in his fifties during the war of Queen Anne was an officer in his thirties who took a prominent part in the 'Descent on England'.

The intelligence agents and propagandists who had worked so long and so hard for William were also handsomely rewarded. Carstares remained one of William's most intimate advisers for the rest of the reign. In 1689 he became Moderator of the General Assembly of the Church of Scotland, and took a leading part in establishing a national presbyterian church that could live peaceably with an episcopalian monarchy south of the Border. The great compromise, by which patronage was introduced into the Kirk, was his doing, and the whole pattern of moderate presbyterianism, with its great influence on the Scottish eighteenth century, takes its origin from his work. In due course William added to Carstares the further honour of Principal of Edinburgh University. Both as Moderator and as Principal he worked in close co-operation with his old opposite number James Stewart, for that devious man had been quick to make his peace with the new order, and William made him Lord Advocate. For years after the Revolution the two sparring partners of the pre-revolutionary underworld continued to correspond about Scottish politics and patronage in cipher.

James Johnston's first task after the Revolution was a journey as special envoy to Berlin, carrying the Garter which William had promptly awarded to his indispensable ally, the Elector of

Brandenburg. On his return Johnston, like Carstares, went to help with the new whig government of the Northern Kingdom. In 1692 he was made Melville's colleague as Joint Secretary of State for Scotland, a post he held for four years. He lived, and continued to exercise influence in Scottish politics, far into the following century. The veteran agent who had written so cheerfully that it was important to 'trust God Almighty (though generally speaking He only takes care of people that take care of themselves)', survived to the age of eighty-two, as almost the last survivor of those who had taken a prominent part in the overthrow of James II.

Dr Hutton, the former herd-boy, graduate of Padua, and concocter of invisible inks, had followed William from Holland, and was installed in a special apartment on the backstairs of Whitehall Palace in preparation for Mary's arrival just before the end of 1688. He went with his master to Ireland and was present at the Boyne. Medical honours showered upon him— Fellow of the Royal College of Physicians in 1690, M.D. of Oxford in 1695, Fellow of the Royal Society in 1697; and he grew rich. He too gravitated to his native Scotland, and in the last of Queen Anne's parliaments he appears as member for Dumfries.*

One Scot who had worked abroad for William who did not follow the common pattern was Gilbert Burnet. His lot had been cast with the Anglican Church, and quite soon after the Revolution he received his reward, the bishopric of Salisbury. There, occupied in writing his invaluable but inaccurate history, he seems to diminish. It becomes hard to believe that this worthy, chatty, diocesan was the supposed target of assassination plots. William had found him useful but had never thought highly of him; and had other channels for communicating with the English clergy, who had done more than any other organised force except his own soldiers to bring him to the throne.

For if peerages and military promotions flowed strongly in these glorious years, preferment in the Church was even more abundant. Seven of James II's bishops—including five of those

* Perhaps Dr Stanley should also be included in the intelligence group: at any rate he was well looked after. In 1689 he was made a canon of St Paul's and in 1692 Archdeacon of London—a key post in organising the metropolitan clergy. Thence he went on to be Master of his old college at Cambridge, Corpus, and ended his career as Dean of St. Asaph.

who had stood up so boldly against the dispensing power, decided they could not in conscience change their allegiance. William, advised by Compton and Lloyd, did his utmost to avoid their abdication, even offering to let them retain effective possession of both their sees and their incomes without taking the required oaths, but they refused. With them and the four hundred clergy who followed their lead disappeared the old spirit of the Tudor and Caroline Church.

The consequent opportunities for preferment were considerable. Within three days of William's coronation Trelawny was promoted to Exeter, left vacant by Lamplugh, and ended his career in the even richer see of Winchester. But the greatest rewards went to the London clergy. When Sancroft insisted on stepping down it was Tillotson who took his place at Lambeth. Soon afterwards Stillingfleet and Symon Patrick were promoted to Worcester and Chichester respectively. Patrick's joy at his good fortune is celebrated as heralding the authentic note of the next century: 'Particularly I ought to acknowledge,' he wrote in his journal on learning he was to be a bishop, 'as it is in the Psalm for this day, that He hath put a new song in my mouth for our wonderful deliverance in these Kingdoms from popish tyranny, by an unexpected hand and in a peaceable manner.' At the same time Fowler became Bishop of Gloucester, and Tenison Bishop of Lincoln, as a preliminary to further advancement on Stillingfleet's death in 1694 and a reign at Lambeth that lasted until the House of Hanover was safely on the throne. Lloyd of St Asaph, who had done so much to further the Revolution, had to wait rather longer. It was not until 1692, after three years' energetic work re-organising the Church, that he was translated to Coventry and, after seven more years, to Worcester. He lived to be ninety, unpopular with his clergy for his extreme latitudinarianism, and the very pattern of a political bishop.

But there is another side to this picture of the post-revolutionary Church. There was no attempt to purge it, even of those who had flirted with romanism to please James II. Lamplugh, whose flight from Exeter had brought him the Archbishopric of York from James's almost powerless hands, was left undisturbed. Sprat, Crewe, and even Watson, who had been so closely identified with almost every step of James's ecclesiastical policy, were allowed to keep their sees. There could hardly be better examples of William's principle that security of tenure should, as far as possible, be safeguarded by his régime.

In the appointments where parliament, with its whig majority, had a greater interest, the picture was very different. Of the judges on the bench at the end of James's reign only one out of fourteen was reappointed: the judiciary paid the penalty for their approval of the dispensing power. Jeffreys and Wright had both died in prison during the spring. One was replaced by commissioners; the other was pursued by parliament beyond the grave, and was one of the few excepted by name from the Act of Indemnity. Henry Powle, having replaced Sir John Trevor as Speaker of the House of Commons, replaced him also as Master of the Rolls. The Chief Justiceship was offered to Mr Justice Powell, the hero of the Seven Bishops trial, who had been dismissed by James, but that prudent judge was content to accept no more than restoration as a puisne. No fewer than five of the twelve new appointments to the bench were made from the ranks of the majority in the Convention, and the judiciary assumed a decidedly whiggish, or even cromwellian appearance.* Old Sir Nicholas Lechmere, raised to the bench in his seventy-sixth year, had sat in the Long Parliament and in the parliaments of the Protectorate. Most of the new judges had learned their law in the 1650's.

*   *   *

This short account of some obvious immediate effects of William's military adventure enables us to see connectedly the chain of necessary events and combinations of forces which made that adventure a success. A more detailed analysis of careers would, without doubt, throw still more light on the inner springs of this extraordinary event. For it cannot be said of the English Revolution, as has been said of other celebrated revolutions, that it was the inevitable consequence of deep-seated, long-term, social, economic, and intellectual trends. It was, on the contrary, an artificial event, mainly produced by the judgments and misjudgments of individuals acting in a unique combination of

---

* Powle, Holt, Eyre, Pollexfen, and Ventris were all members of the Convention. Dolben, Gregory, and John Powell had been judges before, but had been dismissed. Atkyns was the one judge of James II's bench to survive the Revolution.

domestic and international circumstances. The effective decisions, moreover, were taken outside the British Isles.

Pre-eminent among these circumstances was the political, financial, and domestic situation of William himself, combined with his peculiar gifts, his particularist outlook, and his unquenchable perseverance. Yet with all his gifts, and all his resources, William would not have been able to take advantage of the misjudgments of Louis* and the domestic policy of James if it had not been for three developments in the European scene of the sixteen-eighties. The first, and most striking of these was the triumph of the Emperor Leopold against the Turks, the establishment of the Dual Monarchy on a secure basis, and the consequent alteration in the balance of power to France's disadvantage both in the West and in the Mediterranean. But the two others were at least equally important. These were the reconciliation between the republicans and the Orangists in the Netherlands, and the decision of the Great Elector to associate Brandenburg with William's foreign policy. The first of these, which was largely the work of Fagel, destroyed the basis of French policy in the Low Countries. D'Avaux records how his old republican friends in Amsterdam told him, in the autumn of 1688, with tears in their eyes, how plainly they saw the dangers to their own country which might result from William's success in England; but that they no longer had any choice in the matter, and were bound to give him their support.

The Brandenburg alliance was absolutely indispensable to the whole invasion plan, for without it an effective covering force for the Netherlands could not have been provided, and the Amsterdam republicans could not have been retained effectively in the Orangist coalition. It is the participation of Brandenburg, the extent of which is so generally overlooked, that finally establishes the descent on England—from the military and diplomatic point of view—as the work of a northern and central European reaction to the challenge of France.

* The Imperial Ambassador in London, Hoffmann, expressed the fatal link between Louis and James with considerable shrewdness. 'France,' he wrote to Vienna on 24 December 1688, 'without whose friendship he [James] allowed himself to be persuaded that he could not maintain himself, has brought all these troubles on him. She has lit a fire which she hoped to have time to put out, but now, to her own regret, matters are beyond remedy'. (*Campana de Cavelli*, II. p. 424).

In this situation, and with these allies, William possessed two instruments which he used with great skill, and without which his intervention in England could not have succeeded. One was the Anglo-Dutch Brigade, and the other was a propaganda machine unequalled in Europe. Both were needed for the effective exploitation of the state of affairs created by James's domestic policy. It is noteworthy, and a subject that deserves further study, that Scotsmen played an outstanding part in both these apparatuses.

I have given pride of place in this analysis to external factors, because these provided the dynamic of the Revolution. The internal situation in Britain produced by James's policy of centralisation at home and non-alignment abroad, and above all by his failure to comprehend the implications of his proposals for religious toleration, was ideally suited for external exploitation. It is rare for a country, especially an inward-looking country such as Britain, to accept enthusiastically a solution to its grievances that is imposed by external authority. But James never grasped the nature of the enthusiastic support he had received at the beginning of his reign, which was rooted in a longing for stability. In seeking to win the landed gentry over to the paradox of a state religion being treated as one of several sects, he produced a polarisation of opinion against his régime that made external intervention tolerable to a majority of the possessing and educated classes.

Should we say, then, that the English Revolution, being a military adventure and the product, largely, of forces outside Britain, does not deserve to be called a revolution at all? Macaulay claimed it as a 'conservative revolution', and a later historian as a 'respectable' one. Modern historiography has shown a tendency to emphasise the continuity on either side of 1688, rather than the break which the word 'revolution' has come to imply. But it would be far from logical to suppose that because the causes of 1688 were diplomatic, military, and political, or because they brought about no manifest change of social structure, that the consequences of 1688 were not far-reaching. On the contrary, William's victory was of the utmost importance not only to Britain but to Europe and to the world.

It has often been said that the Revolution was most creative in the constitutional field. Even today it would not be an exaggeration to say that the twenty years following 1688 saw the fundamental constitutional decisions of British history. Since William landed no year has been without a meeting of parliament, and the monarchy has owed its title to parliament. The liberties of the Bill of Rights, the immovability of judges, toleration (if not non-discrimination), the independence of the universities—all these followed from the Revolution and would not have been achieved without it. Yet William was as formidable a politician (and as power-loving a one) as had sat on the throne since the days of Elizabeth, and neither he nor his closest advisers can be described as liberal. What happened was that William's old-fashioned particularism fused with the tissue of English privilege to produce a durable pluralism that gave first place to personal and corporate rights.

Looking a little wider, the Revolution also hastened the union of the three kingdoms over which James had reigned. Although union with Scotland was still nearly twenty years away, William called himself King of Great Britain, and is so described on his coinage. The extent to which his inner circle of advisers was drawn from Scottish emigrés, and the subsequent establishment of so many of these men in positions of influence in Scotland, was in itself a major step towards union. James had sought to play his kingdoms off against one another: William, for political purposes, wanted unity. A compliant government in Scotland, and a British ascendancy in Ireland, were necessities in the struggle against France, while the national feeling of both the smaller countries was a dangerous asset on the side of his domestic enemies.

Economically the Revolution released the forces of expansion that James had perceived and hoped to harness. The latent financial strength of England suddenly proved to be enormous. To the money-starved governments of Charles and James it would have seemed inconceivable that Britain would be able to finance nearly 200,000 men in the armed forces (the figure reached in 1711 at the height of Marlborough's war), or that money would be raised in London by foreign governments, as happened for the first time in 1706 with the Imperial Austrian loan. The sixteen-nineties and the reign of Anne reek of commerce and business enterprise. The country became fascinated by the possibilities of trade, and sophistication of the commercial and financial systems rapidly followed. The National Debt, the Bank of England, the elaboration of the currency structure, the beginning of an organised stock market, the development of economic thought and economic statistics, are all features of the post-revolutionary era.

William's invasion symbolises above all the new and much closer relationship between Britain and Europe that was to be characteristic of the next two and a half centuries. From being a secondary, peripheral power Britain became, with surprising speed, a major political and economic force in Europe—a change marked, among much else, by the disappearance of the age-old requirement, which James had tried to maintain, that anyone of importance should seek official permission before leaving the country. The Revolution, in fact, heralds Britain's emergence as a great power. Within two decades of 1688 British fleets were dominating not only the Narrow Seas but the Mediterranean and the Atlantic. British armies were to cross Germany and themselves win victories on the Danube, and to campaign on France's southern flank in the Peninsula. But—and here is the double significance of the Revolution—the new nation-state had been established on the basis, not of authority but of pluralism.

The consequences for the whole world, even today, have been very great. It is difficult to see what force, short of a nation-state established in Britain, could at the end of the seventeenth century have frustrated Louis' dream of a predominance of France in western and southern Europe as the enduring basis for the economic and material developments which were then opening for European man. In the 1680's the inhabitants of France were probably more numerous than the inhabitants of Britain, the Low Countries, and the Empire combined: today they are perhaps a fifth of the total living in that area. Much else has contributed to this extraordinary change, but the Revolution certainly marks its beginning.

Nor were the consequences limited to Europe. Just at the moment when competition for the settlement and exploitation of the North American mainland by the powers of Western Europe was beginning, a decisive shift in the economic and political balance of power took place; and at the same time, as the natural consequence of the conservative pluralism established by the Revolution in England, James's tidily assembled, monolithic Dominion of New England was dissolved into its former components. The old charters, the old proprietors and assemblies, were speedily restored to the provinces which were in due course to constitute seven of the thirteen original states of the United of America. Between the arrest of James's Governor Andros in April 1689, and the death of Queen Anne, the population of the British colonies on the mainland of North America increased from just over 200,000 to nearly 350,000—almost seventy-five per cent in twenty-five years. The pace was to gather still more strongly as the eighteenth century progressed. By the time of the American Revolution there were two and a half million English-speaking North Americans—ten times the number a century earlier.

Judged by its consequences, then, the Revolution was a far-reaching event, even though it was not a social upheaval of the kind the word 'revolution' describes today. It is likely that those who coined it for the events of 1688 were using it in the stricter etymological sense of a circle returning to itself, a return to normality in the course of events. But it was not quite in this sense that the 'Glorious Revolution' was built up as the foundation of political life, as propagandists and historians speedily proceeded to do. The fact that the party of continuity had been defeated in the debates of February 1689; the conferment of the crown by a vote of parliament; and the asseveration of an original contract between King and people—all this was built into the popular imagination. Among so much else 1688-9 marks the great discovery that a Revolution is as effective a myth about the origins of political institutions as a sun-god or a Trojan hero. The title chosen by Lawrence Echard for his account of the Revolution, which long remained the orthodox version, tells much: 'The History of the Revolution and the Establishment of England in the year 1688.'

Appendix A

Distribution of Support for James II

The returns from the magistracy of England and Wales during the winter of 1687 in response to the King's three questions are a not unreasonable measure of the degree of support and opposition to James II. They are remarkably comprehensive, covering thirty-three of the forty-three English counties, and the whole of Wales. They are preserved in Rawlinson MSS (Bodleian Library) and are printed in extenso in Sir George Duckett's two volumes *Penal Laws and the Test Act* (1882–3). Duckett's purpose, however, was primarily genealogical, and the returns have never, so far as I know, been tabulated. Had they been, King James could readily have seen the dangers in persisting with his religious policy.

In preparing the following tabulation only the answers to the first two questions (would you, if elected to parliament, vote for repeal, and would you vote for a candidate pledged to repeal?) have been taken into account. All but one eccentric replied positively to the third question (Will you support the Indulgence policy by living peaceably with people of all persuasions?). Unqualified affirmatives to both questions have been counted as 'consent'—as have entries of 'catholic' against a name. 'Refusal' is taken as covering any answer containing a distinct expression of opposition to complete repeal of both the Penal Laws and the Test Act. The 'doubtfuls' are mainly those who said that if elected they would consider the arguments put forward in parliament. Many of these answers were couched in what were clearly prearranged formulae. Under the heading 'Absent &c' I have included not only those who did not reply at all, either in person or by letter, but those who gave completely unrevealing answers (e.g. 'he begs to be excused from answering'), and those against whom the Lord Lieutenant marked 'sentiments known to his Majesty', or some such phrase. This last group (not a very numerous one) probably includes a majority who had pledged their support.

The questions were administered at county meetings convened by the Lieutenants at one or more centres during the winter of 1687, when the questions were put orally to each magistrate in turn. Some absentees sent in their answers by letter. Some Lieutenants included former as well as active magistrates in their canvass, and these answers have been included in the tables.

Some magistrates (especially in Wales) were in the commission for more than one county. I have excluded those names against which the Lieutenant has noted 'answers in another county', but even so the figure for absentees, and consequently the total of the sample, is somewhat inflated, at any rate for Wales. On the other hand bad winter communications and Welsh caution clearly contributed to the poor response of the Welsh magistrates (only 54 per cent as against 78 per cent in England). On the whole, however, absence does not suggest support.

With these qualifications a total of 1,511 names is virtually a 10 per cent sample of the 16,560 estimated by Gregory King as the total of Lords, Baronets, Knights, esquires and gentlemen in 1696. Its main bias is probably the inclusion of a certain number of catholics who would not have been within Gregory King's definition; on the other hand the absence of a return for Lancashire, where the catholic gentry were strong, is an offsetting factor. On the whole the sample seems not unrepresentative.

The returns have been arranged in three tables. Table I analyses the thirteen English counties where consent was above the national average of 26.7 per cent of all magistrates in the sample. Table II analyses the twenty counties where 'consent' was relatively weak, and shows the respective weights of flat refusal and doubt. Table III summarises the whole, bringing in Wales.

It will be seen from Table III that consent commanded just over a quarter of the magistracy of England, and just under that fraction for England and Wales combined. Twenty-seven per cent in England, and just under 30 per cent in England and Wales combined, entered direct refusals. Thus more than half the total were prepared to be specific one way or the other, with a slight majority of distinct refusals despite the obvious pressures. This belies Macaulay's statement that a doubtful answer 'far more provoking than a direct refusal, because tinged with a sober and decorous irony which could not well be resented, was all the emissaries of the court could extract from most of the country gentlemen.' (*History of England*, Chapter Eight). The 'doubtfuls' constitute exactly a quarter of the sample, though no doubt, like the absentees, they were mostly potential opponents of James's proposals. The inference is, therefore, that although James had a not inconsiderable body of support, he had something like two-thirds of the landowning classes against him, and half of these were not afraid to say so.

The other two tables indicate in more detail the degree and distribution of support and opposition. From Table I it can be

TABLE I

English Counties where rate of Consent was above National Average

	County	Con-sents	Re-fusals	Doubt-ful	Absent, No Reply etc.	Total	% Consent
1	Kent	57	13	18	19	107	54·0
2	Northumberland	13	2	11	0	26	50·0
3	Worcestershire	16	3	8	5	32	50·0
4	Herefordshire	23	8	2	18	51	45·0
5	Lincolnshire	12	13	3	0	28	43·0
6	Oxfordshire	8	3	12	0	23	35·0
7	Yorkshire, N. Riding	9	1	16	0	26	34·5
8	Durham	1	0	2	0	3	33·3
9	Bristol	2	3	0	1	6	33·3
10	Gloucestershire	18	16	5	17	56	32·0
11	Staffordshire	15	9	13	14	51	29·5
12 13	Cumberland and Westmorland	13	3	24	8	48	27·0
	TOTALS	187	74	114	82	457	41·0

inferred that support for James was strongest in three areas: Kent; the extreme North (Cumberland, Westmorland, Northumberland, Durham and the North Riding); and the West Midlands (Worcestershire, Herefordshire, Gloucestershire, Oxfordshire, and Bristol). Support in this last area was non-conformist and old-style cavalier rather than catholic. Lancashire, London, and Middlesex, for which there are no returns, would probably also have shown foci of support for James.

Table II is interesting as showing not only the distribution and strength of the opposition, but its tactics. Dorsetshire, significantly, comes at the top, with nearly eighty per cent flat refusals. William landed in the right quarter. Refusal was also the absolute

TABLE II

Other English Counties, showing rate of Direct Refusal

County	Con-sents	Re-fusals	Doubt-ful	Absent, No Reply etc.	Total	% Refuse
1 Dorsetshire	6	26	1	0	33	79·0
2 Derbyshire	6	14	2	1	23	61·0
3 Norfolk	9	37	3	14	63	59·0
4 Hampshire	12	27	6	2	47	56·0
5 Shropshire	9	24	0	11	44	54·0
6 Leicestershire	7	17	2	13	39	44·0
7 Buckinghamshire	12	23	2	17	54	43·0
8 Bedfordshire	2	11	13	2	28	40·0
9 Northamptonshire	11	20	5	16	52	39·0
10 Huntingdonshire	5	8	5	3	21	39·0
11 Berkshire	7	10	10	3	30	33·0
12 Sussex	9	16	23	6	54	29·5
13 Somersetshire	10	13	9	14	46	28·0
14 Monmouthshire	7	6	1	11	25	24·0
15 Essex	17	12	35	0	64	18·0
16 Nottinghamshire	1	3	10	5	19	16·0
17 Wiltshire	6	7	21	13	47	15·0
18 Yorkshire (E. & W. Ridings)	7	0	27	0	34	—
19 Cornwall	1	0	15	10	26	—
20 Devonshire	9	0	53	8	70	—
TOTALS	153	274	243	149	819	
%	(19·0)	(33·0)	(30·0)	(18·0)	100·0	

Table III
Summary

	Consent	Refuse	Doubtful	Absent, etc.	Total	
Thirteen English Counties where consents were above national English average of 26·7 per cent.	187 (41·0)	74 (16·2)	114 (25·0)	82 (17·8)	457 (100·0)	
Twenty other English Counties	153 (19·0)	274 (33·0)	243 (30·0)	149 (18·0)	819 (100·0)	Note (1)
Total England	340 (26·7)	348 (27·3)	357 (28·0)	231 (18·0)	1276 (100·0)	
Wales	29 (12·0)	87 (37·0)	11 (5·0)	108 (46·0)	235 (100·0)	Note (2)
Total England and Wales	369 (24·5)	435 (29·0)	368 (25·0)	339 (22·0)	1511 (100·0)	

Notes
(1) No returns are available for ten English counties (Lancashire, Cambridge, Warwickshire, Middlesex, London, Cheshire, Middlesex, Surrey, Suffolk, and Rutland).
(2) The figure for absences is probably inflated, since large numbers of Welsh J.P.'s were in the commission for more than one county.

majority (including absentees) in the important counties of Norfolk and Hampshire, and the eastern Midlands were also fairly emphatic in their rejection of James's policy. The lower end of the table shows the counties where, although support for James was virtually non-existent, the tactics of opposition were more cautious, and took the form of massive 'doubtful' votes. These 'cautious areas' lay in the far south-west (Somerset, Devon, and Cornwall), where recollections of Monmouth must still have been strong, and the two southern ridings of Yorkshire. The same picture is visible in Essex, but here there was also a fairly strong element of support for James—probably non-conformist.

The picture in Wales is different again. Here the main tactic was absenteeism. But that the Principality as a whole was strongly opposed to James's policy is evident. There was a strong 'refusal' vote, and one of the weakest 'consent' votes in the country.

Appendix B

The Cost of William's Operations

Estimates among the Portland MSS in Nottingham University Library allow an assessment of the finance William devoted to his invasion, and so throw considerable light on the cost of military operations in the late seventeenth century.

The troops taking part in the expedition (apart from William's household troops) were paid for by the United Provinces up to the time of embarkation, after which they became the responsibility of William's personal treasury. Bentinck's Estimate for land forces (P.W.A. 2187) allows, on the basis of 42 days' pay and rations, for the command organisation and land army of seventeen cavalry regiments, seventeen infantry regiments, two regiments of dragoons, and supporting arms (artillery, engineers, medical, and provost). To this is added the cost of transport for 30 days—the difference of 12 days being presumably to allow for the sea journey. The assumption of 30 days for the duration of the land campaign was surprisingly accurate, though the delays in starting after the troops were embarked meant that the troops were dependent on William for considerably longer than the budget allowed. By the time he reached Hungerford he must have been under considerable financial strain.

The provision made can be summarised as follows:

	£	s	d
Commands and Staff	18,573	6	8
Cavalry	100,012	10	0
Infantry	187,732	10	0
Dragoons	35,929	0	0
Artillery	7,797	0	0
Engineers	420	0	0
Medical	815	0	4
Provost	1,164	0	0
Transport (30 days only)	31,690	0	0
Total	384,133	7	0

From this it may be calculated that when William's army was fully operational, it was costing just under £10,000 a day, or about 13s 4d per combatant. The figure may be slightly exaggerated by the very large salaries and expenses given to senior officers: it appears, for instance, that Schomberg was being paid at the rate of £10,000 a year plus expenses. He had mentioned to Bentinck as recently as October that very advantageous offers were reaching him through French intermediaries (letter of 1.10.1688, Portland MSS P.W.A. 1125). But these salaries form only about 5 per cent of the Estimate, and the effect can only be marginal. The significant point about the calculation is that since it was William's policy to pay for everything his army needed (in which respect he was behaving very differently from most commanders of the time) the figure of 13s 4d may be taken as an approximation to a coefficient of 'real cost per combatant' for a balanced force of the period.

The total cost of the expedition can also be computed approximately as follows:

	£
Pay and Rations for Land Forces from 6 October to 31 December	870,000
Purchase of Stores	18,000
Hiring of Sea Transport	140,000
	1,028,000

This takes account only of bills preserved (exchanging guilders at the rate of 6.6 to the £) and is therefore almost certainly an under-estimate even for the costs borne by William (or ultimately the English Exchequer, from whom he recovered them). And no allowance is made for the cost of the battle fleet, most of which was borne by the Dutch Treasury. Allowing for these factors the total cost cannot have been far short of £1.5 million—a figure equivalent to three-quarters of the annual revenue of James II's government.

One can go on, still more hazardously, to compute the cost of the entire operation, including the covering armies under Waldeck and Schöning. The Dutch contribution to these last, which met far the greater part of their cost, was almost £1 million. So a reasonable figure for the total cost of the Williamite military operations for the last three months of 1688 might be £2.25 million.

The econometric hazards of applying a multiplier to a money

figure for a year as long ago as 1688 in order to arrive at 'present-day values' are considerable. Nevertheless I conclude by doing this in order to suggest a point about the impact of war on economies at different stages of development which is not, I think, invalidated by these objections.

Taking a multiplier of twelve (one as large as twenty would not invalidate the point that is to be made) the cost of the operations described in this book during the last three months of 1688 can be put at about £27 millions of our money: in other words they represented war expenditure at a 1967 rate of about £108 millions a year. Such expenditure would not be a heavy drain on the economy of even a comparatively small modern state. It is, for instance, less than one-third of one per cent of the G.N.P. of this country in 1967. The 1688 figure corresponding to £108 millions—i.e., £9 millions—represented a far greater proportion of the 1688 British G.N.P. Although such a G.N.P. figure is not, of course, exactly ascertainable, it cannot have exceeded £100 millions, so that the annual burden represented by William's invasion expenditure must have approached, or even exceeded, 10 per cent of G.N.P. The *relative* effort can therefore be judged by considering the impact on our economy if defence expenditure were approximately doubled. The *actual* effect of diverting so large an effort to war purposes out of economies in which most of the population lived at very low standards was, of course, even more severe than this comparison would suggest, as Louis XIV was to find.

References

The *first* reference to a source gives the full title of the work. Subsequent references to the same work are in italic, and normally abbreviated to the name of the author or editor. Conventional abbreviations have been used without explanation e.g. B.M. for British Museum, H.M.C. for Historical Manuscripts Commission, E.H.R. for English Historical Review. The references are confined to sources actually quoted.

CHAPTER ONE

1 Rousset, E., Histoire de Louvois, I, p. 212 (Louvois to Vauban, 4 and 13 October 1676)
2 Pontbriant, A., Histoire de la Principauté d'Orange, p. 101
3 Correspondance Administrative Sous la Règne de Louis XIV, III, p. 700
4 Temple, Sir William, Works (1770), I, p. 170
5 An Historical Account of the British Regiments . . . in the Formation and Defence of the Dutch Republic, (1794), p. 36
6 King, Gregory, Two Tracts (edited by J. H. Hollander, 1936), p. 55
7 Gérin, E., Révocation de l'Edit de Nantes, p. 387. The remark was made on 11 January 1683
8 The Hearth Tax 1662–1689 (Public Record Office Publication 1962)
9 *Rousset, I, p. 421 (Louvois to Barillon, 19 December 1686)*
10 Barillon to Louis, February 1681. P.R.O. 31/3/147

CHAPTER TWO

1 Stewart Transcripts in Wodrow MS (National Library of Scotland)
2 Erskine of Carnock's Journal 1683–1687 (Scottish Historical Society, 1891), p. 112
3 Maitland Club, vol. 71, i, p. 167: Caldwell Papers, p. 168
4 McCormick, Joseph, State Papers and Letters Addressed to William Carstares (1774), p, 160

CHAPTER THREE

1 Louis XIV's Memorandum for his grandson, quoted by Pierre Goubert, Louis XIV et Vingt Millions de Français (1966) p. 47.
2 *Pontbriant, p. 138*
3 *Stewart Transcripts (Stewart to Carstares 24 September 1687)*
4 *Temple, II, p. 386*
5 Blencowe, R.W. (Editor) Diary of the Times of Charles II, I, p. 130
6 Campana de Cavelli, Les Derniers Stuarts à St Germain en Laye (1871), I, p. 152

7 Conversations Inédites de Madam de Maintenon (1828)
8 St-Simon, Memoires (1791), II, p. 70

CHAPTER FOUR

1 Fox, C. J., History of the Early Part of the Reign of James II, Appendix p. 79 (Barillon to Louis XIV, 17 May 1685)
2 *Fox Appendix p. 13 (Louis XIV to Barillon, 19 November 1685)*
3 *Ferguson pp. 536–41*; Dalrymple, Sir John, Memoirs of Great Britain and Ireland (1753), Part One, Book II, Appendix, p. 23 (James to William, 3 July 1685)
4 *Dalrymple, Part One, ii, Appendix p. 23 (James to William, 30 June 1685)*
5 Prinsterer, G. van, Archives ou Correspondance Inédite de la Maison d'Orange-Nassau, II, v. p. 589 (William to the Prince of Nassau-Dietz, 30 March 1685)
6 *Erskine of Carnock, s. d. 31 October 1685*
7 Lavisse et Rambaud, Histoire Générale, VI, p. 296

CHAPTER FIVE

1 Duckett, Sir George, Penal Laws and the Test Act (1882–3), I, p. 196
2 Luttrell, Narcissus, A Brief Historical Relation (1857), I, p. 371
3 Caldwell Papers, I, p. 146
4 *Erskine of Carnock, s.d. 5 February 1686*

CHAPTER SIX

1 Burnet, Gilbert, Travels (1724), pp. 270–1
2 *Ibid., p. 288*
3 *Ibid., p. 302*
4 *Erskine of Carnock s.d. 19 and 20 February, 11 March, 7, 8, 9, 12, and 13 July.* Erskine makes it clear he talked to Leven
5 *Ibid. s.d. 17, 22, 24, 26, 29, and 30 July.* Erskine's party included Baillie, Hume, and Lockhart
6 *Ibid. s.d. 3, 4, and 5 August*
7 Mazure, F. A. J. Histoire de la Révolution de 1688 en Angleterre (1825), II, pp. 161–3
8 *Mazure, II, p. 175 (Mordaunt to Bentinck, 12 October 1686)*
9 Life of James II King of England (1703), p. 158 gives the full text
10 D'Avaux, Jean Antoine de Mesmes, Count, Negotiations (1754), IV pp. 100–2
11 Burnet, Gilbert, A History of His Own Time (1838), p. 441

CHAPTER SEVEN

1 *D'Avaux, IV, p. 110*
2 *Dalrymple, Part One, V, Appendix, p. 52*
3 Japikse, N. (Editor), Correspondentie van Willem III en van Hans Willem Bentinck, II, ii, p. 749 (William to Fagel, 30 March and 13 April 1687)
4 *Japikse, II, ii, p. 750*
5 *Dalrymple, Book V, Appendix, p. 70*
6 *Ibid., p. 54 (William to King James, 17 June 1687)*
7 *Japikse, II, ii, p. 757 (Carstares to Bentinck, 1 and 2 August 1687)*
8 *Ibid., I, ii, p. 18*
9 *Ibid., I, i, p. 33 (William to Bentinck, 21 September 1687)*

CHAPTER EIGHT

1 Portland MSS (Nottingham) P.W.A. 2103 (Johnston's report of 25 November 1687)
2 Bramston, Sir John, Autobiography (Camden Society), p. 300
3 Memorials of the Life of Mr Ambrose Barnes (Surtees Society, Vol. 50), pp. 218 and 177–9
4 Their Highness's the Prince and Princess of Orange's Opinion about A General Liberty of Conscience, London, 1689
5 Portland MSS (Nottingham) P.W.A. 2101b (Johnston's report of 18 November 1687)
6 *Duckett, I, p. 280*
7 *Ibid., I, p. 214*
8 *Ibid., I, p. 48*
9 *Campana de Cavelli, II, p. 156*
10 *Japikse, II, ii, p. 772 (Clarendon to William, 15 December 1687)*
11 Calendar of Treasury Books 1688, p. 2053 (Albeville to the Treasury, February 1688)
12 Blencowe, R. W. (editor), Diary of the Times of Charles II, by Henry Sidney, II, p. 265 (Schomberg to Sidney 25 September 1687)
13 *Japikse, I, ii, p. 7 (Sidney to Bentinck, 8 December 1687)*
14 *Duckett, I, p. 195*
15 Information about Brent is extremely meagre, and much of what there is is coloured by hindsight. He is not in the D.N.B. The particulars in this paragraph are gleaned from The Pension Book of Gray's Inn, II, p. 92 and H.M.C., VII, Report, p. 509
16 *Bramston, p. 304*
17 H.M.C. Lindsey p. 270

CHAPTER NINE

1 *D'Avaux, IV, p. 132 (s.d. 25 November 1687)*
2 *Dalrymple, V, Appendix, pp. 138 and 142 (Barillon's despatches of 18 December 1687 and 5 January 1688)*
3 Portland MSS (Nottingham) P.W.A. 2112 d
4 Clarendon, Earl of, The State Letters of Henry, Earl of Clarendon (1765), II, p. 174. This was on 15 January. Terriesi had noticed sceptical rumours as early as his despatch of 23 December
5 *Campana de Cavelli, I, p. 156 (Terriesi to the Tuscan Secretary of State, 23 December 1687)*
6 *Dalrymple, V, Appendix, p. 171*
7 *Ferguson, p. 544*
8 *Ibid., p. 555*
9 Macpherson, James, Original Papers (1775), I, p. 289 (Letter from Colonel Ambrose Norton)
10 *Dalrymple, V, Appendix, p. 122 (Cardinal d'Estrées to Louvois, 18 December 1687)*. The genuineness of this letter is, however, seriously in doubt.
11 *Japikse, II, ii, pp. 756–62 and II, iii, p. 36*
12 Calendar of State Papers Colonial (America and West Indies) 1685–1688, p. 506. The Governor considered that Mordaunt's story of a treasure hunt 'might be a veil for other designs'.

CHAPTER TEN

1 *Japikse, I, i, p. 36 (William to Bentinck, 29 April 1688)*

2 Portland MSS (Nottingham) P.W.A. 2159 (Johnston's report of 4 April 1688)
3 *Ibid.* P.W.A. 2161 (Johnston's report of 23 May 1688)
4 Gutch, J. L. Collecteana Curiosa (1781), I, pp. 299–308
5 Portland MSS (Nottingham) P.W.A. 2149 (Johnston's report of 10 March 1688)
6 *Gutch, I, pp. 335–40*
7 *Japikse, I, i, pp. 40–41 (William to Bentinck, 4 and 7 June 1688)*
8 Portland MSS (Nottingham) P.W.A. 2164 and 2167 (Johnston's reports of 27 May and 13 June)
9 B.M. Add. MSS 34512 f. 131 (Van Citters to the States General, 28 June 1688)
10 *Japikse, I, ii, p. 603 (Johnston to Bentinck, undated)*
11 H.M.C. Portland, III, p. 404
12 *D'Avaux, IV, p. 182*
13 Portland MSS (Nottingham) P.W.A. 2167 (Johnston's report of 13 June 1688)
14 Lord Campbell, Lives of the Chief Justices (1856) quotes extensively from the trial in his life of Wright.
15 Portland MSS (Nottingham) P.W.A. (Johnston's report of 2 July 1688)
16 *Dalrymple, Book V, Appendix, p. 106*

CHAPTER ELEVEN

1 *Japikse, I, i, p. 54 (William to Bentinck, 4 September 1688)*
2 *Ibid., I, i, pp. 604–6*
3 *Ibid., I, i, p. 46*
4 *Ibid., II, iii, 37 (William to Fagel, 29 August)* and I, i, p. 48 (*William to Bentinck, 29 August*)
5 *Ibid., I, i, p. 48 (William to Bentinck, 29 August 1688)*
6 *Ibid. loc. cit.*
7 *Ibid. loc. cit.*
8 L. von Pastor, History of the Popes (1940), xxxii, p. 386
9 *Japikse, I, i, p. 56 (William to Bentinck, 14 September 1688)*
10 *Dalrymple, Book V, Appendix, p. 194 (James to William, 18 September 1688)*
11 *Ibid., p. 201* (James to William, 27 September 1688)

CHAPTER TWELVE

1 Pepys to Captain Killigrew 3/13 September 1681: 'The King has for now about 14 or 20 daies been greatly awakened, and indeed little less than surprised' by William's preparations (quoted by Tanner, Naval Preparations of James II in E.H.R. for 1893)
2 *Japikse, I, i, p. 97 (William to Bentinck, 26 September 1688)*
3 *Burnet, p. 483–4*
4 H.M.C. Dartmouth, V, p. 166 (Pepys to Dartmouth, 17/27 October 1688)
5 Torrington Memoirs (Camden Society New Series, vol. 46), p. 27
6 *Japikse, I, ii, p. 607 (Van Leeuwen's report)*
7 *Ibid., I, i, p. 606*
8 *Ibid., p. 610*
9 *Ibid., p. 613*
10 *Gutch, I, p. 409*
11 Müller, P. L., Wilhelm III von Oranien und Georg Friedrich von Waldeck (1880), II, p. 111 (William to Waldeck, 2 October 1688)
12 H.M.C. Dartmouth, V, p. 138; H.M.C. Lindsey, p. 423
13 *Gutch, I, pp. 410–13*

14 *D'Avaux, IV, p. 204*
15 H.M.C. Dartmouth, V, pp. 260–1 (Dartmouth to the King, 22 Oct./
1 Nov. 1688)
16 *Gutch, I, pp. 422–4*
17 *Japikse, I, ii, p. 603*
18 *Ferguson, p. 566*
19 H.M.C. Dartmouth, V, p. 178 (Albeville to Sunderland, 31 October 1688);
Rapin de Thoyras, Histoire d'Angleterre, X, p. 125
20 *Müller, II, p. 116 (William to Waldeck, 2 November 1688)*; Burnet to
Herbert, 2 November 1688 in E.H.R. 1886, p. 527
21 H.M.C. Dartmouth V. p. 261 (Dartmouth to the King, 24 Oct./3 Nov.
1688)
22 *Gutch, I, p. 425*
23 H.M.C. Dartmouth, V, pp. 201–2 (Albeville's despatch copied to
Dartmouth)
24 H.M.C. Dartmouth, V, p. 262. (Dartmouth's despatches of 29 Oct./
8 Nov. and 30 Oct./9 Nov. 1688)
25 *Tanner, loc. cit.* (Captain Tennant to Pepys)
26 *Rapin, X, p. 126*
27 *Tanner, loc. cit.* (Mr. Bastick to Mr. Frowde)
28 H.M.C. Dartmouth, V, p. 185

CHAPTER THIRTEEN

1 *Rousset, IV, p. 164*
2 H.M.C. Dartmouth, V, p. 184 (Pepys to Dartmouth, 6 November 1688)
3 *Ibid.*, p. 264 (Dartmouth to the King, 30 October 1688)
4 *Japikse, II, ii, p. 53 (William to Herbert, 14 December 1688)*
5 *Müller, II, p. 118 (William to Waldeck, 26 November 1688)*
6 *Mazure, III, p. 180–81*
7 H.M.C. Dartmouth, V, p. 272 (Dartmouth to the King, 12/22 November
1688)
8 *Ibid.*

CHAPTER FOURTEEN

1 Reresby, Sir John, Memoirs (1875), p. 415
2 Clarendon, Earl of, State Letters etc. (1765), pp. 255–6
3 *Torrington Memoirs*, p. 20
4 H.M.C. Dartmouth, V, p. 219 (William to Lord Dartmouth, 28 November/
8 December 1688)
5 Ibid., p. 276 (Dartmouth to the King, 3/13 December 1688)
6 *Clarendon, II*, p. 65
7 *H.M.C. Dartmouth, V, p. 226* (the King to Lord Dartmouth, 10/20
December 1688)
8 *Rousset, II, p. 151 (Louvois to M. de Beringham, 1 January 1689)*
9 *Müller, II, p. 119 (William to Waldeck, 19 December 1688)*
10 Foxcroft, Life of George Savile Marquis of Halifax, II, pp. 57–59
11 Cambridge Historical Journal, V, p. 108
12 H.M.C. Dartmouth, V, p. 22
13 *Clarendon, II, p. 268*
14 *Ibid., p. 269*
15 The account of the anonymous eye-witness is in B.M. Harleian MS 6852
16 *Clarendon, II, p. 274*
17 Symon Patrick, Works (1858), IX, p. 514

CHAPTER FIFTEEN

1 *Müller, II, p. 119 (Waldeck to William, 28 December 1688)*
2 *Foxcroft, Halifax, II, p. 58*
3 *Rousset, III, p. 164*
4 *Foxcroft, Halifax, II, p. 59*
5 *Clarendon, II, pp. 282, 284*
6 Commons Journals, X, p. 9
7 *Foxcroft, Halifax, II, p. 202*
8 *Müller, II, p. 126 (William to Waldeck, 25 February 1689).* The words quoted are especially significant, since they are added in William's own hand to a letter dictated to a secretary.

INDEX